T0361140

THE AMERICANISATION OF
EUROPEAN BUSINESS

After the Second World War, US economic and political influence in Europe was considerable. This influence is probably best exemplified by the Marshall Plan. This volume analyses how, and to what extent, the American example shaped the way in which European business was organised and managed. It contains a number of in-depth case studies and also assesses how management knowledge is transferred between countries.

The book examines the mechanisms and channels through which American managerial know-how and US management models were transferred to Europe after 1945, as well as the actual influence on European industries, companies and regions in the 1950s and 1960s. It explores the role of the European Productivity Agency, business leaders, US multinationals, regional networks and institutions, as well as the actual transfer process and potential political, cultural or institutional barriers. The final section contains the cases of three European companies which adopted American management methods to a considerable extent during the 1950s and 1960s.

This book features contributions from an international selection of experts and will be of great interest to business and economic historians as well as management scholars.

Matthias Kipping is Lecturer in Business and Management at the University of Reading, Department of Economics. **Ove Bjarnar** is a Senior Research Fellow at the Møre Research Centre in Molde, Norway.

ROUTLEDGE STUDIES IN BUSINESS
HISTORY
Series editor: Geoffrey Jones

THE AMERICANISATION OF EUROPEAN BUSINESS

The Marshall Plan and the transfer of US management models

Edited by Matthias Kipping and Ove Bjarnar

Routledge
Taylor & Francis Group

LONDON AND NEW YORK

First published 1998
by Routledge
2 Park Square, Milton Park, Abingdon, Oxon, OX14 4RN

Transferred to Digital Printing 2005
Simultaneously published in the USA and Canada
by Routledge
711 Third Avenue, New York, NY 10017
Routledge is an imprint of the Taylor & Francis Group, an informa business
First issued in paperback 2013

Typeset in Garamond by Routledge

British Library Cataloguing in Publication Data
A catalogue record for this book is available from the British Library

Library of Congress Cataloguing in Publication Data
The Americanisation of European business : the Marshall Plan and the transfer
of US management models / edited by Matthias Kipping and Ove Bjarnar.
p. cm.
A collection of 12 papers by international authors.
Includes bibliographic references and index.
1. Industrial management–Europe. 2. Industrial management–United States.
3. Corporations, Europe. 4. Technical assistance, American–Europe. 5. Marshall
Plan. I. Kipping, Matthias. II. Bjarnar, Ove, 1951– .
HD70.E8A46 1998
658'.0094–dc21   97-45919
                                                                        CIP
ISBN 978-0-415-17191-5 (hbk)
ISBN 978-0-415-86252-3 (pbk)

CONTENTS

ILLUSTRATIONS

Figures

Tables

CONTRIBUTORS

Rolv Petter Amdam is Professor and Head of the Department of Strategy and Business History at the Norwegian School of Management in Oslo. He has published widely on Norwegian business history and the transfer of organisational and management knowledge. He edited *Management, Education and Competitiveness: Europe, Japan and the United States* (Routledge, 1996).

Ove Bjarnar is Senior Research Fellow at the Møre Research Centre in Molde, Norway. His main research areas are business history and organisational history. He has been Visiting Research Fellow at the Norwegian School of Management and the University of Reading. His publications include books and articles on the history of education, organisational history and regional history.

Bent Boel is a Lecturer at the Department of History, University of Copenhagen. He is currently finishing a doctoral dissertation about the European Productivity Agency.

Ludovic Cailluet is a Lecturer in the Department of Economics at the University of Reading. He holds a PhD from the University of Lyon and has devoted his research to the history of the European aluminium industry, its strategy and management practices. His publications include articles on marketing and accounting history and the evolution of corporate organisation in French industry. He has also published *Chedde, un siècle d'industrie au Pays du Mont-Blanc* (Presses Universitaires de Grenoble, 1997).

John H. Dunning is Emeritus Professor of International Business at the University of Reading and State of New Jersey Professor of International Business at Rutgers University, New Jersey. He has been researching into the economics of international direct investment and the multinational enterprise since the 1950s. He has authored, co-authored or edited a large number of books on this subject and on industrial and regional economics.

His latest publications, all in 1997, include *Alliance Capitalism and Global Business* as well as two edited volumes on *Globalization, Governments and International Business* and *Globalization and Developing Countries*.

David W. Ellwood is Associate Professor of International History at the University of Bologna and Adjunct Professor of European History at the Johns Hopkins School of Advanced International Studies, Bologna Center. His major publications include *Italy 1943–45: The Politics of Liberation* (1985), *Rebuilding Europe: Western Europe, America and Postwar Reconstruction* (1992), and the edited volume *Hollywood in Europe: Experiences of a Cultural Hegemony* (1994). He has written extensively on the political, economic and mass-cultural relations between the United States and Europe, with particular reference to the Second World War, the Marshall Plan and the theme of Americanisation.

Henrik Glimstedt is Assistant Professor at the Institute of International Business, Stockholm School of Economics. His main research areas are business history, the political construction of markets, industrial governance and globalisation. He has mainly published on the automobile industry, including *Between Technology and Society: State, Market and Production in Swedish Automobile Production 1930–1960* (University of Göteborg, 1993). He also co-edited a volume in Norwegian (with Even Lange) on *Globalisation in Historical Perspective* (Fagboksforlaget, 1998).

Matthias Kipping is Lecturer in Business and Management at the University of Reading. He has published in English, French and German on industrial policy, the steel producing and using industries, and the role of business interest groups in European integration, including *Zwischen Kartellen und Konkurrenz: Der Schuman-Plan und die Ursprünge der europäischen Einigung 1944–1952* (Duncker & Humblot, 1996). His current research focuses on the international transfer of management know-how in an historical perspective, namely the role of business education and management consultants.

Christian Kleinschmidt is Research Assistant in the Department of Social and Economic History at the Ruhr-University in Bochum. He is the author of a study on rationalisation within the iron and steel industry in the Ruhr area: *Rationalisierung als Unternehmensstrategie. Die Eisen- und Stahlindustrie des Ruhrgebiets zwischen Jahrhundertwende und Weltwirtschaftskrise* (Klartext, 1993). At present he is working on a research project, financed by the Volkswagen Foundation, on the perception by German managers of foreign management and production methods between 1950 and 1980.

Jacqueline McGlade is Assistant Professor of American Business, Economic

History and US Foreign Relations, and Acting Associate Dean of the School of Science, Technology and Engineering at Monmouth University, New Jersey. She has written articles on technical assistance, the history of business-government relations in the United States, business education and aircraft production.

Ruggero Ranieri is Jean Monnet Lecturer and Research Associate in the Department of History, University of Manchester. He gained his doctorate at the European University Institute in Florence and has since published widely in the field of the history of the European Coal and Steel Community and of the Italian and European steel industry after 1945. He is co-author of *The Frontier of National Sovereignty, 1945–1992* (Routledge, 1992) and has edited the memoirs of Gian Lupo Osti, *L'industria di stato dal successo al degrado – Trent'anni nel gruppo Finsider* (Il Mulino, 1993). He is currently researching a book on the first generation of wide strip mills in Europe in the 1940s and 1950s.

Nick Tiratsoo is Senior Research Fellow in the History Department at Luton University and Visiting Research Fellow at the Business History Unit, the London School of Economics. He has written extensively on the history of the Labour Party and is currently researching British management 1945–1990.

Jim Tomlinson is Professor of Economic History and Head of the Department of Government at Brunel University. He has written exten-sively on the economic history of twentieth century Britain, his most recent publication being *Democratic Socialism and Economic Policy: the Attlee Years* (Cambridge University Press, 1997).

PREFACE

This book originated from the idea to commemorate the fiftieth anniversary of the Marshall Plan. This American initiative, first announced in 1947, undoubtedly shaped the subsequent evolution of Western Europe in many different ways. Our objective was to find out what influence it had on European business. We therefore invited a number of scholars who had worked intensively on this subject to Reading for a conference on 'The Response of European Industry to the US Productivity Drive, 1948–60', held on 13 and 14 December 1996.

We would like to express our gratitude to all who responded to our call and attended the conference. This includes not only those who presented papers, but also those who commented on these papers, namely Rolv Petter Amdam, Patrick Fridenson and Steven Tolliday. We also gratefully acknowledge the financial support for the conference received from the Department of Economics at the University of Reading, the Møre Research Centre in Molde, Norway and the British Academy. In addition, we would like to highlight the contribution of the supportive environment in which this conference took place, i.e. the Centre for International Business History (CIBH) at the University of Reading, including its Director Geoffrey Jones and the PhD students who provided indispensable logistical support. And last but not least, we would like to thank the whole Jørgensen Bjarnar family who hosted a memorable Norwegian evening, which was the concluding – and crowning – event of the conference and of the year they had spent in Reading.

For the book, we invited a number of additional contributions. Many thanks to John Dunning, David Ellwood, Henrik Glimstedt and Christian Kleinschmidt who responded to our invitation and completed their chapters under considerable time pressure. We would like to thank all the contributors for their positive response to our numerous suggestions during the editorial process and for their valiant attempts to write their chapters in the Routledge house style. Our gratitude also goes to Jonathan Zeitlin for his support and suggestions, Ann Prior who helped with the language editing of several chapters and to the Møre Research Centre and the Norwegian Research Council, who sponsored the editorial work of Ove Bjarnar, namely two trips to Reading.

Matthias Kipping came up with the idea of organising a conference on the productivity drive and put together the list of participants for this volume. But neither the conference nor this book would have ever seen the light of day without the involvement and the collaboration of Ove Bjarnar who was at the University of Reading as a Visiting Fellow in 1996. Ove Bjarnar would like to thank all those who made it possible for him to spend a year in Reading, namely the Norwegian Research Council, which provided financial support under the Coastal and Rural Development Programme, and the Centre for Business History at the Norwegian School of Management, which generously facilitated the necessary contacts with the CIBH. On behalf of himself and his family, a special thanks goes to all his colleagues in Reading, especially to an excellent and supportive host, Geoffrey Jones, and his secretary at the time, Lynn Cornell.

Matthias Kipping and Ove Bjarnar

ABBREVIATIONS

AACP	Anglo-American Council on Productivity
BDI	Bundesverband der Deutschen Industrie
BPC	British Productivity Council
BSI	British Standards Institute
CED	Committee for Economic Development
CEIF	Council of European Industrial Federations
ECA	Economic Co-operation Administration
ECSC	European Coal and Steel Community
EPA	European Productivity Agency
ERP	European Recovery Programme
FBI	Federation of British Industries
IRI	Istituto per la Ricostruzione Industriale
JTUAC	Joint Trade Union Advisory Council
MH	Materials Handling
MSA	Mutual Security Agency
MTM	Method–Time–Measurement
NAM	National Association of Manufacturers of the United States
NICB	National Industrial Conference Board
NMC	National Management Council
NPC	National Productivity Centre
NPI	Norwegian Productivity Institute
OECD	Organisation for Economic Co-operation and Development
OEEC	Organisation for European Economic Co-operation
OSP	Off-Shore Procurement
RBP	Restrictive Business Practice
SEEA	Swedish Engineering Employers' Association
SME	Small and Medium-sized Enterprise
SMWU	Swedish Metal Workers' Union
SQC	Statistical Quality Control
USTA&P	United States Technical Assistance and Productivity Programme

1

THE MARSHALL PLAN AND THE TRANSFER OF US MANAGEMENT MODELS TO EUROPE

An introductory framework

Ove Bjarnar and Matthias Kipping

Over the last decade, the transfer of management models across national borders has attracted considerable attention both in academic research and from policy makers. This interest was initially triggered by attempts to transfer apparently successful Japanese management practices to the United States and Western Europe.[1] The current transition in Central and Eastern Europe from a centrally planned to a market driven economy provides another example of such a transfer, highlighting both its problems and its crucial importance. In the long run, once foreign advice and funding have ceased, the development of local managerial skills, the establishment of sound industrial relations and, sometimes, the support of local as well as national authorities will determine to a large extent the outcome of the transformation process. But, as recent OECD studies show, public authorities in many Western European countries also place great emphasis on the transfer of technological and managerial know-how. Over the last few years, many governments have established specific programmes to facilitate such a transfer.[2]

None of these efforts, however, not even those currently under way in the former Eastern bloc, can rival the European Recovery Programme, or ERP, more widely known as the Marshall Plan. On 5 June 1947, US Secretary of State George C. Marshall announced the intention of the United States to help European countries overcome the consequences of the Second World War. In addition to providing immediate relief and funding for reconstruction, the ERP aimed at improving the productivity of European industry through the transfer of American technology and managerial know-how. Because of their unmatched scale and scope as well as the wealth of available information, the

Marshall Plan and the productivity drive provide a unique opportunity to study the transfer of management models across national borders in depth.

Our volume will undertake such a study, focusing on the one hand on the role of the different institutions, channels and actors involved in the transfer, and on the other on the resulting changes in different industries, companies and regions. It will highlight the diversity of US management models and, at the same time, the wide range of responses across Western Europe. It will also help to understand the mechanisms of both the transfer process and the translation of these new models into practice. Against this background, the purpose of this introductory chapter is threefold. First, it gives an overview of the current state of research on the Marshall Plan and the productivity drive. Second, it introduces some key concepts which will allow us to identify and compare patterns of Americanisation across a number of cases. Third, it briefly summarises each of the following chapters and their contribution to the overall research question.

A new research perspective

The declared intention of the Marshall Plan was to remedy acute shortages in the participating countries and to provide means for reconstruction which would make Europe eventually independent of US assistance. From the outset, however, these motives were questioned in the context of the beginning of the Cold War, especially when the Soviet Union decided not to participate in the aid programme and forced its satellites to do the same. In April 1948, the remaining Western European countries established the Organisation for European Economic Co-operation, or OEEC, designed to distribute ERP funds and to co-ordinate national plans for reconstruction.

As a consequence, much of the earlier academic discussion concentrated on the political motives and political implications of the Marshall Plan.[3] It concerned not only the voluntary, or possibly wanted, exclusion of the Soviet Union, but also the pivotal role of West German reconstruction, which was resented in some of the allied countries. The economic consequences of the ERP, on the other hand, have received attention rather belatedly. In this respect, the debate has focused largely on macroeconomic aspects, especially the importance of US financial assistance for the rapid recovery of Western Europe in general and the German 'economic miracle' in particular. Regarding the latter, a long debate opposed and continues to oppose those who see the Marshall Plan as a key factor for the postwar growth in West Germany with others who argue that most conditions for this expansion had been in place earlier.[4] Alan Milward has in turn even questioned the significance of the ERP as a whole, highlighting instead the crucial importance of West Germany as a trading partner for the other European countries.[5]

Research on the impact of the Marshall Plan at the microeconomic level started much later. This research is largely based on the so-called Technical

Assistance Programme, and has been facilitated recently by the opening of the relevant archival material in the United States.[6] Between 1948 and 1958, several thousand missions with participants from industry, labour and government from all the OEEC countries visited the United States to explore the reasons for the superior performance of its economy. At the same time, a large number of American experts and consultants toured European factories in order to identify the causes and possible remedies for the apparent productivity gap between the United States and Europe. In 1953, a European Productivity Agency, or EPA, was established to co-ordinate these efforts.[7]

So far, most of the research has remained on the level of 'ideology' rather than the practical implementation of the US model. Especially concerning the alleged superiority of US management, several authors have noted the enthusiasm of the returning visitors and the subsequent diffusion of American managerial terminology and fashions.[8] More recent work has, however, questioned the alleged ease with which these were disseminated in Europe. Richard Kuisel, for example, who has studied the reports of the French productivity missions to the United States in detail, points out that a majority of missionaries considered the application of the American experience in France to be unfeasible or even 'undesirable'.[9] Jonathan Zeitlin has highlighted the rather hostile reaction of many British engineers and managers towards American-style mass production, both before and after the Second World War. In the few available case studies, it appears indeed that US technology and, more importantly, the American methods of shop floor organisation encountered significant resistance in European firms.[10]

These authors have so far concentrated almost exclusively on mass production and Fordism, which they perceive as the core of Americanisation.[11] Only recently have they started to examine the transfer and implementation of what they see as the American mass production model and its related elements to Japan and Europe in more detail.[12] However, at the moment, there is only one element of the American model, management education, where the transfer process as well as its outcome have been studied in depth. Robert Locke was the first to show how the existing educational traditions shaped the speed and the extent to which US-type business schools and general management as a subject were introduced in Britain, Germany and France after the Second World War.[13] His work has been followed by a number of more detailed studies on the evolution of management education in Europe which also included other countries and highlighted the role of non-governmental institutions, such as the Ford Foundation, in the attempted transfer of the US model.[14]

However, without questioning the crucial role of management education, we should not forget that it is only one among many other possible transfer mechanisms and that even the introduction of US-type business schools tells us in the end very little about the actual adoption of American management models in different industrial or service sectors, companies or regions. It seems

3

therefore appropriate and necessary to focus our attention on a much wider range of institutions, channels and actors involved in the possible Americanisation of European business, and to study the response to the US management models in a number of cases in depth.

The transfer of management models

The transfer of organisational innovations and learning from best practices is a complicated process, especially when it occurs between different countries. The following section will suggest a few basic concepts for the analysis of the transfer of management and organisational models as part of the attempted Americanisation of European business after the Second World War.

Our aim is not to provide a comprehensive theoretical framework, but to put forward some key concepts which can be helpful in identifying the lessons from the different case studies in this volume. Taken together, these individual cases thus contribute to an enhanced understanding of the entire process of knowledge transfer, from the sources of managerial know-how to the receiving end, be it whole sectors, companies or regions. In order to facilitate a tighter integration of the case studies, three concepts seem to be of special value: the *channels* or *conduits* used in the transfer; the actual transfer *process*, namely the role of the sender and receiver; and, last but not least, the *translation* or *transformation* of the information received into practice.

Transfer channels

This rather complex concept is widely used in the literature on the diffusion of innovations. Diffusion can be defined as 'the process by which an innovation is communicated through certain channels over time among members of a social system. It is a special kind of communication, in that the messages are concerned with new ideas.'[15] Channels are connecting actors and institutions in such a way that messages are communicated between them. Mass media channels for example, are useful in creating knowledge of innovations, 'whereas interpersonal channels are more effective in forming and changing attitudes towards the new idea, and thus influencing the decision to adopt or reject a new idea.'[16]

Comprehensive studies have established a typology of the different intermediaries, or 'linkers', and their interplay in the diffusion process.[17] Among these linking roles, three prove especially useful in the context of this book. There are first the so-called *conveyors*. They intervene in the transfer of knowledge from its producers, such as researchers and experts, to its users. Such a role can be carried out, for example, by agents, trainers, demonstrators, system engineers, scientific experts and teachers. *Consultants* on the other hand, are seen to assist users in the identification of problems, in establishing a link with the appropriate resources for their solution and in the implementation of this solution. Thus, they act primarily as 'change agents', which includes the roles of facilitators, objective observers and process analysts. An especially prominent position in the diffusion process can be attributed to the *leaders* who are executives either of companies, whether in the private or public sector, or of trade associations. Unlike conveyors or consultants, they are 'insiders' in the receiving system, and as such not only have a powerful influence on their own organisation, but can also provide an important example for others.

These 'linkers' have to be seen as part of *social networks* which influence and determine their relationships to both producers/senders and users/receivers of knowledge. It is therefore crucial in the analyses of the transfer process to go beyond anonymous institutions and structures and include the study of informal personal relationships and contacts, the role of reference groups as well as the social strategies pursued by different actors at different stages in the dissemination and adoption process. For example, the extent of the social network of a manager, rather than his or her formal position, might be a key factor for the introduction of new management models in a company. Similarly, a small but socially and politically influential group can pave the way for a widespread diffusion of technological or organisational know-how in a given country or region.[18]

On the other hand, it is important to note that not only actors but also companies and institutions play an important role in the transfer process. Multinationals or trading companies, for example, play significant roles in disseminating management know-how across national borders, notably by acting as successful examples in their host countries.[19] The same is true for global providers of professional services such as accountants or management consultants who try to implement similar models and techniques worldwide.[20] In this context, it should be noted that companies in certain countries sometimes play the role of intermediaries, 'translating' American methods into 'European terms' and thus facilitating their wide-spread dissemination across the Continent.[21]

When it comes to the role of institutions, these can act as channels themselves or, more importantly, facilitate the establishment of direct contacts between the different actors involved in the transfer process. In this respect, American initiatives for the creation of both national and transnational institutions in the immediate postwar period played a unique and innovative role. During the 1950s, institutions such as the National Productivity Centres or the European Productivity Agency brought together European opinion leaders, managers, trade union leaders, professionals, teachers and so on. In this way, they certainly facilitated the transfer of management models, not only from the United States to Europe, but also between different European countries.

The transfer process

Recent research has highlighted the role of national institutional settings in determining the outcome of the diffusion of American-inspired ideas. Any successful Americanisation depended on the strength of the US efforts and on the institutional circumstances in recipient countries open to American ideas.[22] The nation state is seen as a so-called 'structured setting' for a variety of solutions, driven by political, economic, technological and institutional factors. These factors determined whether the US models were transmitted at all, and also influenced the extent of their adoption. Moreover, the national institutions allowed countries to take part actively in the transfer process by searching for new knowledge themselves, by selecting what should be transferred and by adapting it to the national systemic context.[23]

Detailed studies within the field of management education have highlighted the role of institutional constraints and opportunities at a national level, in order to understand why imported ideas are absorbed differently in different national contexts.[24] When it comes to the transfer of US management models after the Second World War, the same is likely to apply to a variety of institutional forces at the national or regional level. These range from politically or ideologically motivated hostility towards 'anything American' to nationally determined frameworks for wage determination. At the time, and probably to an even larger extent today, some of these constraints originated at an international level before being applied to the national context. This is true of, for example, the increasing liberalisation of trade and the integration of markets in Europe.

In addition, studies of the diffusion of innovations argue that it is possible to identify decentralised dissemination systems within the national, regional or local context, where adoption decisions concerning an innovation are more widely shared by clients and potential adopters, and where horizontal networks among the clients are the main mechanism through which innovations spread.[25] It is important to note, however, that decentralised systems and networks do not exclude conflicts of interest and power struggles at the various levels.

While not disputing the value of an analysis at an international, national or regional level, this volume shows that actors, whether individuals or organisations, played an important part in determining the outcome of the transfer process. Actors were not compelled to 'buy' one big American model. Instead, it seems that they tried to pick up specific techniques from an ideologically defined 'American' set of models and attempted to mould them into existing institutions and business practices. As a matter of fact, the 'grand' political and institutional level seems to have played a less significant role in this process than the social relations and networks of actors. Together, these factors will help explain why quite similar processes had rather different outcomes, for example in different companies within the same industry.

Thus, most of the contributions in this volume will demonstrate that the real struggle over Americanisation took place at the transformation stage. Many elements in the transfer process came together at this point; international inspirations as well as national and local institutional arrangements were mixed with ideological and political concerns. All affected the individual actors or organisations and influenced their different linking roles in different channels. The crucial question of applicability was often decided when it actually came to the transformation of US-inspired models or techniques into practice.

Translation and transformation

Recent analyses of the diffusion of management methods from Japan to the West, including both the study of successful Japanese practices by Western firms and the active learning that goes with their implementation, suggest that the outcome of the transfer process is related to how ideas or models are 'packaged' and to the demand or supply driven nature of the transfer process.[26] The distance between the sender and the receiver is not only geographical but also mental, due to differences in culture, society and history as well as strategic paradigms. The distance can be reduced if concepts, models, tools, propositions and illustrative examples are packaged in a way which makes them applicable to the receiver. By interpreting and applying the different elements of the package over several 'learning cycles', the receiver gradually translates these into the national or local context and actual practice. As a result, the foreign model becomes part of the local learning process.

Management tools with very clear-cut applications which require very little packaging can simply be copied from one country to another. Such simple copying is not possible, however, with more complex managerial and organisational models. Thus the widespread failure of Western companies to implement Japanese management methods can be explained as the result of simplistically copying, imitating or translating complex organisational models into a context dominated by very different management paradigms and principles.[27]

Concerning the nature of the transfer and translation processes, they will never be predominantly demand or supply driven, but will emerge as context-specific blends of both elements. These concepts are nevertheless important, because they help clarify terms like 'active receivers'. Transfers of complex models are likely to take place more effectively when an active exporter is faced with an active importer.[28] Efforts at both ends will influence the applicability and the actual implementation of these models. Accordingly, the extent to which the transfer process is demand and/or supply driven plays an important role in its outcome. As many of the case studies in this volume will show, actors, organisations or companies searched for those American-inspired models which they considered helpful in solving problems defined locally, or useful in pursuing their *own* strategies and ambitions.

The role of these actors is also important when it comes to the barriers that might slow down, obstruct or prevent the transfer of knowledge between two systems.[29] These barriers can result from the personal or social implications of the required changes on individuals, and from interpersonal problems between those involved in the transfer process. However excellent or objectively superior a new idea might be, it will be difficult to introduce if it challenges the status of an established business leader, for example. In addition, those not involved in the transfer process directly but concerned with its outcome, in our case namely the middle managers and workers, may play an important role for the adoption or rejection of US management models.

It therefore seems no longer possible to sustain a view according to which American models were transferred from the United States in an 'imperialistic' fashion, imposed on passive receivers. Individual actors and organisations involved in this process actually played an important role, not only as channels for the transfer, but also for its outcome, because the content of what was intended to be transferred was based to a large extent on their perception and choice.

In this respect, it seems likely that the set of choices was not unrestricted, neither in a demand nor in a supply driven process after 1945. At the end of the war, the United States had become the predominant political and economic power, a sort of 'reference society'.[30] The American economic power was apparently largely based on mass production and management as a science, defined later by scholars as a seemingly superior model of managerial, competitive capitalism.[31] While not necessarily an accurate reflection of reality, perceptions of American superiority in these areas must have influenced actors, organisations and institutions in recipient countries, limiting the range of options and models at hand.[32]

The different contributions within this framework

Through an analysis which incorporates the basic concepts outlined above, we will be able to understand how and to what extent US management models were modified and moulded into the existing institutions and traditions in the receiving countries, regions, industries and companies. The contributions in this volume analyse all of the different stages in the transfer and diffusion process, from the origins of the US models to their actual implementation. The individual chapters differ nevertheless in that they highlight specific aspects of the apparent Americanisation of European business, which makes it possible to group them according to the three concepts of *channel*, *process* and *translation*.

In this framework, the contribution of Jacqueline McGlade stands out, as her chapter (Chapter 2) deals exclusively with the perspective of the sender, the United States. McGlade studies in depth the political and institutional context of the postwar American aid policy and shows how the productivity drive emerged from an intricate and complex set of factional struggles over the content and objectives of American assistance to Western Europe. One of the key questions was whether it should concentrate on the simple reconstruction or focus on the reform of European business. In the end, the Marshall Plan came to offer European industry financial assistance as well as know-how.

At the same time, however, the political struggle in the United States about the objectives of American aid overshadowed possible conflicts over the underlying models to be exported. This became abundantly clear in 1949, when the productivity drive was formalised and institutionalised into a massive attempt to export American-inspired productivity and management models, creating a substantial push. Nevertheless, this new supply-driven phase inherited the diversity of objectives from the process leading to its formation. Thus, the detailed picture of the sender perspective presented by McGlade demonstrates that even after adopting a more active stance in 1949, the Americans could hardly have pushed either a homogenous set of objectives or one specific US model through any of the channels at their disposal.

Transfer mechanisms and channels

The following four chapters deal with the role of institutions, whether transnational, national or regional, business leaders and multinational companies as channels in the diffusion of US management models.

In his study of the European Productivity Agency, or EPA, Bent Boel highlights the ambiguous character of the objectives and ideas embedded in the 'politics of productivity', as they were perceived in the recipient countries (Chapter 3). While the creation of the EPA and most of its initial programmes were strongly influenced by the Americans, the institution never became an important channel for the diffusion of US management models. At the same time however, the Agency acted as a catalyst and facilitator for a wide range of transfer mechanisms. Many channels and informal networks between business or labour representatives, experts in various areas and politicians, both between Europe and the United States as well as within Europe, gravitated around the EPA. Thus, while weak and divided at an institutional level, the EPA helped create or support a variety of channels which contributed to spreading American models, notably in the areas of productivity, management education and industrial relations.

This need to discriminate between different channels and different levels is illuminated further in the detailed study of the so-called 'Operation Impact' by Matthias Kipping (Chapter 4). This unique and large-scale operation was carefully designed to convert European business leaders to an all-encompassing American creed. While correct in identifying top managers and industry representatives as possible catalysts for the diffusion of the productivity gospel in Western Europe, the Americans underestimated the potential problems in such a process. In trying to convince representatives from the very upper echelons of European business about the superiority of the US model of capitalism, the organisers challenged influential people, not primarily as business executives, but first and foremost as leaders in their national institutional settings and social networks.

Ultimately, a number of inter-system barriers as well as intra-system barriers were activated. For example, it proved impossible to find a solution for one of the fundamental questions concerning the first type of barriers mentioned, namely to find a common 'language' for translating the American ideas. Furthermore, the European delegates could easily reject US efforts to 'sell' American industrial relations and business practices with the argument that they were not, or not yet, applicable in Europe. As a result, the necessary consensus between the sender and the recipient was not established around the core elements of a transferable American management model, but around a vague, transatlantic 'community of values'. At the same time, Kipping highlights the diversity of opinion about some of the elements of the US model within European business, notably concerning cartels and competition, which was not reflected in the select group of European representatives participating in 'Operation Impact'.

The necessity to decompose the transfer mechanisms and channels is further highlighted by the next two contributions. In Chapter 5, John Dunning focuses on the UK subsidiaries of American multinationals in the manufacturing industries. Through close contact with their parent companies, these subsidiaries were constantly exposed to American management models. However, they experienced and adopted these not as one grand design but as a number of specific techniques, including for example the organisation of production, accounting standards, personnel policies and marketing methods. As a result, the continuous relationship between the subsidiaries and their US parents provided a very effective direct channel for the transfer of the latest American management know-how. But even if some independent UK companies imitated these subsidiaries, this channel seems to have been of limited influence for the wider diffusion of US management models in Britain, since it did not challenge British management culture and business traditions on a larger scale. In a broader context, as revealed by Tomlinson and Tiratsoo (see below), the Americanisation of British industry as a whole cannot necessarily be considered a success story.

In Chapter 6, based on examples from the Møre and Romsdal region in Norway, Rolv Petter Amdam and Ove Bjarnar highlight the complexity of the transfer process and especially the interplay between different diffusion channels. At a regional level, a variety of channels were activated in the dissemination of productivity models through a long lasting process. Facing an industrial structure in Norway with a comprehensive SME (small and medium-sized enterprises) sector, one important strategy of the Norwegian Productivity Institute or NPI, set up in 1953, was to introduce productivity models that would enable this sector to achieve economies of scale by applying a model of business networking between independent firms. Opening up a business networking channel thus appeared as an important step in the diffusion process in the 1950s and no doubt the Americans had a substantial influence at this stage via their role in establishing the NPI.

Since much of the SME sector was located in the different regions, this strategy had already in the 1950s connected the national productivity drive to regional preferences, not the least by setting up a number of local branches of the NPI. This process accelerated in the 1960s, when regional political concerns acquired a growing importance in the general industrial and welfare policy. By disseminating productivity efforts through a local municipality cooperative channel and, increasingly, an educational channel at regional level, both the networking strategy and the concept of productivity were widened. On the one hand, this strengthened the productivity drive as a movement in its own right, strongly influenced by national and regional institutions as well as the – earlier – American inspiration. On the other hand, the productivity movement as a distinctive institutional framework was weakened, since productivity-enhancing efforts were included into other policy areas. The decline of the productivity drive in Norway in the 1970s was partly rooted in this paradox.

The transfer process

The next three contributions focus mostly on the process of diffusion of different elements of the American management model. They highlight the role of the context and potential barriers influencing the adoption of specific managerial techniques.

Jim Tomlinson and Nick Tiratsoo demonstrate that an improvement in the productivity of British industry did not necessarily require the adoption of American-style mass production (Chapter 7). Instead, British productivity missions identified a number of management techniques, such as standardisation, statistical quality control and materials handling, which could have been adopted in Britain with little effort and expense. However, while the usefulness of these techniques was widely recognised, later studies clearly show that they had been introduced only to a very limited extent.

Neither an alleged lack of competition, nor the fragmentation of export markets together with the domination of the Commonwealth, nor the character of the governmental response seem to offer a sufficient explanation for this puzzle. The two most important reasons for the apparent failure of British industry to successfully introduce simple and marginal improvements probably lie in the transfer process and the nature of the recipient culture and environment. Although the British received a lot of information on productivity, Tomlinson and Tiratsoo show that the transfer mechanisms were in fact rather weakly developed. The management culture in British industry was, furthermore, not particularly receptive to new management ideas. The two factors combined explain the weak demand for managerial innovations in Britain and a supply side which was not able to establish viable transfer channels and mechanisms. The failure of Americanisation of British industry appears therefore largely as a story of an insufficiently structured transfer process.

Henrik Glimstedt's analysis of the Americanisation process at the Swedish truck and car producer Volvo (Chapter 8) also highlights the need to see the outcome of the transfer process as a result of the process itself. His chapter focuses on the attempts to implement a system of payment by results of US origin, the so-called Method–Time–Measurement or MTM system at Volvo. While motivated by a changing competitive environment, the MTM system came in to conflict with strong perceptions of good Swedish engineering practice and, later on, a strategy based on the production of high-quality and safe cars. In addition, by introducing the MTM system more or less single-handedly, Volvo challenged existing industrial relations within the company and the framework within which wages were usually set. As a result, a number of labour and employers' organisations and associations became involved in the transfer process.

But, despite considerable resistance from these institutions, Volvo succeeded in introducing the MTM system and seemed to be a fairly 'Americanised' company in the late 1950s. However, the detailed analysis reveals a picture of unevenness and ambiguous responses. One of the main conclusions to be drawn from Glimstedt's chapter is that the Americanisation at Volvo was never an in-depth process. Beyond the superficial Americanisation, we can see actors who managed to find a formula combining US inspiration with Swedish traditions, which allowed Volvo to merge high-quality products, value-added production and socio-technical approaches to strategy formation. A closer look at the transfer process, therefore, highlights the limits of Americanisation at Volvo that would otherwise probably not have been identified.

The contribution of David Ellwood (Chapter 9) adds to this picture of the complexity of the transfer process. It also highlights the importance of discriminating between the different levels of channels in which actors were operating. Ellwood demonstrates how the political debate about the Marshall Plan and the 'politics of productivity' was somewhat removed from the transformation level in the Italian region of Emilia–Romagna. At a policy level, the perceptions of the receivers were characterised by a mixture of support and hostility. On the one hand, this case study of a communist-dominated region suggests that the American authorities in Italy concentrated on building the 'myth' of the Marshall Plan and an allegedly superior US model rather than providing actual assistance. Most of their practical suggestions seemed in fact rather inappropriate for this region, characterised as it was by agriculture and small and medium-sized enterprises (SMEs). On the other hand, Ellwood shows that these SMEs nevertheless managed to take advantage of the

American aid and the productivity drive. However, it would be mistaken to speak of full-scale Americanisation in Emilia–Romagna. As in the cases of Norway or Volvo for example, traditions at the micro level interacted with changing market opportunities and different institutions in a way that enabled a selective use of American funding and a partial application of US management models.

Translation and transformation

In many ways, the ultimate test for the real extent of the Americanisation of European business can be found at the company level where the actual transformation and implementation of US management models took place. The final three chapters in this volume provide in-depth case studies at this level.

Christian Kleinschmidt's study of the Vereinigte Glanzstoff Fabriken AG in the 1950s (Chapter 10) reveals a largely demand-driven search for applicable American models of production and organisation at this major West German textile producer. Kleinschmidt makes it clear that the company had shown a keen interest in American product innovations, production technology and market developments from the 1920s, which was slowed down but never completely submerged by the autarchic Nazi policy and the war. After 1945, Glanzstoff copied many elements of the American model, following closely its competitors in the United States.

The company's management acted on the belief that West Germany would eventually become very similar to the American example and, in doing so, might have accelerated such a tendency. At the same time, the company maintained a certain distance to the US model and adopted American techniques rather pragmatically. Overall, this case study highlights the key role of individual leaders as actors in the transformation process, and the effect of long-term personal and inter-company relations and networks. Not unexpectedly, in terms of Americanisation, the company and its leadership exercised an influence which extended well beyond Glanzstoff into the West German business community as a whole, notably regarding further training for existing managers.

Both the long-term perspective and the crucial role of individuals are further elaborated in the contribution of Ludovic Cailluet, who analyses the Americanisation of the French aluminium and chemicals producer Pechiney (Chapter 11). Cailluet clearly shows that the company had entertained close relations with its American counterparts from the late nineteenth century. The first actual transfer of American managerial know-how occurred, however, only in the 1930s with the implementation of scientific management, assisted by a consultant. Similarly, in the immediate post-1945 period, Pechiney used another US consultant for a complete overhaul of their corporate organisation. The process of Americanisation at Pechiney therefore appears to have been largely demand driven. At the same time, the actual translation of the different American models into management practice was controlled by the company itself. A few actors were in fact able to play the roles of leaders within Pechiney and of conveyors in a wider national context, because of their central positions in the relevant networks. Within the company, they operated a selection process, helping to adapt the US management models to the specific circumstances.

The role of individual actors and wider networks is also highlighted in the contribution of Ruggero Ranieri (Chapter 12). At the same time, he demonstrates that Americanisation at the Italian public sector steel producer Finsider extended well beyond the adoption of large-scale production technology from the United States. While this dimension appears predominant at the origins of the Americanisation process, other elements of the US model were copied subsequently, namely corporate organisation and industrial relations practices. The extent to which these were implemented resulted from a close co-operation between Finsider management and an American steel producer. At the same time, the company executives also occupied a central position within the national framework, which enabled them to access US sources of funding and technology and to fend off considerable opposition from other, privately owned parts of the Italian steel industry. The strength of their position both at a micro and a macro level allowed these actors to fulfil the roles of leaders, conveyors and consultants in the Americanisation process.

The long-term development within the Italian steel industry reveals an apparent paradox, however. The speed and the comprehensiveness of the Americanisation process was one of its major strengths, but was at the same time one of its greatest disadvantages in that it eventually challenged established traditions, market relations and institutional settings in a very fundamental way. Thus, the most Americanised among the companies analysed in this volume was also perhaps the least successful.

It appears indeed that the ultimate success of the Americanisation process resulted from a selective and partial adaptation of different elements of the US management model rather than a fully-fledged adoption. In this respect, the case studies in the book provide a new and enhanced understanding of both the strength and the limits of the Americanisation of European business.

Acknowledgements

The authors would like to thank Patrick Fridenson, Hallgeir Gammelsæter and Jonathan Zeitlin for helpful comments and suggestions on an earlier draft of this introductory chapter. The usual disclaimer applies.

Notes

1 See, for example, M. Kenney and R. Florida, *Beyond Mass Production. The Japanese System and its Transfer to the U.S.*, New York, The Free Press, 1993.

2 For example, OECD, *Impacts of National Technology Programmes*, Paris, 1995; and OECD, *Boosting Business Advisory Services*, Paris, 1995.
3 It is impossible to mention even a small part of the vast literature on the Marshall Plan. For recent overviews, see C.S. Maier (ed.), *The Marshall Plan and Germany*, New York, Berg, 1991, especially his introduction; and C.S. Maier (ed.), *The Cold War in Europe*, Princeton, Markus Wiener, 1996.
4 K. Borchardt and C. Buchheim, 'The Marshall Plan and Key Economic Sectors: A Microeconomic Perspective', in Maier (ed.), *The Marshall Plan*, pp. 410–51; W. Abelshauser, 'American Aid and West German Economic Recovery: A Macroeconomic Perspective', ibid., pp. 367–409.
5 A.S. Milward, *The Reconstruction of Western Europe 1945–1951*, Berkeley, University of California Press, 2nd edn, 1987; and A.S. Milward, *The European Rescue of the Nation-State*, London, Routledge, 1992.
6 See the contributions in M. Lévy-Leboyer and René Girault (eds), *Le plan Marshall et le relèvement économique de l'Europe*, Paris, CHEFF, 1993; J. McGlade, *The Illusion of Consensus: American Business, Cold War Aid and the Reconstruction of Western Europe 1948–1958*, unpublished PhD dissertation, George Washington University, Washington DC, 1995; and, as a background, C.S. Maier, 'The Politics of Productivity: Foundations of American International Economic Policy after World War II', *International Organization*, Fall 1977, vol. 31, pp. 607–33, reprinted in various volumes.
7 International Cooperation Administration, *European Productivity and Technical Assistance Programs: A Summing Up (1948–1958)*, Paris, 1958.
8 For example, L. Boltanski, *The Making of a Class: Cadres in French Society*, Cambridge, Cambridge University Press, 1987, pp. 97–144; A.B. Carew, *Labour under the Marshall Plan: The Politics of Productivity and the Marketing of Management Science*, Manchester, Manchester University Press, 1987; R.F. Kuisel, *Seducing the French: The Dilemma of Americanization*, Berkeley, University of California Press, 1993, pp. 70–102.
9 ibid.; and R.F. Kuisel, 'The Marshall Plan in Action: Politics, Labor, Industry and the Program of Technical Assistance', in Lévy-Leboyer and Girault (eds), *Le plan Marshall*, pp. 335–58.
10 J. Zeitlin, 'Americanization and Its Limits: Theory and Practice in the Reconstruction of Britain's Engineering Industries, 1945–55', *Business and Economic History*, Fall 1995, vol. 24, no. 1, pp. 277–86; V. Guigueno, 'L'éclipse de l'atelier. Les missions françaises de productivité aux Etats-Unis dans les années 1950', unpublished DEA dissertation, Ecole Nationale des Ponts et Chaussées – Université de Marne-la-Vallée, 1994.
11 This has to be seen as part of a debate about the move from mass production to flexible specialisation, initiated by M.J. Piore and C.F. Sabel, *The Second Industrial Divide: Possibilities for Prosperity*, New York, Basic Books, 1984.
12 Papers presented at a conference on 'Americanization and its Limits: Responses to US Technology and Management in Postwar Europe and Japan', organised by Jonathan Zeitlin and Gary Herrigel at the University of Madison-Wisconsin in March 1997. Most of these papers, to be published in a volume with the same title, dealt with the steel, automobile and mechanical engineering industries.
13 R.R. Locke, *Management and Higher Education since 1940: The Influence of America and Japan on West Germany, Great Britain, and France*, Cambridge, Cambridge University Press, 1989; for a summary, see R.R. Locke, 'Educational Traditions and the Development of Business Studies after 1945: An Anglo-French-German Comparison', *Business History*, January 1988, vol. 30, no. 1, pp. 84–103.
14 R.P. Amdam (ed.), *Management, Education and Competitiveness: Europe, Japan and the*

United States, London, Routledge, 1996; T. Gourvish and N. Tiratsoo (eds), *Missionaries and Managers: United States Technical Assistance and European Management Education, 1945–1960*, Manchester, Manchester University Press, 1998; V. Zamagni and L. Engwall (eds), *Management Education in an Historical Perspective*, Manchester, Manchester University Press, forthcoming.

15 E.M. Rogers, *Diffusion of Innovations*, New York, The Free Press, 4th edn, 1995, p. 5.

16 ibid.

17 See especially R.G. Havelock *et al.*, *Planning for Innovation: A Comparative Study of the Literature on the Dissemination and Utilization of Scientific Knowledge*, Ann Arbor, University of Michigan, 1969, chapter 7; for an overview see also P. Fridenson, 'La circulation internationale des modes manageriales', in J.-P. Bouilloud and B.-P. Lecuyer (eds), *L'invention de la gestion. Histoire et pratiques*, Paris, L'Harmattan, 1994, pp. 81–9.

18 Such aspects are analysed in different kinds of literature, for a few examples see Havelock, *Planning for Innovation*; Rogers, *Diffusion of Innovations*; and M.F. Guillén, *Models of Management: Work, Authority and Organization in a Comparative Perspective*, Chicago, The University of Chicago Press, 1994.

19 G. Jones, *The Evolution of International Business*, London, Routledge, 1996, chapter 7.

20 There are, however, indications that they have at least partially adapted their services to the national context in which they operate; see M. Kipping, 'The U.S. Influence on the Evolution of Management Consultancies in Britain, France, and Germany since 1945', *Business and Economic History*, Fall 1996, vol. 25, no. 1, pp. 112–23.

21 For example, for the 'translation' of statistical quality control methods by the British during the Second World War, subsequently used by French industry, see P. Fridenson, 'Fordism and Quality: The French Case', in H. Shiomi and K. Wada (eds), *Fordism Transformed*, Oxford, Oxford University Press, 1996.

22 Guillén, *Models of Management*.

23 There is, however, a long-standing debate in the academic literature between those who argue that the outcome of this process will be a convergence among these practices, due to the imitation of institutions and organisations perceived as successful, and others who highlight the role of the national context in shaping the adoption of new managerial models and thus helping to maintain and even reinforce the existing differences. For an example of the former see W.W. Powell and P.J. DiMaggio, *The New Institutionalism in Organizational Analysis*, Chicago, The University of Chicago Press, 1991; for the latter, among many others, R. Whitley and P.H. Kristensen (eds), *Governance at Work: The Social Regulation of Economic Relations*, Oxford, Oxford University Press, 1997.

24 Amdam (ed.), *Management, Education*, pp. 10–11.

25 Rogers, *Diffusion of Innovations*, p. 7.

26 P. Lillrank, 'The Transfer of Management Innovations from Japan', *Organization Studies*, 1995, vol. 16, pp. 971–89.

27 ibid., p. 982.

28 R.H. Parker, 'Importing and Exporting Accounting: The British Experience', in A.G. Hopwood (ed.), *International Pressures for Accounting Change*, Hemel Hempstead, Prentice Hall, 1987.

29 See for details Havelock, *Planning for Innovation*. With respect to the transfer of programmes for management training and education, for example, a number of barriers are identified by R. Holtzer, *Management Education for Small and Medium-Sized Enterprises in the European Communities*, Berlin, CEDFEOP, 1989; S. Gil,

J. Allesch and D. Preiss-Allesch, *Improving SMEs Access to Training: Strategies for Success. A Report on Best Practice in EC Member States*, Berlin, CEDFEOP, 1994.

30 Guillén, *Models of Management*, p. 290. It should, however, not be forgotten that the Soviet model constituted a theoretically possible but practically excluded alternative for Western Europe. While politically very different, it was based on similar economic principles, such as mass production and Taylorism.

31 See, for example, A.D. Chandler, *Scale and Scope: The Dynamics of Industrial Capitalism*, Cambridge, MA, Harvard University Press, 1990; and W. Lazonick, *Business Organization and the Myth of the Market Economy*, Cambridge, Cambridge University Press 1991.

32 According to recent theories, actors in organisations tend to perceive new institutional models that enjoy general popularity as 'natural' and 'necessary', and as a result seldom question them openly. Therefore, new trends and 'prototypes' will frequently be adopted uncritically and become 'institutionalised'; see Powell and DiMaggio (eds), *The New Institutionalism*. However, as the contributions to our volume show, the role of conflicts of interest and power struggles as well as the influence of commitment, values and basic norms in shaping and altering institutions and organisations should not be underestimated.

2

FROM BUSINESS REFORM PROGRAMME TO PRODUCTION DRIVE

The transformation of US technical assistance to Western Europe

Jacqueline McGlade

In 1948, the administrators of the European Recovery Programme or ERP launched a new programme, the United States Technical Assistance and Productivity Programme, or USTA&P, intended to introduce American-style business practices into Western Europe. Over the next ten years, the programme would grow from exchange visits into a massive production drive aimed at European industry. When studied as a whole, the USTA&P serves as an important microcosm through which the many dramatic shifts that occurred in American aid objectives and relations with Western Europe during the early Cold War years can be examined.

Existing accounts of the USTA&P, however, tend to review the programme only in its first few years of operation or submerge it within a larger study of the ERP.[1] In addition, recent interpretations by Michael Hogan and Melvyn Leffler present the whole process of US policy making concerning postwar European aid as a synthetic, seamless event. They suggest that a consensual arrangement of American attitudes and objectives arose by 1948 and prevailed in the planning of European aid. As a result, their works fall short in explaining the complex panorama of administrative conflict, international compromise and policy change that marks the history of the USTA&P.

Instead of consensus, this chapter highlights division as the driving force in the shaping – and reshaping – of US aid policies and practices in Western Europe after the Second World War. In particular, it traces the contiguous rise of two divergent leadership factions in the early postwar years of American foreign aid policy making. While both groups saw technical assistance and productivity as an important tool by which the United States could exert greater authority over European economic affairs, they diverged sharply on the central goals and direction of its administration. Instead of converging upon the formation of the ERP in 1948, these factions continued to split apart over the appropriate path for assistance to European business, and entered into a contentious struggle for control of overseas aid. In the end, this contest not only reshaped the thrust of technical assistance into Western Europe, but also influenced the entire fabric of American government–business relations and foreign economic policy making as reconfigured by the coming of the Cold War. The roots of this struggle between the two factions can be traced to the early arrangement of American international aid policy at the end of the Second World War.

Old pundits and new prophets of international aid

In 1945, few American policy makers recognised the need to provide Western Europe with economic and technical assistance. Conservatives in the 80th US Congress paid little attention to worsening economic conditions overseas, choosing instead to concentrate on domestic issues. Despite a 'cogent plea' by State Department officials Eugene Rostow and Dean Acheson before the House Committee on Foreign Relations in early January 1945, they flatly rejected the idea that an American aid plan be drafted for the 'reconstruction of European economies'.[2] Mirroring the isolationist mood of Congress, President Truman moved to terminate all wartime aid offered under Lend-Lease and dismantled its funding agency, the Foreign Economic Administration, or FEA, in August 1945.[3] In light of such actions, US and European aid advocates lost hope, as they departed the United Nations charter meetings in the fall of 1945, that an American assistance package would be created to supplement the rapidly depleting funds of the last wartime relief agency, the UNRRA.[4]

New fears over Soviet aggression in 1946, however, cast the question of European economic recovery in a different light. In a speech on 9 February 1946, Stalin announced his intentions to build postwar Soviet recovery, not upon the foundation of international economic co-operation established by the Bretton Woods Conference and the United Nations, but through the revival of the 'Soviet social system'. US officials also watched with concern as the Soviet government extended military aid to communist groups in Poland, Romania and Hungary and refused to withdraw troops stationed in Manchuria. As noted by the historian Melvyn Leffler, the perception that Stalin had mapped out a postwar strategy for Soviet expansion based on 'opportunism' stemming from the 'systematic disintegration' of Europe 'sent shock waves through Washington'. The revelation in February 1946 that the Soviet government had formed an atomic spy ring further reinforced the resolve of the Truman White House to block any further expansion of Soviet might.[5]

It is at this point that American policy makers began to tie European economic problems to the threat of Soviet expansion. Initially, the countries of

Western Europe had seemed capable of mounting a rapid postwar recovery without additional US assistance. By December 1945, European industrial production had been restored to 60 per cent of its prewar levels. By the spring of 1946, production in France, Belgium and the Netherlands had reached nearly 90 per cent of prewar levels, with Great Britain and Norway even exceeding such levels by 10 to 15 per cent. However, severe shortages in resources and raw materials, especially coal and steel, soon plagued Western European attempts to sustain this recovery. Due to the ongoing disruptions in the British and German coal markets, European steel production fell by over 40 per cent in 1947. European farmers also faced shortages in agricultural machinery, fertilisers and manpower and, as a result, struggled to meet the growing food demands of a starving continent. A devastating winter followed by a lengthy drought in 1946–7 further crippled European agricultural production and precipitated a dramatic 20 to 30 per cent decline in cereal, grains, meat and milk supplies by the spring of 1947.[6] Stagnating financial conditions in Europe and Britain also greatly inhibited postwar recovery efforts. Wartime destruction of transatlantic shipping, tourism, export and investment markets left European nations without the revenues necessary for domestic recovery. In addition, constricted currency supplies, trade imbalances, disrupted tax bases and prolonged patterns of black market profiteering sent inflation rates spiralling upward in many countries.[7]

Despite their growing resolve, American policy makers remained badly divided in 1947 over the appropriate course of action to stem European distress and Soviet aggression. In the prewar years, the ideological and political direction of US internationalism had largely been determined by one individual, Franklin D. Roosevelt.[8] Upon Roosevelt's death in 1945, US internationalists began to splinter into two distinct camps. Led by former New Deal planners, 'progressive' businessmen and free traders, one camp espoused supra-nationalist visions of a permanent world peace achieved through global adoption of the US model, which they saw as consisting mainly of economic growth and democratic reform. By contrast, the second camp focused on national security, anti-communism and trade protection. Its proponents advocated the hegemonic advance of American power – both military and economic – as a direct counter to Soviet aggression.

While subtle, these ideological differences continued to fragment US internationalists to the point that, by 1946, a tangled web of government–business interests and associations had emerged to replace the former consensual arrangement achieved by such groups before and during the Second World War. Aligned in these new configurations, conservative internationalists tended to view postwar US foreign involvement solely in the light of political hegemony and military security, while liberal internationalists envisioned American leadership as a conduit for global social reform and unlimited economic expansion. The need for swift action in 1947 would force a brief reconciliation of these factions and lead to the creation of a new overseas aid package, the European Recovery Programme, or ERP. However, conservative and liberal internationalists continued to remain divided, sometimes violently, on the aims of the ERP and its administration after 1948. It is important to re-examine this rivalry as it acted to shape the initial direction of the ERP as a business reform programme and spur its later transformation into a military production drive.

The business reform objectives of the ERP

When the ERP was first proposed in 1947, the absence of direct Soviet military threat worked to the advantage of business progressives and liberal internationalists intent on capturing early control of the programme. Upon taking office as Secretary of State in January 1947, George Marshall had been counselled by his longtime friend and confidante Bernard Baruch 'not to be hurried by clamorous propagandists' and view the ERP as a plan for 'an economic reorganization of Europe as a whole' and not as a tool for Soviet containment. Baruch also warned Marshall that any further impasse in US–Soviet relations over postwar Allied recovery 'would react against all who want peace', and he feared the outbreak of another world war.[9]

Renowned as the 'architect of American victory' during the Second World War, Marshall had already surprised both conservative and liberal internationalists by insisting that peaceful negotiation, not military containment, served as the best defence against Soviet aggression.[10] In light of his long and distinguished military career, Marshall's repeated attempts to bring moderation into US–Soviet negotiations and policy making served as a source of frequent concern for American conservatives and hope for liberal internationalists in 1947–8. Nevertheless, Marshall initially rejected the liberal notion that an aid programme be created with the intention of sponsoring European economic and business reform. Upon leaving for the Moscow Conference of Foreign Ministers in April 1947, he had expressed strong doubts as to the effectiveness of such a European aid programme declaring that he was 'opposed to indefinite American subsidy' of foreign nations.[11] While reticent to act, Marshall also recognised that US action was necessary to stem the tragic and disturbing escalation of European economic problems.

As Marshall prepared to go to Moscow in April 1947, millions of Europeans faced starvation and death as a result of ongoing shortages in food, clothing, energy and housing. The Moscow meeting proved a historic one, as it inspired Marshall to reverse his views on overseas aid. On his trip, Marshall witnessed firsthand the misery wrought by European distress as well as the challenge posed to American world leadership by Soviet non co-operation. As a result, he abandoned the idea that the United States would be able to reach a peaceful settlement with the Soviet Union over postwar issues and moved to secure passage of a massive aid package for European recovery.

Mindful of Baruch's advice to 'let the new global sights guide you',

Marshall instructed his Policy Planning Staff in late April 1947 to draft a plan for the 'revival of the Western European economy' which concentrated on the 'deeper meaning' of the 'submerged and protracted causes of Europe's debility' beyond 'the Soviet menace'.[12] Encouraged by the non-aggressive tone of Marshall's statement, liberal internationalists lobbied hard for the adoption of economic reform as the main goal of a US aid programme to Western Europe.

Among the liberal internationalists, the so-called 'business progressives' took the lead in the autumn of 1947 in promoting the creation of a European economic aid programme. In the American business community, 'progressive' executives had first risen to prominence as supporters of Franklin Roosevelt's New Deal administration in the 1930s.[13] In 1942, these executives formed the Committee for Economic Development, or CED, which actively worked with government administrators on the formation of US economic and social policies. By doing so, the CED broke with the older, isolationist pattern of government–business relations previously established by such business groups as the National Association of Manufacturers of the United States, or NAM, and the National Industrial Conference Board, or NICB. As a result, conservative business groups like the NAM and the NICB often disagreed with the CED and its involvement in governmental matters and social issues, which were perceived as lying beyond the scope of traditional business concerns.

Seen as 'moderate, even liberal in its political outlook', the CED had nevertheless attracted to its membership 'a small business elite from all parts of the country who shared [a] broad economic vision'.[14] As CED Chairman, Studebaker Motorcar President Paul Hoffman had enticed several noted business executives to join the organisation, including Marion Folsom of Eastman Kodak, meat-packing mogul Jay Hormel, Harrison Jones of Coca-Cola, Clarence Francis of General Foods, Charles Kettering of General Motors and Will Clayton, who would later serve as a close aid to Secretary of State Marshall.[15] By 1942, the 'broad vision' shared by most CED members rested in New Deal theories on social improvement gained through greater national economic planning. Shunned and reviled by many business executives, Franklin Roosevelt and his New Deal administration eagerly embraced the support offered by the CED business progressives. As a result, the CED stood by 1945 as the strongest business lobby in American politics.

The close partnership of the CED with the Roosevelt Administration enabled many of its business supporters to attain powerful government positions during the Second World War. As wartime bureaucrats, business progressives widened their political influence through key positions on the War Production Board, or WPB, in the Foreign Economic Administration, or FEA, and as diplomats and military production co-ordinators overseas. As a result, several top CED leaders including Paul Hoffman, GE President Philip Reed, SFK Industries President William Batt and pressed metals producer William Foster stood in a position to strongly influence the direction of US foreign economic policy after 1945.

As early as the summer of 1947, these business progressives and others began to lobby hard for a European Recovery Programme that would not only restore war-torn industries but also spread US models of economic and corporate activity overseas. Progressive executives argued that recovery would come swiftly for those European countries which adopted the American economic strategy of 'liberalism of abundance', a strategy which encouraged economic growth through greater trade integration, production activities tied to expanding consumer markets, and non-intrusive government policies in support of private enterprise and its expansion.[16] Encouraged by Marshall's assertion in his Harvard address of June 1947 that US aid should serve as a 'cure, not a palliative' for overseas woes, progressive executives stepped up their efforts to frame the ERP as a business programme intended to spur an economic overhaul or 'reconstruction' of Western Europe.[17] As members of the Harriman Committee, which was formed by President Truman in the fall of 1947 to examine the European relief question and its remedy through an aid package, progressive executives remained true to their business reform agenda and succeeded in excluding from the original ERP legislation any provisions for overseas military rearmament. Wary of the liberal thrust of the ERP, conservative internationalists continued to block its passage and lobby for the inclusion of Western defence aid.

At this point, George Marshall's leadership as Secretary of State played a crucial role in re-unifying the divergent positions of internationalist groups towards the passage of the ERP. Since the summer of 1947, conservatives as well as liberals had been steadily touting Marshall as the new prophet of postwar US internationalism, casting him in the role of a global leader parallel to that of Franklin Roosevelt. When Marshall announced his support in January 1948 for the ERP, as drafted largely by the Harriman Committee, anti-Soviet opponents including his own Assistant Secretary of State, Dean Acheson, had little choice but to support the programme. Passage was finally secured in April 1948 when several key Republicans, led by Arthur Vandenburg as chair of the Senate Foreign Relations Committee, agreed to usher in the aid package.

Although an initial consensus had been forged on the ERP, conservative and liberal internationalists began to fight almost immediately over the aims of the programme and its organisation. From its outset, then, the ERP would be continually plagued by the persistent ideological divisions and political competition among the rival internationalist factions.

Business reformers and their conservative critics

The signs of conflict first re-emerged over the appointment of a director for the ERP's newly-formed administrative agency, the Economic Cooperation Administration, or ECA. The battle over the ECA Administrator provides early evidence of the ensuing disparity in official visions of the ERP and its management. When President Truman first revealed his intentions to appoint Dean Acheson, a Democrat and staunch Cold Warrior, to head up the ECA, Republicans and ERP business supporters recoiled in horror at his initial choice. Republican Senator Arthur Vandenberg went as far as to publicly voice the fear that, under Acheson, the ECA would adopt a 'Machiavellian philosophy of obstructing Soviet recovery' instead of helping 'Europeans formulate and carry out a plan for . . . genuine recovery'.[18] Upon learning of Truman's next choice, former business executive-turned State Department aide Will Clayton, Vandenburg sent a scathing complaint to George Marshall that 'it was Congress' desire' that the ERP Administrator come 'from the outside business world with strong industrial credentials and *not* via the State Department'.[19] Acting on Vandenburg's suggestion, Marshall persuaded Truman to appoint CED Chairman Paul Hoffman to serve as the founding administrator of the ECA.

From the beginning, Hoffman envisioned his new job running the ERP as that of 'an investment banker'.[20] True to his purpose, Hoffman began to fashion the ECA as a kind of 'business advisory' agency for ERP recipient nations. By 1949, Hoffman and his ECA staff would create an extraordinary array of programmes aimed at European financial reform, technical modernisation and the revival of business activity. Unfortunately, Hoffman's insistence that the ECA operate as an overseas 'economic reorganization' agency did little to satisfy the Truman White House and its push for the build-up of anti-Soviet defence in Western Europe.

In addition to setting a contradictory course for the ECA, Hoffman further alienated the Truman Administration by selecting an administrative staff committed to an economic reform agenda for the ERP. Intent on organising the ECA in a 'business-like manner', Hoffman and his staff 'induced' over 400 business, labour and government executives in less than ninety days to take part in the 'largest peacetime operation of the United States'.[21] Hoffman's economic platform and hiring biases soon drew a personal reprimand from Truman who, on 9 August 1947, warned that 'it is customary for the President to have at least [some] representation' in executive agencies such as the ECA.[22] For the next two years, Hoffman continued to aggravate the Truman Administration. His expansive personality and management style of the ECA often ran counter to government bureaucratic standards, which in turn, only added to White House frustrations over the direction of the ERP and the absence of a military rearmament programme for Western Europe.

The liberal policies forged by Hoffman and others in the ECA also upset trade protectionists within the American business community. While extremely reluctant to endorse the ERP in 1948, business protectionist groups such as the NAM and the NICB had gone along with its progressive economic agenda, mainly because of a lack of alternative strategies for the structure of the aid programme. Nevertheless, American business conservatives and protectionists continued to strongly criticise the ECA and its mission to foster

European economic recovery over military defence. The ECA's goal to build an integrated and liberalised European trade environment clashed especially with the sentiments of American business protectionists. Many executives who had anticipated lucrative profits flowing out of the ERP subsidies became deeply disturbed over ECA policies which set out to restrict, not expand, US business and export trading opportunities overseas.

In particular, protectionists voiced extreme 'concern and disappointment' over ECA export regulations aimed at the American pulp and paper, tobacco, tuna, aluminium, hand tools and livestock industries, and the placement of a 50–50 quota on all US–European shipping activities. Disgruntled business groups such as the NAM and the National Foreign Trade Council, or NFTC, accused the ECA of consciously discriminating against US transatlantic trade interests. On the whole, recession-weary producers did not understand in 1949 that the 'ERP was not designed, [nor] administered, as a vehicle for increasing American exports abroad'.[23] As a result, these business groups began criticising the ECA for fostering 'the growth of certain policies and trends in participating countries which threaten not only the success of the recovery program . . . but the creation as well of permanent barriers to an expanding world trade.'[24]

As early as 1949, then, business protectionists had rallied and emerged as persistent and ardent critics of the ERP as run by progressive executives and liberal internationalists. They soon joined forces with government officials and 'Cold Warriors' who were already concerned over the lack of anti-Soviet defence measures in the ERP. Together, business protectionists and Cold War advocates began to exert strong opposition to the economic reform agenda of the ERP. In line with such sentiments, the Truman White House took its first steps to amend the non-aggressive direction of the US foreign policy in Europe by championing the formation of the North Atlantic Treaty Organisation, or NATO, and the passage of a Military Defence Assistance Act, or MDAA, in the spring of 1949.

When initially faced with these pressures, Paul Hoffman refused to veer the ERP away from its original business reform agenda towards European remilitarization. Instead, he encouraged his aides to expand and accelerate the activities of ECA programmes involved in European business reform and reconstruction. In this way, Hoffman and others in the ECA hoped to preserve the founding spirit of the ERP – to encourage overseas industrial revival and reform through acts of European self-initiative rather than as an outcome of American aid directives. Despite the ECA's continuing commitment to European economic reform, the entire focus of the ERP and the primary arrangement of its programmes did indeed change after 1949.

While providing civilian and monetary relief had previously dominated the activities of the ECA, the political shifts in late 1949 also elevated industrial production as a central US aim for European recovery. As a result, a new array of ECA industrial assistance programmes, some of which were quite minor in importance prior to 1949, were ushered into the spotlight of the ERP. One programme in particular, the United States Technical Assistance and Productivity Programme, or USTA&P, would emerge as one of the premier vehicles in the ECA's new thrust to stimulate and expand European production.

The USTA&P and the changing emphasis of the ERP

When founded in the autumn of 1948 by a joint committee of American and British industrialists and policy makers known as the Anglo-American Council on Productivity, or AACP, the USTA&P was intended to serve as a 'goodwill' project, not as a systematic reform programme.[25] As first designed by the AACP, the principal responsibility of the USTA&P was to forge increased interaction and co-operation between American and European firms and industries. It was anticipated that USTA&P activities such as the team visits would foster the re-emergence of transatlantic business ties and serve as a stimulus for industrial reform in Europe. By the end of 1949, however, programme administrators began to rethink the co-operative focus of the USTA&P, and took steps to bring it in line with the ECA's new mandate to immediately raise European levels of industrial production.

Initially, the ECA looked to the AACP for recommendations regarding the USTA&P and its reorganisation. In a meeting in April 1949, the AACP reviewed the programme and concluded that neither the co-operative visits nor the transfer of new technologies offered under the ERP's European Industrial Projects Programme, or EIP, had managed to bridge the 'productivity gap' between the United States and Western Europe. Several AACP members had suggested that a massive drive aimed at workplace reorganisation and workforce retraining be created under the aegis of the USTA&P as a way to stimulate European business reform. In late 1949, the ECA began promoting the recommendation of the AACP that the USTA&P sponsor a greater 're-orientation' of European industry and business in line with the operation of American firms.[26] Abandoning the ideal of overseas initiative, ECA administrators adopted the alternative notion that a massive transfer of American organisational skills and management techniques was needed to stimulate and insure a 'lasting' revival of European industry. With the adoption of this 're-orientation' stance, the ECA moved to permanently dismantle the original premise of the ERP that European self-initiative, not American direction, serve as the impetus for postwar overseas industrial reform. After 1949 then, the USTA&P and other ERP programmes were retooled to support this new, more active thrust of US efforts to promote change in European industry.

In its revised phase, the USTA&P sought to directly disseminate American business practices and models of workplace relations through a variety of programme vehicles. Most notably, management and labour retraining seminars were created as a support for the existing technical assistance visits and industrial modernisation projects. In early 1950, the USTA&P, in conjunction with the National Management Council, or NMC, and several major US universities, including the Massachusetts Institute of Technology, Stanford, New York University, Columbia, Northwestern and Cal-Tech Universities, restructured the European team visits to include intensive training seminars for managers, labour leaders and business educators.[27] As a follow-up measure, American technical consultants and business advisors were also dispatched overseas to aid European managers to put into practice the techniques they had learned as USTA&P visitors. In addition the NMC, together with NAM, aided the USTA&P in launching 'Operation Impact', a programme which targeted European business leaders for reform.[28] During the next two years, over 1,000 companies in Western Europe received special funding for managers willing to attend training courses at American universities.[29]

Despite the accelerated pace of its industrial reform activities, the ECA continued to lose ground in its fight to preserve the ERP and its business reform agenda in the face of the rising tide of US Cold War conservatism. With the outbreak of the Korean War in June 1950, Hoffman and others in the ECA found that they could do little to stop American 'Cold Warriors' and business protectionists from subsuming the ERP within aid programmes such as the Mutual Defence Assistance Act, or MDAA, and the Additional Military Production Programme, or AMP, which directly supported European remilitarisation.

Beleaguered and exhausted, Paul Hoffman finally resigned in August 1950, throwing the ECA and its administration of ERP programmes into a state of confusion. As Hoffman's successor, William C. Foster, along with a small but influential group of agency officials including former MIT economics professor Richard Bissell and business executive William Batt, led a vigorous fight in the fall of 1950 to retain ECA control over the ERP and MDAA/AMP assistance programmes in Western Europe. Under Foster, ECA officials stepped up their efforts to reorient the USTA&P and other ERP programmes towards the goal of increased European military production. As an initial strategy, the ECA moved to implement new aid restrictions introduced by the Benton–Moody Amendment in July 1950. Under Benton–Moody, European governments were required to create National Productivity Centres, or NPCs, and to promote the spread of 'free enterprise' and its practices in civilian industries, particularly through the exclusion of communist trade unions, or else face a forfeit of further ERP funds. By the autumn of 1950, the ECA had pushed eleven of the sixteen ERP recipient countries to create NPCs and prohibit ERP production assistance to industries which maintained communist unions.[30]

Along with the creation of the NPCs, the ECA started a 'pilot plants' programme which extended special assistance to European firms willing to implement American management and industrial relations practices. Both the NPCs and the pilot plants programme would be managed under the watchful eye of the newly organised European Production Assistance Board, or EPAB, once staffed primarily by European administrators and now guided by ECA and Pentagon officials. The ECA also expanded the number of USTA&P management retraining visits to encompass European firms engaged in military as well as civilian production. As a further refinement, the ECA categorised all of its initiatives in the autumn of 1950 as supporting the ERP's 'new direction' – to stimulate a 'production drive' in Western Europe. Under this 'umbrella', ECA administrators hoped to facilitate the demands of NATO production as well as preserve the ERP's original reform mission towards European civilian industry.[31]

Despite such valiant efforts, the ECA finally succumbed to mounting conservative criticism and was absorbed under the State Department in late 1950. Upon 'annexation', the era in which the ECA had acted as an independent 'business agency' finally came to an end. Also, the agency lost its autonomy as the sole authority over US industrial aid and its administration in Western Europe. Under the State Department, the ECA was forced to accept the inclusion of Pentagon officials on its planning boards and as administrative agents in its overseas offices. While preparing for the final year of the ERP in the fall of 1951, a demoralised ECA staff also watched as the State Department slated many of the ERP's business reform programmes for elimination in 1952.[32] Only a few programmes would survive, including the USTA&P which, under the newly created Mutual Security Agency, or MSA, would continue to spearhead the US Cold War drive for increased European military production.

Triumphant conservatism: the MSA production drive

After the start of the Korean War, national security advocates and trade protectionists had anticipated a swift end to the extension of US assistance to overseas civilian industries. In the fall of 1950, however, American conservatives had nervously watched as the start of NATO military production triggered a devastating 30 per cent drop in the activities of European domestic manufacturing and civilian goods markets.[33] By 1951, many conservatives had become resigned to the unpleasant reality that European civilian assistance must remain as a counterbalance to production drains caused by NATO defence initiatives. As a result, the US Congress provided in late 1951 for the continuation of aid to European civilian as well as military industries under the MSA.

In its first two years of activity, the MSA took on the reactionary lustre of its Cold Warrior Director, former Republican Senator Harold E. Stassen. Under Stassen's leadership, the MSA was fashioned as an 'economic defence' bureau as outlined in the Mutual Defence Assistance Control Act, or MDAC, of 1951. Coupled with the Benton–Moody Amendment, which had prohibited communist-held foreign governments from receiving US aid, MDAC provisions further forbade 'aid to any country that knowingly permits the shipment to the Soviet Bloc of . . . strategic materials', including 'arms and atomic energy'.[34]

Upon its start in 1953, then, the MSA took on the dual role of administering strategic trade controls as well as military production aid in Western Europe. Almost immediately, the MSA's system of strategic trade controls acted to accelerate the growing East–West split in world trade. In particular, MSA trade controls dramatically limited the previous access Western European firms had enjoyed into civilian trading markets in Eastern Europe and Asia. As a result, several European countries, led by France, began placing pressure on the Eisenhower Administration in the spring of 1953 to either ease MSA trade restrictions or increase yet again US levels of civilian and military assistance overseas. While Great Britain settled for increased military aid in 1953, other European countries, particularly France, West Germany and Italy, succeeded in receiving sizeable amounts of civilian as well as military industrial aid through the MSA. Administered largely under the USTA&P, European governments enjoyed an average of 8–10 million dollars in additional civilian production aid per year from 1952 to 1958.[35]

Nevertheless, the largest portion of US support for European industries after 1953 flowed out of the lucrative opportunities offered by the MSA under NATO production contracts. Shortly after taking office in 1953, Stassen and his MSA staff had reorganised the duties of the USTA&P to include the negotiation and administration of 'off-shore procurement', or OSP, contracts with European companies. Under pressure to quickly let out OSP contracts, the USTA&P redirected many of its technical assistance projects to support European firms engaged in military R&D and defence production. As a result, the focus of American technical assistance not only shifted away from the European civilian business sector, but also shifted from small and medium-sized firms towards larger producers. By 1954, big European companies such as Rolls-Royce, Renault, Fiat and others dominated the roster of OSP contractors. On an average, the USTA&P distributed over 370 million dollars annually to such firms for the manufacture of NATO jet aircraft engines and parts, radio-electronics, submarines, field weapons and ammunition as well as land and water transport vehicles.[36] When it was finally ended in 1958, the USTA&P had allocated more than 8 billion dollars in OSP contracts to military manufacturers and suppliers in Western Europe.[37]

Despite its hurried delivery of NATO production contracts, the MSA continued to require European firms receiving OSP contracts to comply with restrictions levelled by the Benton–Moody Amendment and the MDAC in 1950–1. Under this legislation, European businesses were compelled to demonstrate, through signed agreements with the MSA, their willingness to conform with American-style practices in labour relations, industrial organisation and workplace practices. As a result of the combined experience of USTA&P training programmes and NATO procurement contracts, the owners and managers of military and civilian industries in Western Europe received prolonged and intense exposure to American industrial operations, labour relations and business practices. To what extent European business executives took advantage of the unique opportunities afforded through the USTA&P and other Cold War aid programmes is a question deserving of further study.

Conclusion

As the first administrators of the ERP, business progressives had a profound effect on the postwar formation of US foreign aid policy. Led by auto executive Paul Hoffman, progressive businessmen and liberal government officials abandoned the traditional laissez-faire thrust of American economic aid and built instead a massive system of assistance programmes intended to foster industrial reform in Western Europe. Over the protests of business protectionists and military strategists, these early ECA administrators also created policies which supported the independent recovery of Western Europe through greater economic integration, industrial modernisation, business reform and the expansion of consumer markets.

Wary of the economic liberalism of ECA policies, the Truman White House struggled throughout 1949 to bring the ERP in line with its Cold War military objectives. The outbreak of the Korean War, however, provided the opportunity for Cold War policy makers to break the hold of business progressives over the ERP and redirect European aid objectives away from civilian business reform towards increased military production. With the passage of the Mutual Security Act in 1951, Cold War strategists succeeded in subsuming the ERP within the growing framework of US overseas military aid and NATO production programmes.

In a final push to maintain control, ECA administrators did make several important adjustments to the ERP between 1950 and 1952, most notably the launch of a series of 'production drives' into European industry. Through these drives, ECA officials hoped to preserve the original business reform thrust of the ERP while meeting the escalating demands of NATO production. In a desperate attempt to spur immediate overseas business reform, the ECA refashioned and enlarged one programme in particular, the USTA&P, to include intensive managerial retraining seminars, 'pilot plant' projects, consultancy programmes and American industry visits for European firms. The USTA&P also sponsored the creation of National Productivity Centres throughout Western Europe to act as vehicles for the further dissemination of American-style business practices and management education overseas. While ambitious, the USTA&P's productivity drives did little to assuage Cold War critics of the ECA and its business reform agenda.

Even though it was dismantled in 1952, the ECA, under the guidance of progressive business executives, had managed to usher in many important long-term changes in terms of US aid policy making and European relations during the Cold War. Much to its dismay, the Eisenhower Administration encountered strong resistance from several European nations, most notably from France, in its attempts to eliminate civilian business assistance programmes such as the USTA&P. As a result, the United States was forced to maintain high levels of assistance to overseas civilian as well as military industries or risk disruptive relations with its European NATO partners. Taking advantage of such new-found autonomy, European nations increasingly gained control over the direction and administration of industrial aid offered under the USTA&P. Instead of bowing to widespread reform or 'Americanisation' of their firms, European managers stood in a better position to selectively act upon the technical assistance, business opportunities and production contracts extended by the USTA&P until its end in 1958.

Finally, the story of the USTA&P illuminates the often clouded and complex nature of American political and business attitudes regarding postwar European economic reconstruction and the strategic use of foreign aid. Until recently, historians have assumed that US business and military planners had managed to forge and maintain a shared set of goals regarding the ERP and its implementation. This chapter has shown that the liberal economic reform agenda of the ERP, as shaped and guided by ECA business progressives, often conflicted with the military security and defence production aims of Cold War strategists.

When examined in the light of such diverse goals, a more accurate portrayal emerges of the American political pressures and policy decisions that forced the transformation of the USTA&P from a co-operative business assistance programme into a compulsory military production drive for Western Europe. By continuing to chart more closely the changing pattern of USTA&P leadership and administration, historians can also gain further insights into the shifting ideological, political and economic framework of US-European relations during the Cold War.

Notes

1 For more on the USTA&P under the ERP, see A.B. Carew, *Labour under the Marshall Plan: The Politics of Productivity and the Marketing of Management Science*, Manchester, Manchester University Press, 1987; R. Kuisel, *Seducing the French: The Dilemma of Americanization*, Berkeley, CA, University of California Press, 1993; F. Romero, *The United States and the European Trade Movement, 1944–1951*, Chapel Hill, NC, University of North Carolina Press, 1992; and N. Tiratsoo and J. Tomlinson, *Industrial Efficiency and State Intervention: Labour 1939–51*, London, Routledge, 1993. For an overview of the formation of the ERP, see M. Hogan, *The Marshall Plan: America, Great Britain and the Reconstruction of Western Europe, 1947–1952*, Cambridge, Cambridge University Press, 1987; M. Leffler, *A Preponderance of Power: National Security, the Truman Administration and the Cold War*, Stanford, CA, University of California Press, 1992; and A. Milward, *The*

Reconstruction of Western Europe, 1945–1951, Berkeley, CA, University of California Press, 1987.

2 J. Blum, *V Was for Victory: Politics and Culture During World War II*, New York, Harcourt Brace, 1976, pp. 310–12.

3 Dean Acheson had a personal stake in spearheading an administrative campaign for a European recovery assistance programme in January 1945. After wresting control of the FEA away from Henry Wallace in 1943, Acheson went to further control European wartime and postwar economic affairs by negotiating the US position on UNRRA. As head of the FEA, it would have fallen to Acheson in the spring of 1945 to co-ordinate US postwar assistance to Western Europe. As a strong advocate of Soviet containment, he would have been in favour of creating a 'mixed' economic/military assistance format for the ERP. Indeed, the ERP did take a dramatic turn away from its purely 'economic agenda' toward European remilitarization after Acheson succeeded Marshall as Secretary of State in 1949.

4 Prior to the ERP, the US extended approximately $16.6 billion in overseas recovery aid through the UN Relief and Rehabilitation Administration. From 1944–7, UNRRA aid was distributed to Great Britain, France, Italy and Germany in the form of direct recovery grants. The rapid exhaustion of UNRRA funding by its recipients led many US policy makers to call for greater spending accountability measures to be built into the ERP; US Department of Commerce, *Foreign Aid by the United States Government*, Washington, DC, 1955, pp. 16–17.

5 Leffler, *A Preponderance of Power*, pp. 102–4.

6 United Nations, *Survey of the Economic Situation and Prospects of Europe*, New York, 1948, p. 3; Economic Cooperation Administration (hereafter ECA), *Third Report to Congress of the Economic Cooperation Administration*, Washington, DC, 1950, p. 216.

7 For more on European postwar economic distress, see Hogan, *The Marshall Plan* and ECA, *Third Report to Congress*; for an alternative view of European economic conditions in 1946–7, see A. Milward, *The Reconstruction of Western Europe*.

8 For additional insight into the prewar origins of US internationalism, see R. Divine, *Second Chance: The Triumph of Internationalism in America During World War II*, New York, Athenaeum Press, 1971.

9 George C. Marshall Library, Lexington, VA, Papers of George C. Marshall, Box 57, Folders 14–18, Letters from B. Baruch to G.C. Marshall, 1947.

10 F. Pogue, *George C. Marshall: Statesman, 1945–1949*, New York, Viking Press, 1987.

11 US Department of State, Report on the Moscow Meeting of the Council of Foreign Ministers, Washington, DC, 1947, pp. 1–5.

12 H. Price, *The Marshall Plan and Its Meaning*, Ithaca, NY, Cornell University Press, 1955, pp. 23–4.

13 For a more detailed discussion of the rise of business liberalism and its influence in modern US governmental administration, see K. McQuaid, *Uneasy Partners: Big Business in American Politics, 1945–1990*, Baltimore, MD, Johns Hopkins University Press, 1993; and R. Collins, *Business Response to Keynes, 1929–1964*, New York, Columbia University Press, 1981.

14 W. Sanford, *The American Business Community and the European Recovery Program, 1947–52*, Westport, CT, Greenwood Press, 1987, pp. 73–4.

15 'Committee on Economic Development Trustees Roster', in *Community Handbook on the Special Problems of Small Business*, New York, 1944, p. 1.

16 For more on the foreign policy views of the CED, see the Hagley Museum and Library, Wilmington, DE, Papers of Philip Reed; M. Hogan, *The Marshall Plan* and C. Maier, 'The Politics of Productivity: Foundations of American

International Economic Policy After World War II', *International Organization*, 1977, vol. 31, pp. 607–33.

17 Secretary of State George C. Marshall first applied the term 'reconstruction' to describe US aid objectives for a Western European aid programme in his Harvard Commencement address delivered in June 1947; see US Department of State, *Bulletin*, 15 June 1947, p. 1159.

18 Price, *The Marshall Plan and Its Meaning*, p. 73.

19 Sanford, *The American Business Community*, p. 102.

20 Price, *The Marshall Plan and Its Meaning*, p. 74.

21 ibid., p. 77.

22 United States National Archives and Records Administration, Washington, DC and College Park, MD (hereafter NARA), Record Group (hereafter RG) 469, ECA, Office of the Administrator (hereafter OA), Box 3, Letter from H. Truman to P. Hoffman, 9 August 1948.

23 Sanford, *The American Business Community*, p. 131.

24 Hagley Museum and Library, Wilmington, DE, Accession 1411, National Association of Manufacturers, International Relations Report, 1948, p. 4.

25 For more on the formation of the AACP, see Carew, *Labour under the Marshall Plan*; Tiratsoo and Tomlinson, *Industrial Efficiency*.

26 NARA, RG 469, ECA, Productivity and Technical Assistance Division (herafter PTAD), New York Office, Subject Files (hereafter SF), Box 6, Speech to Society of American Management, 15 December 1949, pp. 3–4.

27 The USTA&P start-up of overseas higher management training resulted in a dramatic postwar expansion of foreign student education in American universities. By the 1950s, leading centres of US scientific and business education had started exchange programmes such as the MIT's Foreign Student Summer Project or FSSP, which helped host the postwar education of thousands of young European scientists and industrialists; see MIT Archives, Papers of the FSSP, 1948–1970. For an in-depth discussion of the impact of US business education and 'management science' on business education and training in Western Europe, see R.R. Locke, *Management and Higher Education since 1940: The Influence of America and Japan on West Germany, Great Britain, and France*, Cambridge, Cambridge University Press, 1989.

28 See for details the contribution of Matthias Kipping in this volume (Chapter 4).

29 NARA, RG 469, Mutual Security Agency (hereafter MSA), Deputy Director for Technical Services (hereafter DDTS), Office of Industrial Resources (hereafter OIR), Industrial Training Division, In-Plant Training Branch, Boxes 5 and 6, Work Study Program, 1954–58.

30 *Mutual Defense Assistance Program: 1950, Joint Hearings*, 81st Congress, 2d session, 1950.

31 NARA, RG 469, Office of the Special Representative to Europe (hereafter OSR), PTAD, Labor Program Branch, General SF, Box 2, PTAD Conference – Paris, September 1953, pp. 43–4.

32 See J. McGlade, *The Illusion of Consensus: American Business, Cold War Aid and the Recovery of Western Europe, 1948–1958*, unpublished PhD dissertation, George Washington University, Washington, DC, 1995.

33 MSA, *Worldwide Enforcement of Strategic Trade Controls*, Washington, DC, 1953, pp. 20–1.

34 ibid.

35 International Cooperation Administration, *European Productivity: A Summing Up*, Paris, 1958, p. 43.

36 NARA, RG 469, Agency for International Development, DDTS, OIR, Industrial Procurement Division, Box 6, 'Procurement Programs'.
37 NARA, RG 469, AID, Office of the Deputy Director for Management, Office of the Controller, Budget Division, Box 7, 'Military – Miscellaneous Papers'.

Part I

TRANSFER MECHANISMS AND CHANNELS

3

THE EUROPEAN
PRODUCTIVITY AGENCY

A faithful prophet of the American model?

Bent Boel

For eight years, during the period of 1953–61, the European Productivity Agency, or EPA, a semi-autonomous organisation within the framework of the Organisation for European Economic Co-operation, or OEEC, initiated a vast array of activities aimed at promoting productivity in Western European countries. It was partly designed as a means to transfer American techniques, know-how and ideas to Western Europe. While much of the recent historical literature has highlighted the limits of US power in Western Europe after the Second World War, the EPA could be construed as an illustration of American influence.[1] However, as the following chapter will show, while certainly an American creation, the agency increasingly became a framework within which the member countries looked for European solutions to European problems.

The US productivity drive and the creation of the EPA

The EPA grew out of the American postwar technical assistance programme in Western Europe. While the first technical assistance projects started with the Marshall Plan in 1948, it was only in 1949 that productivity became a key word in the rhetoric of the US aid policy towards Western Europe. Increasing productivity came to be seen as an economic necessity if Western Europe's structural economic problems were to be tackled, their economies made competitive and the dollar gap closed. The 'politics of productivity' were more generally thought of as a means to recast Western European societies in an American mould. 'Feudal' management practices and 'socialist' labour attitudes were to be jettisoned, questions of income distribution to be depoliticised and treated as technical matters concerning the best ways to improve output and collective bargaining between social 'partners'. If Europeans adopted American ways of doing things, they would gain access to the longed for 'American way of life'. As such, the 'politics of productivity' were part of anti-communist endeavours during the Cold War and of the American attempts to stabilise Western Europe politically and socially after the Second World War.[2]

The European reactions to this American inspired productivity drive were ambivalent. Many European governments welcomed a drive for modernisation. Some of them had already taken steps of their own immediately after the war to modernise their economy. Nevertheless, in many European circles the productivity drive met with reluctance. Some governments feared the socially and politically destabilising effects which the campaign might have. Business interests and, in some cases, trade unions mistrusted governmental interference in the life of private enterprises. In Northern European countries, including the United Kingdom, there was scepticism towards moves furthering European integration as well as a widespread feeling that nothing much was to be learned in matters of productivity from anybody. Some even suspected the Americans of being driven by low mercantile motivations.[3]

The American technical assistance during these first years was essentially bilateral in nature.[4] It aimed at promoting national productivity programmes implemented by organisations specifically set up for that purpose. This institutionalisation of the productivity campaign within a national framework did achieve some success. In 1952, eleven OEEC countries had created National Productivity Centres, or NPCs, at US prompting. However, some countries were hesitant in taking these steps and the US was far from happy about the quality of the work done by many of the productivity centres. This situation was – together with a general desire to further European integration – a strong incentive for the Americans to encourage multilateral endeavours in the productivity field. Similar efforts had already been undertaken within the framework of the OEEC since 1949. While the idea of strengthening the role of the OEEC in a European productivity drive left most European governmental decision makers cold, it found resolute support in some small expert circles associated with the work of the OEEC in this field. These experts induced the OEEC to go considerably further in co-operating on common productivity policies than the member countries originally intended.[5] However, quite often their enthusiastic efforts were only half-heartedly supported by their national governments, to the extent that these governments were aware of them at all. They would certainly not have resulted in the creation of the EPA if the US had not taken the lead.

The initial productivity increasing projects within the OEEC consisted in the organisation of international productivity missions to the US, the dispatch of American consultants to the member countries and the financing of productivity studies and other activities in co-operation with the horizontal committees of the OEEC. These multilateral activities were modest and rather uncoordinated. In 1951–2 the US administration was thus pondering, not too convincingly and without making too much headway, different ways of creating a truly European productivity movement.[6]

The decisive impulse came from the US Congress in the form of two amendments. The Benton Amendment was adopted in 1951 and reflected the dissatisfaction in Congress with the Administration's perceived 'softness' in its dealings with the Europeans. It placed the whole American aid policy towards Western Europe under the sign of the 'politics of productivity'. The US aid was henceforth to promote free private enterprise, discourage restrictive business practices, or RBP, encourage competition and productivity and strengthen the 'free' (i.e., non-communist) trade unions as the collective bargaining agencies of labour within aid-recipient countries. This amendment gave a certain impetus to the Technical Assistance drive, but the sums allocated to it by the Administration were considerably lower than originally envisaged. Noting the failure of the Administration to carry out the Benton Amendment, Congress in 1952 voted the Moody Amendment which earmarked 100 million dollars to further the Benton Amendment objectives and 2.5 million dollars which were to be used for the same purpose by the OEEC. This aid was conditional on the European recipient countries furthering the Benton Amendment objectives. It led to arduous negotiations concluded by bilateral agreements between the US and eleven individual Western European countries on the implementation of a national productivity campaign.

Parallel to these bilateral discussions, the OEEC countries discussed an American proposal to set up a European Productivity Agency to administer the US donation to the OEEC. While the idea of a European institution did not arouse much enthusiasm, US assistance was obviously welcome. And since the latter was conditioned on the former, the choice was not hard to make. On 24 March 1953 the OEEC countries decided to establish the European Productivity Agency to 'seek, develop and promote the most suitable and effective methods for increasing productivity in individual enterprises, in the various sectors of economic activity in the Member countries, and over the whole field of their economies.'[7] As the chairman of the OEEC Council, Hugh Ellis-Rees, stated, 'the creation of the agency was not entirely a matter of free will'.[8] Upon American insistence, the EPA pledged that it would fight restrictive business practices and support share-out clauses as well as co-operation between management and labour organisations. These ideas were not to the taste of all OEEC countries, but it was clear that they were central to the US aid policy and they were quickly agreed upon.[9]

The initial capital of the EPA was almost exclusively of American origin. In addition to the 2.5 million dollars which the US provided directly to the agency, the OEEC countries receiving Moody aid accepted an American request that they pay 8 per cent of the counterpart funds of this aid into the agency, which amounted to 7.5 million dollars. The resulting capital fund of 10 million dollars was supplemented by yearly American and European contributions. After the end of the first experimental three-year period of existence, it was agreed to continue the EPA at least until 1960 and to 'Europeanise' its finances. In 1960–1, European payments represented two-thirds of the yearly contributions to the agency. However, during the whole period 1953–61, direct or indirect American funding represented two-thirds of the total 30 million dollars contributed to the EPA.[10]

To sum up, the EPA was the product of American ideas, actions and money. Although a group of enthusiastic European productivity experts played an important role as well, most Western European governments seem to have been largely passive. The American hope was that the agency would serve the threefold purpose of furthering European integration, improving labour–management relations and increasing productivity in Western European countries. The US thus tried to use the leverage which its financial assistance gave it to mould the EPA's organisational set-up, its spirit and its programming.

American ambitions and European reactions

The EPA as an instrument to promote European integration

One of the central motives behind the creation of the EPA was the American policy goal to further co-operation and integration in Western Europe. The US saw it as 'highly desirable that movement towards higher productivity evolve in European context and not confined within national boundaries'. Such a development was moreover seen as 'important to basic US policy of strengthening OEEC as force towards European integration'.[11] This could seem an overly ambitious goal, since until then the OEEC had hardly proved an efficient integration instrument. The American vision of the EPA as a strong and autonomous organisation for European co-operation was far from being shared by all OEEC countries. The two extremes in the debate were represented by the French and the British. The former advocated a strong and independent EPA outside the OEEC framework, while the latter favoured an EPA closely monitored by the OEEC's Secretary General. In the end, the EPA was created as a semi-autonomous organisation within the framework of the OEEC under the authority of the Secretary General and of the OEEC Council. It was agreed that the agency would in practice enjoy a high degree of freedom of action.

During the subsequent years, the EPA suffered from the perverse effects of both positions. On the one hand, the continuation of the EPA remained fundamentally dependent on the goodwill of the member countries acting not only through the agency's governing body but also through the OEEC Council. In fact, its survival was often questioned. Several countries viewed it mainly as an experimental entity or, more cynically, as a device useful so long as US technical assistance was available. The persistent uncertainty of its prospects made long-term planning almost impossible and created a permanent recruiting problem for the agency. Qualified applicants were either discouraged from applying or tempted to abandon the ship before it sunk.[12]

The EPA enjoyed a large degree of autonomy, which benefited the agency less than its single components. To a certain extent the agency became a conglomerate of sections largely working out their own projects. These two opposing tendencies made for a weak and fragmented agency, plagued by constant disputes about its legitimacy, structure and role.

While the agency never gave up its federating role, many member countries were extremely sensitive to the tiniest hint of interference in their national sovereignty. They successfully turned down American proposals to let the EPA take over responsibility for all bilateral technical assistance programmes and to provide 'leadership and co-ordination to the total European productivity effort'.[13] The agency was sometimes dismissed as a 'cheap travel agency'.[14] However, at the same time one may argue that in this very capacity the EPA played a unique and innovative role in the 1950s in bringing together European opinion leaders – managers, trade union leaders, teachers and so on. It also furthered the creation of numerous national and transnational organisations. The effect of such network building can not be quantified, but it seems reasonable to assume that it contributed to what may be termed a process of European *social* integration.[15]

The EPA and labour–management relations

Another ambition of the US was to turn the EPA into a tripartite organisation for labour, business and governments in Western Europe and thereby to strengthen the 'free' trade unions, especially in Southern European countries.[16] Some member countries endorsed this idea and indeed defined the EPA as a 'joint "management–labour–government" organisation'.[17] But in its boldest version, this objective was defeated from the outset. The American proposal for a strong EPA management board, composed of labour, business and government representatives, was vetoed by several European member countries. While it was decided to create a committee composed of representatives from management, labour and agriculture, it remained restricted to a purely advisory function. The British in particular insisted that its role should be modest since 'the Advisory Board was likely under US influence to suggest overambitious or inappropriate projects'.[18] As a concession to the American view, it was decided to appoint several prominent business and trade union leaders to this otherwise powerless entity. The result was an unhappy and frustrated Advisory Board which entertained a rather conflictual relationship with the rest of the agency. Its prestigious members indeed found that their opinions ought to be taken seriously, which they rarely were.

In this respect, the EPA as a tripartite organisation at a European level was a failure. The influence of the Advisory Board, which was the formal link between the European professional organisations and the agency, always remained limited. However, contacts were made, and in some cases labour and business representatives within the Advisory Board achieved a high degree of agreement in defending their common interests vis-à-vis the agency. This was particularly the case from 1957, when the EPA and several big European countries decided to increasingly switch the emphasis of EPA programmes from productivity enhancement in its most narrow sense to science, technology and aid to underdeveloped areas. The Council of European Industrial Federations, or CEIF, and the Joint Trade Union Advisory Council to the OEEC, or JTUAC, found a common interest in countering this threat against the 'traditional' activities of the agency in the fields of industry, distribution and commerce.

However, the EPA also offered an area where trade unions and employers' associations learned to confront each other at a European level. In this battlefield, labour was more successful than the employers.[19] The trade unions got a far greater say in the EPA than could have been expected, considering their relatively weak stand and lack of governmental political support in Western Europe in the 1950s. In the area of labour–management relations the EPA instituted less a model of co-operation than a spoils system where business got one part of the cake while labour got another. But the system had an oddity. Only labour was really interested in having its share. To a large extent, business let the agency run the business management activities on its own, and often had to be talked into accepting the EPA projects. The situation was very different with the trade union programme, which was worked out in close co-operation between the agency, the European trade union movement and American advisors.

The interest of the European trade union movement in participating in the EPA projects was not surprising. The agency dispensed money, and the recognition of the European trade union movement by the OEEC/EPA was a source of prestige and as such particularly useful in those countries where the non-communist trade unions were weak. It is apparent however, that quite a few trade unions, especially in Northern Europe, had to be convinced of the EPA's usefulness. One of the agency's successes was that it actually managed to 'sell' itself to the unions, which ended up being among its fiercest supporters.[20] The strength of the trade union position within the EPA was clearly not due to the fact that it had imposed itself upon the agency, nor that the national trade union movements had forced their governments into pressuring the EPA to adopt such a stance. It was, first of all, the result of the American wish to see the EPA give high priority to the trade union question. This view seems to have been accepted, although probably never really understood, by the EPA leadership. The result was that the European trade union movement got its trade union programme as a segregated area where it could operate largely autonomously within the EPA.

One must therefore conclude that, while the US did not manage to turn the EPA into a joint management–labour–government organisation, it did to a certain extent succeed in associating European trade unions with productivity enhancing endeavours. Considering the strong suspicions nourished by many trade unions towards the productivity campaign in 1953–4, this must be considered no small achievement.[21]

Attempts to 'Americanise' European business

As mentioned earlier, the EPA was not a unitary actor trying to sell a ready-made package – the 'American model' – to European business, labour, universities and other groups. Rather, it was characterised by fragmentation and by the extreme diversity of the projects it initiated.[22] However, much of the agency's activities were clearly inspired by the US, and the Americans also used their funding to influence the agency's activities. From 1953 to 1957, US annual payments were tied to specific EPA projects, either projects in Europe which the US wished to encourage or projects involving dollar costs. After 1957 the American contribution was paid directly into the accounts of the EPA and allocated to specific chapters of the agency's programme which the Americans wished to encourage, notably the trade union programme and the programme for areas in the process of economic development.[23] In 1959, the US decided not to earmark any part of its aid for specific activities, but stressed that it presumed that the EPA programme previously presented would not be altered by the governing body, as such action 'might affect the US attitude towards continuing the practice of not earmarking funds with respect to future programs'.[24] The strings were cut mainly because the EPA did in any case implement such activities for which the US might have approved funds. The US also helped shape the programme in other and more discrete ways, notably through close contacts with the agency's secretariat and through the numerous American experts employed by the agency.[25] The US thus encouraged the high priority given to labour and management activities, and later the emphasis on assistance to areas in the process of economic development as well as training of scientific and technical personnel.[26]

The EPA could only implement activities in which the member countries were interested.[27] Many American proposals for EPA activities were either welcomed by the Europeans or viewed as inoffensive. However, the strong US influence on the EPA programmes sometimes resulted in a strained US–European relationship within the agency's framework. This was, for example, the case with EPA activities concerning restrictive business practices, management education, trade unions and the support for areas in the process of economic development.

Since fighting restrictive business practices, or RBP, in Western Europe had been one of the main elements in the Moody Amendment, the US insisted that the EPA made this fight its own.[28] In general, however, European governments were reluctant to accept the US view on RBP. They denied, for instance, that cartels were necessarily a nuisance and were wary that attacks on RBP would create domestic political turmoil.[29] The hostility in many industrial circles towards this part of the EPA programme was reinforced by the fact that, as the CEIF saw it, the 'EPA obstinately refuses to deal with trade unionist restrictive practices and only wants to deal with employers' RBP'.[30] The result of this sceptical European attitude was that the EPA's modest activities in the field of RBP were essentially lip service paid to the American demands, confined to a limited effort of documentation.[31] However, the pressure from the US for European action in the field of RBP remained throughout the EPA's existence. In 1960, it was reported to the CEIF that 'some Americans found that the purely symbolic activities of the EPA in the field of RBP was a violation of the agreement between OEEC and the US in the sense that it is much too limited'.[32]

In the field of management education, the inspiration for the agency's activities was obviously American.[33] The idea of professionalising training for leading positions in companies clashed in many cases with a widespread view within industrial circles that business leaders were 'born and not bred', especially as far as the top management was concerned. This contributed to shaping the rather reserved attitude among European employers towards the activities of the EPA. However, the EPA's management education activities did achieve some success. One of the central aims of this programme was the creation of European centres for management training and the 'Europeanisation' of the content of the training given. Towards the end of the agency's existence, the first results of these efforts could be seen in the fact that an increasing number of teachers used in the courses organised by the EPA were European.[34]

The EPA's trade union activities were also clearly American-inspired, since they had their immediate roots in the Moody Amendment which made it an official goal of US policy to encourage 'free' trade unionism in Western Europe.[35] While the agency tried to downplay its political role, there was never any doubt in the EPA's trade union section that its main function was to strengthen non-communist trade unions in the member countries.[36] The training of trade union leaders took many forms, including courses in Europe and the US as well as seminars and conferences where European and American trade unionists would meet. As explained above, while this programme enjoyed a large degree of autonomy within the EPA, it had strong connections to American trade unionists. It was viewed with suspicion by European employers, who disliked the fact that the trade unions were building their own empire within the EPA. In addition, they resented US influence and particularly the emphasis by American trade unions on tough salary bargaining as a means to pressure employers into increasing productivity. As the Director of the Swedish employers' federation said in 1957, 'as far as industrial relations are concerned, the differences between the US and Europe are so big that no real comparison can be made: the systems are so far apart from each another that they can hardly be seen as part of the same civilisation.'[37]

The origins of the programme of aid to underdeveloped areas are difficult to trace, since several former EPA officials claim parenthood. The programme was developed at a time when the US began to press the Europeans for more generous assistance to underdeveloped countries as a weapon in the Cold War. Pressures for the creation of such a programme were also mounting inside the EPA. Within the Secretariat of the agency as well as within the Advisory Board, it was argued that such a programme was necessary to prepare for market liberalisation in Europe. Some member countries with less developed areas considered that they did not profit sufficiently from the activities of the EPA, which were narrowly aimed at increasing productivity, and therefore claimed that a programme adapted to their special needs would have to be developed. The programme for the underdeveloped areas took many forms. The single most important project in this programme was the Sardinian pilot area. Here, the American input existed mainly in the inspiration provided by the New Deal's Tennessee Valley Authority project.[38] American experts only played a minor role, and several among them seem to have been perceived as naive and out of touch with the Sardinian realities by those responsible for the project.

The gradual Europeanisation of EPA activities

The powerful American influence exerted on the agency was partly due to the weakness of a new and inexperienced Secretariat, which felt that it had to show quick results.[39] It was worsened by the dearth of proposals from member countries, since this meant that the main source of proposals was the US.[40] On their side, the Americans did not hide their interest in shaping the programme and in participating in its implementation. At one stage an official even asserted that 'there would be no US financial contribution unless US experts [were] employed' by the EPA.[41] The Europeans were quick to express qualms about the situation. As early as November 1953, King warned the Secretary General of the OEEC, Robert Marjolin, that the programme of the agency was about to be 'too much dominated by American projects'.[42] A similar criticism was forcefully voiced by Ellis-Rees:

> The Americans, having put up most of the money for the agency, were obviously in a favoured position to influence the Director and at a late stage of the preparations we discovered that they had persuaded him to include in the programme a large number of grandiose, ill-considered and expensive projects costing something like £300,000, which is a large slice of the available funds. But a point of special interest was that these projects provided for the employment of between 40 and 50 American experts travelling round Europe lecturing on management, labour relations and distribution. Fortunately, and after a great effort, we have done something to reduce the size of this invasion and we hope that some at least of these projects will develop on sound European lines.[43]

Resentment was fed by an overpowering American presence which was not always felt necessary and therefore created suspicions of Americans pursuing selfish interests:

> The Americans have no inhibitions about trying to sell their goods: for example the Technical Assistance mission no. 142 – a team of Americans employed travelling round Europe training retailers in modern methods of food distribution – is accompanied by a large caravan full of the latest types of American refrigerating equipment, and since last June they have been doing it at the agency's expense.[44]

It is also clear that while many European industrialists welcomed American assistance, the concrete forms in which this was given did not always raise enthusiasm. Looking back on the achievements of the EPA in 1958, Fritz Beutler, Secretary General of the Federation of German Industry (BDI, or Bundesverband der Deutschen Industrie), said that as a consequence of the EPA's activities, German employers had 'observed a stream of American consultants, most of whom left a rather negative impression with his industries'.[45] As Peter Angelkort, Head of the EPA's Business Management Division, stated in February 1959, the strong American influence was one of the reasons explaining the 'rather lukewarm' attitude towards the agency among European industrialists.[46]

As early as December 1953, to counteract this American influence, King urged the member countries to put forward their own proposals to complement the American projects in the second annual programme.[47] Three months later, he called for Europe to 'stand on its own feet', meaning that the activities of the EPA should be 'Europeanised' and that the EPA should develop a 'European programme providing for European self-help and limiting European requests for American assistance to those matters in which the US possessed special skills, techniques or experience beyond those available in Europe.'[48] This call for a Europeanisation of the programme of the EPA was backed by Prince Guido Colonna, Deputy Secretary General of the OEEC, who envisioned the agency as an institution for European self-help, 'the channel through which the knowledge gained by the more highly developed European countries would be directed towards the less advanced countries to help them in their economic and social recovery programme'.[49]

As an example of the more 'sound European lines' along which the EPA's programme should be developed, Ellis-Rees mentioned that it was 'absurd that Europeans should go to the US, as they have done in the past, to learn about banking methods or cost accounting'. Such considerations were obviously not devoid of national self-interest. Believing that trade followed consultants, the UK advocated a greater use of European, preferably British, consultants.[50] Ellis-Rees in particular urged the British to consider the economic advantages which could be reaped if the EPA member countries could be persuaded to look more to the UK for technical leadership. In his opinion, the main rivals of the UK, the Americans and the Germans, threatened to take over leadership in the EPA. He therefore urged the UK to play a more active role in the agency, using it as a means to penetrate European markets and assert British influence over technical development in Europe. Ellis-Rees thought that, for instance, 'if the wool industry were ready to expose its latest techniques through [the EPA], orders for British textile machinery would increase.'[51] More strategic motives also played a role, namely the fear that Europe was being left behind by the two superpowers. Europeans would have to stand on their own feet if their continent was to play any major political and economic role in the world. The result of continued technological and economic lagging behind both the US and the Soviet Union would indeed be 'to confirm the decline of Europe compared to that of the two big powers.'[52]

The Europeanisation argument was considerably strengthened after 1956, when the European contributions to the EPA were increased and the American contribution reduced. It was further strengthened by the improved knowledge in productivity matters, i.e., the achievements of the productivity drive. Some Europeans also argued that constant regards to availability or non-availability of American funding unduly influenced productivity-enhancing projects in Western Europe. As a consequence, US aid was counterproductive since it led in some cases to the adoption not of the most promising or efficient projects, but of the projects most likely to receive US support.[53] Such a situation meant not only a diminished efficiency of the EPA's activities, but also resulted in the wasting of the EPA's energy in trying to ensure US funding.[54] The 'American connection' had further been a liability for many national productivity centres which, according to G.L.G. de Milly, Vice-Chairman in the PRA Committee, had been 'handicapped in prestige, finances, staffing, etc. because they are considered as (post-war) temporary phenomena for spending US money and not worth incorporating in national institutional structure'.[55] For all these reasons, a Europeanisation of the agency was not only necessary but, as EPA Director Roger Grégoire stated in 1956, also healthy.[56]

One sign of the increasing self-reliance of the Europeans was the early call for an Atlantic 'partnership' in the productivity field. Already, in 1954, the idea had been formulated that the technical assistance programme need not be a one-way story; America could learn from Europe as well. Although the EPA continued to play a role as a channel for US technical assistance to Western Europe, there were examples of know-how or ideas flowing in the opposite direction across the Atlantic, thereby making the EPA a mutual technical assistance agency.[57] In 1957, the idea that the EPA could be used as an instrument for joint European–American productivity promotion led to the proposal by OEEC Working Party no. 16 that the US and Canada become full members of the EPA – though not of the OEEC – with full voting rights. The offer was politely declined by the Americans, who thought their influence on the EPA might be greater from outside than if they became members of the EPA, where they would be only one of eighteen or nineteen members.[58] In 1958, just a year later, the idea of US membership of the EPA was revived and, in June 1959, the US seemed at last to be considering this proposal seriously.[59]

In the end, ironically, the story turned out quite differently. In December 1959, the US decided to join the OEEC countries in a reorganised organisation and, in 1961, it co-founded the OECD. But the price for this development was the winding up of the EPA. During the OEEC reorganisation talks, many EPA countries wished to see the EPA's activities continued within the framework of the new OECD. While in some cases this was motivated by the desire to keep the reorganised OEEC as a strong link between the six member countries of the European Economic Community, created by the Treaty of Rome in 1957, and the other OEEC members, it also reflected a generally positive assessment of the EPA's activities. However, the US made it plain that it did not wish the EPA to continue, not even as a field of activity confined to the European countries. It did not consider that Western Europe needed further American technical assistance to increase its productivity relative to that of the US. At a moment when the American balance of payments situation was worsening, it seemed tactically unsound to help Europe improve its productivity – especially when this had the appearance of helping the Europeans with American taxpayers' money. Not only was the US unwilling to co-operate in this field, but it opposed any continuation of this work by the reorganised OEEC.[60]

Conclusion

As the detailed analysis in this chapter has shown, the productivity campaign in general, and even more so its institutionalisation at a European level, was viewed with much scepticism by several European countries. Nonetheless, the EPA was created and rapidly began to implement a strongly American-influenced programme. Even during the later phase, when both the funding and programme were being 'Europeanised', the American inspiration was obvious. This, of course, was hardly a triumph for the US. The EPA operated in a 'low politics' area which did not involve any fundamental questions of national sovereignty for the member countries, and the sums involved were modest compared to the Marshall Plan as a whole.

However, the numerous and sometimes vehement conflicts between member countries about the EPA's existence and role testify to the fact that the agency was not devoid of importance. Although the story of the EPA is one of many failures and much frustration, it is also one of success. While the real economic impact of its activities is impossible to assess, the EPA was perceived by many member countries to play a positive role both politically and economically from the mid-1950s onwards. By the time it was wound up in 1960–1, it had quite a few convinced supporters.[61] One may also argue that it was successful in trying to make itself superfluous through the creation of several national and transnational institutions in numerous fields of activities. Thus to a large extent, the story of the EPA is the story of the 'Europeanisation' of an institution and of a productivity campaign initially conceived by the Americans.

Overall, the EPA could hardly be a faithful prophet of the 'American model' since it did not try to sell one single well-defined package. Instead, it was offering access to a wide range of techniques, know-how and ideas, many of which originated from the US. The question one may ask, however, is whether the EPA was perceived by contemporaries to be at least a channel for the 'Americanisation' of Western Europe. The answer must be ambivalent. The EPA was perceived to be 'faithful' in the sense that it to a large extent did transfer American techniques and ideas across the Atlantic Ocean. It became 'unfaithful' because, from a very early stage, it tried to stand on its own feet, to find European solutions to European problems and to use European consultants to work out such solutions. But this 'unfaithfulness' had to a large extent been planned. The whole idea of the EPA was to further European co-operation and self-reliance, including in the field of productivity. That the Americans were not necessarily happy with all aspects of this new European assertiveness was understandable; however, they cannot be exonerated from a certain degree of responsibility for it.

The European countries were initially ambivalent towards the American productivity gospel and always remained wary of American 'dictates', 'coups' and 'invasions', suspicious of any pursuit of selfish interests and ironic towards what was perceived as American naiveté. But the frequent European tributes to the American technical assistance were more than the weak bowing down before the powerful. This homage also reflected the fact that, in many ways, the EPA was seen by the Europeans as a useful conveyer of American ideas to their countries.

Table 3.1 Allocations per chapter in the EPA's operational programme, 1954–60 (in million French francs)

Chapter	1954–5	1955–6	1956–7	1957–8	1958–9	1959–60
Business management	115	86	246	299	344	260
Human factors	–	–	–	–	72	75
Social factors	120	110	205	195	–	–
Trade union programme	–	–	–	–	174	141
Applied research	90	32	56	74	91	39
Building	80	55	114	39	–	–
Agriculture	200	158	231	179	226	190
Economic factors	40	33	40	47	–	–
Distribution	80	45	166	–	–	–
Combined actions	5	20	–	–	–	–
Economic development	–	–	180	213	260	230
Information	35	30	28	50	–	–
National activities/information	–	–	–	–	165	142
Audio visual aids	35	66	38	33	–	–
Miscellaneous activities	–	–	–	–	51	48
Total	800	635	1,304	1,129	1,383	1,125

Source: B. Boel, The European Productivity Agency: Politics of Productivity and Transatlantic Relations, 1953–61, PhD dissertation, University of Copenhagen, forthcoming.

Note: During the financial years 1955–6, 1956–7 and 1957–8, one-third of the 'social factors' activities were considered 'human factors' activities, while two-thirds were classified as 'trade union programmes'. From 1957–8 onwards, the projects concerning 'distribution' were merged with those concerning business management.

Notes

1 For example, R.T. Griffiths, 'The European Integration Experience', in K. Middlemas (ed.), *Orchestrating Europe: The Informal Politics of European Union 1973–1995*, London, Fontana Press, 1995, p. 3; see also C. Wurm, 'Early European Integration as a Research Field: Perspectives, Debates, Problems', in C. Wurm (ed.), *Western Europe and Germany: The Beginnings of European Integration 1945–1960*, Oxford, Berg, 1995, pp. 9–26.

2 C.S. Maier, 'The Politics of Productivity: Foundations of American International Economic Policy after World War II', in C.S. Maier, *In Search of Stability: Explorations in Historical Political Economy*, Cambridge, Cambridge University Press, 1987, pp. 121–52; M. Hogan, *The Marshall Plan: America, Britain and the Reconstruction of Western Europe, 1947–1952*, Cambridge, Cambridge University Press 1989; A.B. Carew, *Labour under the Marshall Plan: The Politics of Productivity*

and the Marketing of Management Science, Manchester, Manchester University Press, 1987; B. Boel, *The European Productivity Agency: Politics of Productivity and Transatlantic Relations, 1953–61*, PhD dissertation, University of Copenhagen, forthcoming; see also the contribution of Jacqueline McGlade in this volume (Chapter 2).

3 B. Boel, 'The European Productivity Agency and the Development of Management Education in Western Europe in the 1950s', in T. Gourvish and N. Tiratsoo (eds), *Missionaries and Managers: United States Technical Assistance and European Management Education, 1945–1960*, Manchester, Manchester University Press, 1998.

4 In addition to the references in note 2, see J. McGlade, *The Illusion of Consensus: American Business, Cold War Aid and the Industrial Recovery of Western Europe, 1948–1958*, unpublished PhD dissertation, George Washington University, Washington DC, 1995.

5 One of the driving forces was Alexander King. He was elected chairman of Working Party No. 3, a small group of experts set up in June 1949 to co-ordinate the different OEEC productivity missions. In January 1957, he became deputy director of the EPA. Among other prominent experts were Laszlo Rostas, Jean Fourastié and Robert Major (interviews with Alexander King on 23 June 1995 and 3 February 1996).

6 For more details on this and on the creation of the Committee for Productivity and Applied Research in May 1952, see Boel, *The European Productivity Agency*.

7 OEEC, *Acts of the Organisation*, vol. XII, Paris, 1954, pp. 90–95.

8 Public Records Office, Kew (hereafter PRO), CAB 134/1183, TA(L)(54)19, 15 February 1954, Sub-Committee on Technical Assistance (hereafter SCTA), Letter from Ellis-Rees to Strath, 2 February 1954.

9 Udenrigsministeriets Arkiver, Copenhagen (Danish Foreign Office Archives, hereafter UMA), 73.C.41/19i, Box 2, C(53)81(final), 17 June 1953; ibid., OEEC del. CE no. 1754, 22 June 1953.

10 Boel, *The European Productivity Agency*.

11 US National Archives and Records Administration, Washington, DC and College Park, MD (hereafter NARA), Record Group (hereafter RG) 469, Office of the Special Representative to Europe (hereafter OSR), Office of the General Counsel, Subject Files (hereafter SF) 1948–53, Box 58, OSR to SecState, REPTO 1144, 3 October 1952.

12 Archivi Storici della Confindustria (hereafter ASCONF), Box 58/4.2, Gruppo di Lavoro per l'attività EPA, Anno 1958–59, Letter from Arnaud to Mattei, 6 February 1959, attached note by Angelkort, 'Quelques idées sur un programme européen pour le développement de l'industrie et du commerce'.

13 PRO, CAB 134/1183, TA(L)(54)48, 5 April 1954, SCTA, attached PRA 954/23, Letter from Fobes (USRO) to Harten, 12 March 1954.

14 Interview with Werner Rasmussen, 9 December 1994.

15 Concerning social integration in Europe, see H. Kaelble, *A Social History of Western Europe 1880–1980*, Dublin, Gill and Macmillan, 1989.

16 For more detail on this question, see B. Boel, 'The United States, the European Productivity Agency (EPA) and Trade Union Politics in Western Europe in the 1950s', paper prepared for the European Association for American Studies Conference on *American Culture and its Impact 1946–1996*, 21–25 March 1996, Warsaw.

17 UMA, 106.O.21, Box 1, 'Productivity promoting activities within OEEC after 30 June 1960', joint document from Denmark, Norway and Sweden, 26 September 1958.

18 PRO, CAB134/1014, MAC(53) 27th Meeting, minutes of a meeting held on 9 July 1953, 'The Advisory Board of the EPA'.

19 The JTUAC was also a stronger organisation than the CEIF ever was; see also the contribution of Matthias Kipping in this volume (Chapter 4).

20 For details, see Boel, 'The United States'.

21 For a more sceptical view, see Carew, *Labour under the Marshall Plan*, p. 199.

22 For this aspect, see also R.P. Amdam and G. Yttri, 'The European Productivity Agency, the Norwegian Productivity Institute, and Management Education', in Gourvish and Tiratsoo (eds), *Missionaries and Managers*.

23 NARA, RG 469, Office of African and European Operations (hereafter OAEO), SF 1955–59, Box 61, ECOTO ICA/W A-523, 13 November 1957; UMA, 106.P.11, Box 2, OEEC del., no. 2710, 20 June 1956; NARA, RG 469, OAEO, SF 1955–59, Box 81, Letter from Van Dyke to Francis, 28 March 1958.

24 NARA, RG 469, Office of Labor Affairs, Labor Programs Division, Records Relating to the EPA, Box 1, ECOTO Circular A-4, Paris to ICA/W, 20 December 1958.

25 PRO, FO371/150114, M557/11, Note, Ellis-Rees to Owen, 28 March 1960.

26 This evolution is to some extent reflected in the appended Table 3.1, which shows the allocation of resources between different operational activities of the EPA. After 1958, projects concerning scientific and technical personnel were carried out by a separate organisation, the Office for Scientific and Technical Personnel or OSTP, headed by the EPA's deputy director, Alexander King.

27 Most projects could only be implemented if a minimum of five, in some cases seven, member countries were interested. However, a declaration of interest sometimes reflected less sincere interest than 'tactics'. Member countries could back the implementation of a project they were not really interested in, in order to obtain other countries' support for projects they themselves wished to see implemented.

28 ASCONF, Box 58/4.2, CEIF, '2ème réunion du groupe de travail institué pour suivre les travaux de l'Agence Européenne de Productivité, 7 décembre 1957, Compte rendu des décisions'.

29 ibid., and 'Productivity promoting activities within OEEC after 30 June 1960' (see note 17 above); on European attitudes towards cartels, see W. Asbeek Brusse and R.T. Griffiths, 'L'"European Recovery Program" e i cartelli: Una indagine preliminare', *Studi Storici*, 1996, vol. 37, pp. 41–68, as well as the contribution of Matthias Kipping in this volume (Chapter 4).

30 ASCONF, Box 58/4.2, CEIF, '12ème session du groupe de travail institué pour suivre les travaux de l'AEP, réunion des 30 et 31 mai et 1er juin 1960, compte rendu des décisions'.

31 CEIF, '2ème réunion' (see note 28 above).

32 CEIF, '12ème session' (see note 30 above).

33 G. Gemelli, 'American Influence on European Management Education: The Role of the Ford Foundation', in R.P. Amdam (ed.), *Management, Education and Competitiveness*, London, Routledge, 1996, pp. 38–68.

34 Boel, 'The European Productivity Agency and the Development of Management Education'.

35 Boel, 'The United States'.

36 Interview with Preben Hansen on 5 January 1995.

37 ASCONF, Box 70/18.5, CEIF, 'Assemblée générale du 8 novembre 1957'.

38 One of the main driving forces behind the Sardinian project was Philippe Lamour, who was strongly inspired by the TVA project when he created the regional Rhône-Bas Languedoc project. The TVA project had also been an inspiration for the Italian development agency Cassa per il Mezzogiorno.

39 Dutch Ministry of Foreign Relations, The Hague (hereafter MBZ), Box 106, DGEM-archief 66/EPA Algemeen deel 5, note from King, 2 December 1953, 'Notes on a conversation between Marjolin and King on 26 November 1953'; see also MBZ, DGEM-archief 663, letter from Hijmans to Berger and Milly, 9 November 1954, attached 'Toelichting op EPA-programma voor het jaar 1954–1955, De Voorgeschiedenis van de EPA'.

40 PRO, CAB134/1014, MAC(53) 27th Meeting, minutes of a meeting held on 9 July 1953 regarding the Advisory Board of the EPA.

41 PRO, CAB134/1182, TA(L)(53)79, SCTA, 15 February 1953, note by the Secretariat, attached E.R.(P)(53)11(limited distribution), 12 December 1953: OEEC, UK Delegation, 'Program of the EPA'; see also UMA, 73.C.41/19j, Box 1, OEEC del. CE no. 5340, 18 December 1954, 'PRA komité årsrapport, CE nr 5113 af 6.12.1954'.

42 See note 39 above.

43 Letter from Ellis-Rees to Strath, 2 February 1954 (see note 8 above).

44 ibid.

45 Bundesarchiv, Koblenz (hereafter BA), B102/37395 (2), OEEC Delegation (Werkmeister), 1 August 1958, no. 1149, 'Zukunft der EPZ'.

46 Angelkort, 'Quelques idées' (see note 12 above).

47 BA, B102/37052, EPA/D/19, 19 January 1954, 'The Second annual programme of EPA. Declaration by Dr. King at the Administrative Session on 18 December 1953'.

48 Letter from Fobes (USRO) to Harten, 12 March 1954 (see note 13 above); PRO, CAB 134/1183, TA(L)(54) 4th meeting (M), SCTA, 29 May 1954, minutes of meeting of the sub-committee held at the Board of Trade, 10 May 1954.

49 UMA, 106.P.11, Box 1, EPA/ABI/36, January 1955, 'Advisory Board, Draft Minutes of the 4th Session held in London on 3 December 1954'; see also UMA, 73.C.41/19i, box 4, OEEC del. CE no. 1240, 23 March 1954.

50 UMA, 106.P.11, box, PRA/M(57)4, 29 May 1957, 'Minutes of the 54th Session held on 6–7 May 1957'; Letter from Ellis-Rees to Strath, 2 February 1954 (see note 8 above).

51 ibid.

52 UMA, 106.O.21, Box 2, OEEC del., 20 June 1959, no. 2926, 'Referat af mødet den 16 June 1959 med Sir Ellis-Rees om rapporten fra rådets arbejdsudvalg nr. 26 vedr. EPA's fremtid'; MBZ, Box 345, DGES-Archief, 996.256 EPA OEEC/ Deel I, 1955 t/m dec 1957, note of 15 February 1956 from Milly to Grégoire.

53 UMA, 106.O.21, Box 1, OEEC del., no. 4712, 20 October 1958, 'EPA. Governing Body'.

54 Handelsministeriets Arkiver (Ministry of Commerce Archives), 88–5-56, Embassy in Washington (Hoelgaard), 19 December 1955, no. 3255, 'EPAs hidtidige virksomhed og fremtidsmuligheder'.

55 Note of 15 February 1956 from Milly to Grégoire (see note 52 above).

56 ASCONF, Box 70/18.1, CEIF, 'Allocution de Grégoire à l'Assemblée générale du CEIF', 22 Février 1956.

57 Historical Archives of the European Communities, Florence, Archives de l'Agence Européenne de Productivité, RE 5/7/09 Agence E, Letter RS 1833 from Sergent to Dillon, 24 October 1958, attached Note of 24 October 1958, 'United States Contributions to the EPA and the OSTP'.

58 UMA, 106.P.11, Box 5, OEEC del., no. 3214, 5 July 1957, 'Rådet. EPAs struktur'; see also Note of 5 February 1956 from Milly to Grégoire (see note 52 above).

59 UMA, 106.O.21, Box 2, OEEC del., 20 June 1959, no. 2926, 'Referat af mødet den 16.6.1959 med Sir Ellis-Rees om rapporten fra rådets arbejdsudvalg nr. 26

vedr. EPA's fremtid'; cf. also UMA, 106.O.21, Box 1, 18 September 1958, no. 4167, 'EPAs fremtid'; BA, B102/37395 (2), Note (Müller), 9 July 1958, 'Zukunft und Struktur der EPZ, Besprechung im BWM am 7.7. 1958'.

60 Rijksarchief (Dutch National Archives, hereafter RA), The Hague, Box. no. 590, note 1989/101, Strengers to Directorat Generaal voor Europese Samenwerking, 21 March 1960, 'Reorganisatie OEES'; RA, 2.06.061, Box no. 590, Note, Berger, 8 September 1960, 'Bespreking bij Buitenlandse Zaken', 9 September 1960.

61 For a discussion of the perceived impact of the EPA, see B. Boel, 'The Shepherd, the Horsefly and the Milk Cow: The Achievements and Failures of the European Productivity Agency', paper presented at the conference Democracy and Technology: Comparative Perspectives, Centre for Culture and Technology, University of Oslo, 17–19 January 1997.

4

'OPERATION IMPACT'

Converting European employers to the American creed

Matthias Kipping

> The method of the oppressive conqueror is to force upon others
> the acceptance of his own philosophies. At the very least, he says
> 'Copy us; do as we do' and uses his economic power to secure
> compliance. But the method of America is to show by example,
> to give others an opportunity to see and adapt American
> methods to their own very differing conditions.[1]
>
> Sir Norman Kipping, Director-General,
> Federation of British Industries

In the literature on the diffusion and the transfer of know-how and innovations, leaders are among those seen to fulfil an important 'linking role'
between the sources of knowledge and practice.[2] Unlike consultants and
trainers or educators they are 'insiders', i.e., they are themselves part of the
system to which the new ideas or techniques are being transferred. Thus, once
convinced of the need for change, they can accelerate the transfer process
within their own organisation and, depending on their status, act as examples
for other organisations.

At the same time however, a number of barriers can present serious obstacles in the diffusion process. These barriers are likely to be more important
when the message is transferred between countries, as in the case of the
transfer of US management models to Europe after 1945. As Table 4.1 shows,
in such a case sender and receiver can differ not only in the language, but also
in a number of other dimensions including their cultural background and the
social construction of interactions.[3]

As part of the productivity drive after the Second World War, American
politicians and company executives made an effort to reach out to European
business leaders. In the autumn of 1951, they invited a large group of leading
businessmen and industry representatives from seventeen European countries
on a tour of cities and factories in the United States, followed by a joint

Table 4.1 Potential barriers for the transfer of knowledge

Inter-personal barriers	*Inter-system barriers*
Language	Coding scheme
Being 'out-of-phase'	Suspicion of outsiders
Role perception and definition	Local pride
Status discrepancy and ambiguity	Social structures
Self image	Norms, attitudes and values

Source: Adapted from Havelock, *Planning for Innovation*, section 2, pp. 17, 33 and section 6, pp. 7–10

'conference of manufacturers', held in New York. Quite tellingly, the American organisers code-named the whole programme 'Operation Impact'.

'Operation Impact' was obviously not the first occasion when European businessmen were confronted with American management methods. As a large number of detailed studies have shown, US management models exercised a significant influence on European companies during much of the twentieth century, starting with Taylorism.[4] Nor was the conference of manufacturers in New York in 1951 the first meeting where American and European industry representatives discussed topics of common interest; similar meetings had already taken place more or less regularly during the interwar period, mainly but not exclusively within the framework of the scientific management movement. In addition, the 1951 event was followed over the next decade by three more conferences, held alternately in Europe and the United States.[5]

Nevertheless, the 1951 conference and 'Operation Impact' as a whole merit special attention, because they represent the very first conscious US attempt to imbue European business leaders with the 'gospel of productivity' after the Second World War. The following chapter examines the American efforts and the European reaction to 'Operation Impact' in some detail. It is divided into four sections. The first gives a brief overview of the reasons behind the US decision to specifically target business leaders. The second section looks at preparations on the American side, which consisted of the selection of the appropriate message and messengers. The third section shows how the European participants also prepared very carefully and aimed to diffuse any potential conflict, especially regarding the cartel question. The fourth and final section examines the apparent failure of 'Operation Impact' to convince the European business leaders of the superiority and applicability of the US management model. It also highlights some differences in the reaction of industry representatives from some of the major European countries, namely Britain, France and Germany.

'Operation Impact': born out of frustration

An important part of the US productivity drive from the late 1940s consisted of the so-called productivity missions. Between 1948 and 1958, several thousand managers, engineers, workers and, occasionally, civil servants from Western Europe toured the United States and visited factories to identify the reasons for the superior performance of American industry.[6] Upon their return, so it was hoped, they would implement the necessary, very often simple changes in their own companies and countries.[7] Usually, these missionaries came back full of praise for American technology and management methods. They produced reports which were published and disseminated by the national productivity centres in each of the participating countries.[8]

However, as early as 1949 frustration was mounting among policy makers and programme administrators of the Marshall Plan's Economic Co-operation Administration, or ECA, about the lack of concrete results from the productivity missions.[9] These reflections and criticisms were crystallised in a report written by the independent consulting management engineer Arthur R. Mosler in May 1950.[10] After reading the relevant documentation and conducting interviews with a number of ECA officials and US industrialists, Mosler concluded 'that management inertia rather than the lack of technical know-how is the root cause of a low European productivity'. His detailed suggestions, which had a considerable influence on the future direction of the US productivity drive, focused largely on the need to train European managers in American management techniques and to overcome the resistance of both management and labour to the necessary changes.

Subsequently, Marshall Plan officials launched a number of new initiatives designed to influence management attitudes and practice in Europe. They included, for example, the promotion of programmes for the study of business administration at European universities as well as for the further training of existing managers, efforts which were carried out with the help of the European Productivity Agency, or EPA, and the Ford Foundation.[11] In addition, the ECA sent American experts as consultants to Western Europe and instituted so-called pilot plant demonstrations. 'Operation Impact' was another of these attempts to drive the American productivity message home:

> It has become abundantly clear that the full and enthusiastic cooperation of the top industrialists of ECA countries is needed if our efforts to increase productivity are to yield maximum results. We have long been aware that our principal task is to persuade top European management that it would be good business . . . to change from their form of capitalism to the more enlightened, more just and, above all, more efficient free enterprise system of the kind that has grown up in the U.S.[12]

The report summarising the history and the results of 'Operation Impact' also highlights how much it was the result of the frustration with earlier efforts to influence European business, which had focused on the trips of 'younger men' to the United States. 'But', so the report continued, 'it was clear that the lessons learned by these technicians and engineers would only find their way into European business practice very slowly without some support from the top management of industry.'[13]

The idea to focus these attempts on business leaders and a change in their attitude seems to have been first launched in the fall of 1950 by the ECA Mission to France. In a telegram to the ECA in Washington, the Mission proposed to organise a trip of French top executives to the United States 'to confer with dynamic leaders of American business and to observe free enterprise in operation'.[14] Unlike earlier visits, it would not concentrate on technical matters and a single industry or field, but would familiarise French businessmen with the attitudes of their American counterparts through 'close contact with recognised leading executives'. The Mission considered the following subjects to deserve special attention:

A. *What American management is like*: divorce of management from ownership, management training, etc.

B. *Features of American business organisation*: scale of operations, industrial integration, dependence on sub-contracting, functions performed by trade and business associations, nature of business contracts.

C. *The part played by competition*: prevalence and forms of competition, legal and institutional basis, employer incentives.

D. *Employer attitudes toward labor*: high wage–high productivity philosophy, collective bargaining, democracy in industry.

E. *Attitudes toward consumers*: efforts to find out what the consumer wants, advertising, price appeal, consumer credit.

F. *Attitudes toward government*: nature of government restrictions, co-operation with government in adoption of uniform standards, quality testing and business statistics, business influence on legislation, taxes.

From detailed research on American business we know that these characteristics represent a rather reductive and stylised version of American capitalism. However, they provide a concise summary of the views shared by a large group within the ECA. As Charles Maier and others have shown, many of these ideas originated from the experience of the New Deal and were at the heart of the American productivity drive in the postwar period, at least during its initial stages.[15] And, as will be seen in the next section of the chapter, most of these elements were also at the centre of 'Operation Impact'.

In its response to the suggestion from the French Mission, the ECA in

Washington approved the idea in principle, but also highlighted a number of potential problems.[16] One was the language barrier, which the Mission had also identified as problematic. Even more important was the difficulty of finding concrete and meaningful ways to illustrate the US model to the French executives. The ECA rejected a programme based on 'time-wasting formal speeches, banquets, etc., where the ideas expressed are often merely laudatory of the American way or so general as to be useless'. In addition, the selection of appropriate participants was identified as a dilemma difficult to solve. In case they were hostile to the American methods, a trip to the United States 'might prove a total waste of effort unless our programme was felt to be extraordinarily persuasive'. At the other extreme, inviting businessmen sympathetic to the US model, as suggested by the Mission, was also seen as rather unhelpful, since they were often the ones 'who have the least to learn from us'. In the preparations for 'Operation Impact', the ECA tried to address all of these problems.

US organisers: selecting messages and messengers

The decision to organise a visit of top executives on a Europe-wide basis seems to have been made at the end of 1950, following the earlier suggestions of the Mission to France. These plans became more specific during the first half of 1951 with the involvement of the US member in the international scientific management movement NMC, or National Management Council, and the major American employers organisation NAM, or National Association of Manufacturers. Both organisations together submitted a formal proposal in March 1951, which was endorsed by the ECA in May.

A memorandum of 29 May 1951, addressed to the ECA administrator William C. Foster by his assistant William H. Joyce, highlights the similarities between 'Operation Impact' and the proposal of the French Mission in terms of their overall and specific objectives.[17] In addition to technical efficiency, competition and better labour relations, the 'willingness to share the rewards of greater efficiency with workers (higher wages), consumers (lower prices), as well as stockholders' figured prominently among the ideas to be conveyed to the European leaders. At the planned conference in New York, these ideas were translated into six different topics: production policies, marketing policies, employee relations, financial policies, competitive policies and public relations policies. For each of these, both the American and the European participants prepared statements, summaries of which were presented at the conference by a chosen representative, followed by short interventions by delegates from each of the participating countries in alphabetical order which, incidentally, put the representatives from the United Kingdom at the very end.

While not directly addressing the concerns raised in the earlier response to the proposal of the French Mission, the above-mentioned memorandum implicitly suggested that most of them could be avoided by careful preparation and selection of the appropriate participants. Thus, it stated very clearly that the Europeans should only be confronted with 'a very carefully selected group' of US industrialists, characterised repeatedly with the attributes 'enlightened', 'progressive' and 'persuasive'. With these criteria in mind, the organisers chose the venues to be visited on over thirty different tours, the businessmen and ECA officials who accompanied the European executives on these tours and the participants for the manufacturers' conference in New York.

Among those who hosted a group of European visitors at their factories and/or participated at the concluding event were Henry Ford II, Charles E. Wilson of General Motors, Thomas J. Watson of IBM and Philip D. Reed of General Electric. Among the many other firms visited were US Steel, Remington Rand, Burroughs, General Foods, Monsanto and Dow Chemicals. The opening address at the conference was given by another well-known advocate of 'business reform', Paul G. Hoffman, the former head of the ECA who had become director of the Ford Foundation.

The Americans also made considerable efforts to overcome possible barriers and achieve maximum impact. On the one hand, they arranged for simultaneous translation into English, French and German so as to overcome the language barrier. In order to illustrate the considerable differences between American and European goods in terms of the time and the cost of production, a leading US industrial designer was asked to prepare an exhibit showing a detailed breakdown of these costs. In addition, the organisers anticipated one of the reasons given most frequently by Europeans for their inability to achieve the same low cost, namely the differences in market size. Speakers were asked to stress that many US manufacturers actually operated only in limited markets like the Pacific Coast, much smaller than most European countries.

But the Americans not only carefully selected their own delegation and adjusted their message for the invited audience, they were also concerned about the selection of the appropriate European participants. Their declared aim was to invite 'a broad cross-section of industry in each country' and 'men who would have a great influence on the business thinking and practices in their respective countries'.[18] However, while they appear to have had some influence in this respect, the national employer organisations of the participating countries retained the ultimate responsibility for compiling the list of delegates and preparing the responses. As the following section will show, the preparations on the European side were equally careful.

European preparations: anticipating controversies

The preparation of all the statements presented on behalf of European industry by members of national employer organisations was co-ordinated and organised by the Council of European Industrial Federations, or CEIF.[19] The CEIF had been founded in the spring of 1949 following an initiative from Georges Villiers, the head of the French top employers' organisation CNPF, or Conseil National du Patronat Français. The CEIF combined the employer federations of all countries receiving Marshall Plan aid, and intended to represent business interests in the framework of the Organisation of European Economic Co-operation, or OEEC. Villiers became the first CEIF president, a small secretariat was set up in Paris and a steering committee was constituted, which met regularly to discuss issues of mutual interest.

The preparations for the European mission to the United States reflect the intention of the CEIF and its leadership to anticipate and, if possible, counter possible American criticisms of European business. As seen above, competition policy was one of the six topics to be discussed at the conference in New York and it was likely to be one of the most controversial, given the ECA's well-known 'abhorrence' of cartels. This issue probably illustrates best how carefully the European representatives, just like their American counterparts, 'massaged' their messages, and even concealed their true attitudes in order to avoid possible controversies and to depict European business practices in a more favourable light.

The trip was discussed for the first time at the CEIF's general assembly in July 1951. President Georges Villiers correctly predicted 'that the Americans would not fail to question their European visitors in November–December about cartels'.[20] The CEIF therefore established a working party to prepare the document stating the European position on competition policy. It was directed by Pierre Ricard, vice-president and *éminence grise* of the top French employers' organisation. Ricard was a well known and outspoken supporter of cartel agreements, a fact which did not escape American observers.[21] When reporting at the next general assembly on 30 October 1951, Ricard expressed regret that the section on cartels had to be 'reduced to a minimum in order to prevent incidents, viz. considering the presence of the press, . . . despite our conviction that international cartels prepared by national cartels are a necessity in our fragmented Europe.'[22]

It seems that most of the business representatives present at the CEIF meeting agreed with Ricard on the substance of his report. Some even considered his support of cartels 'a little timid'. Discussions evolved around language problems and the possible quantification of restrictive agreements in Europe. Concerning the wording of the document, it proved impossible to find an appropriate translation for the French *organisation professionnelle*, which covered not only legitimate activities of trade associations but also illicit restrictive agreements. Such an encompassing meaning would not be conveyed by the English 'professional organisation'. The euphemism finally used in the statement prepared for the conference was 'commercial accords'.

A somewhat more contentious issue was an attempt made by Ricard to quantify the share of industrial production in France covered by cartel agreements which he put at 5 per cent. Ricard arrived at such a low number due to the exclusion of cartels (nominally) supervised by the French government, such as the steel sales syndicate CPS, or Comptoir des Produits Sidérurgiques. Sir Norman Kipping, director-general of the Federation of British Industries, or FBI, therefore objected to such a quantification as misleading. In his opinion, the percentage was 'probably higher in Great Britain and, without doubt, in Europe as a whole'. It was finally agreed that the report should not state any precise number.[23]

It would be mistaken to interpret this consensus among industry representatives as an expression of the general opinion among European businessmen. In most countries sizeable and influential minorities, mainly in the downstream industries, displayed a more favourable attitude towards competition, because they saw cartels in raw materials as harmful for their own interests. Their representatives intervened – sometimes decisively – in the domestic debates about the introduction of competition laws, which were being discussed in many European countries. Some of them also played an important role in the formulation and the ratification of the treaty establishing the European Coal and Steel Community, which contained very strict provisions against cartels and excessive concentrations of economic power.[24]

In France for example, Jean Constant, the secretary general of the association of mechanical engineering and metal-working industries, repeatedly challenged the positive opinion of CNPF president Villiers towards cartel agreements. At a meeting of the CNPF's directorate in April 1950, Constant reminded Villiers that not all sectors of the French economy considered cartels as 'beneficial' and were opposed to a stricter legislative framework.[25] Subsequently, Constant and the chief executive of the nationalised automobile producer Renault, Pierre Lefaucheux, were among the staunchest supporters of the ECSC, which promised to outlaw domestic and international cartel agreements and thus reduce the price of their major input material, steel. Similarly, in Italy a group of 'modernisers', often from the state-owned industries, advocated a break with the cartelised past.[26]

Very often, these 'dissidents' explicitly used the US example to back their claim that more rather than less competition would be beneficial for European industry. In a hearing before the – purely consultative – French Economic Council, Constant presented the behaviour of the steel industry in the United States as the example to emulate. Unlike their French counterparts, who were most concerned about cartel agreements as well as government support and protection, the American steel producers had made continuous efforts to reduce costs and increase sales.[27] This example is especially telling, because it highlights that in the postwar period the American model became 'instrumentalised' in domestic debates, to an extent that its description sometimes bore little resemblance to reality.[28] As we know from other sources, Constant's view of a vigorous and competitive steel industry in the United States was indeed rather inaccurate.

Given the well-known opinion of Constant, Lefaucheux and others on the benefits of competition, it should come as no surprise that none of them was part of the delegation chosen to represent French industry in the United States. There was indeed a high probability that they would have sided with their American hosts in the condemnation of restrictive business practices in Europe. Instead, the French contingent counted a large number of fervent cartel supporters, notably from the steel industry. Delegations from other countries appear similarly biased. In the Italian case for example, the steel producers were represented by Giovanni Falck, an advocate of cartelised markets and a limited expansion of production.

Overall, the national employers' associations and their European federation CEIF seem to have made every conceivable effort to ensure unity among their delegates and to anticipate possible criticism of European business practices, notably with respect to cartels. However, as the following section of the chapter will show, this careful dissimulation exercise failed to produce the desired effects.

Mission and conference: dialogue between the deaf?

The visit of the European business leaders took place between 19 November and 5 December 1951. After their arrival in the United States, the European participants were combined into small groups of mixed nationality with similar interests and then travelled to different cities, where they visited plants and held discussions with business representatives. Then, on 30 November, all participants convened in Washington, DC where they were received by high-ranking officials of the US government. Finally, on the following day they transferred to New York City for the first international conference of manufacturers, organised by the NAM which also invited the Europeans to join its annual congress, held immediately afterwards.[29]

In terms of the number of participants and the interest, which it generated, 'Operation Impact' was a considerable success. Almost 300 business leaders and industry representatives from seventeen European countries participated in all or part of the visits and in the conference. This attendance by far exceeded the expectations of the ECA. The organisers had at best hoped for 200 participants from Europe, given that all of the visitors had to pay for their own travel across the Atlantic and cover all the costs for their wives who were invited to accompany them, which they did in many cases.

Concerning its declared objectives, the American organisers appeared also very satisfied with the outcome. The NMC, which had been in charge of the field trips during the first phase, concluded that it would be 'no exaggeration to say that Operation IMPACT may well prove to be the most efficient investment of the American taxpayer's dollar in our history'. This evaluation is based on the feedback from American participants and from the volunteers – many of them businessmen themselves – who had accompanied the European visitors on their factory tours across the country. According to the NMC Report, their comments 'amounted to a mass testimonial of IMPACT's accomplishment of its declared purpose'.[30]

There is no doubt that many of the European visitors were impressed with what they saw during their tours of US cities and factories. The elements mentioned most frequently in the reports of the American escorts on these field trips include industrial relations, namely the appearance and the positive attitude of the 'American working man', the extent of training programmes at all levels, public relations and the exchange of information between companies. However, a detailed analysis of the European reactions reveals that in fact very little was accomplished in terms of convincing the visiting business leaders that it would be worthwhile to transfer these and other elements of the American model to Europe.

The dissimulation exercises in which both the Europeans and the Americans had engaged during the preparatory stages proved rather futile. The organisers indeed managed to show their visitors 'American "know-how" at its best'. As a result however, most of the European industrialists realised that they were being 'oversold on the comparative case of adopting U.S. production, distribution, and marketing practices'.[31] What seems to have incensed many of the visitors was the lack of understanding for the European situation, namely the diversity of cultures and circumstances in Europe. They especially criticised the inclination of American businessmen 'to reach sweeping, "black-or-white" conclusions in the face of even the most complex problems'.[32]

Most European participants insisted that the different conditions in Europe constituted almost insurmountable obstacles for the adoption of the US model, at least for the time being. Probably the best expression of this attitude can be found in the report from one of the American escorts:

> Many friendly critics from abroad stated that they envy and, *in the abstract*, endorse our system of maximizing production and distribution, expanding markets, lowering production costs, and increasing wages. In the words of one delegate, however, these and attendant policies constitute 'an ideal only fully realizable in the Europe of the future.[33]

The British delegation appeared the most sceptical regarding the American model and the least enthusiastic about the whole event. This had already become apparent in the preparation of 'Operation Impact'. During a preparatory visit to London in September 1951, NMC president Eldrige Haynes had to 'reinspire [the] Federation of British Industries to co-operate more fully'.[34] British participants openly voiced their doubts about the possibility of applying the US model in Europe. To give but one example, in the session on production policies, Ernest H. Lever, the chairman of Richard Thomas & Baldwins Steel Company, stressed that 'great caution is necessary before applying American production techniques generally to Europe. The indiscriminate adoption of large-scale mechanisation and mass production, he continued, 'can be *highly dangerous*'.[35] Similarly, the report of the UK delegation concluded that, 'although there is much to be learned from the American way of attaining high productivity, they remain convinced that British and European conditions make it impossible for these methods to be copied wholesale as they stand.'[36]

Concerning the different issues debated at the New York conference, as anticipated, the Europeans were faced with considerable criticisms from their American counterparts with respect to restrictive business practices. The discussion about the benefits of competition extended beyond the session dedicated to this topic. Thus, Paul Hoffman focused much of his keynote address on the need for strong competition which he described as crucial for the achievements of the United States in terms of productivity and living standards. But while his judgement of current European practices was quite harsh, he clearly refrained from direct interference:

> It is not for us Americans to say that you should abandon the highly civilized competition that prevails in most of your countries in favor of the very uncomfortable form of competition that we have in the United States. Whether you shift at all, or the extent of the shift, is something that you alone should decide. However if you wish to achieve the leap in productivity that Europe so desperately needs, it seems to me that some shift, perhaps a considerable shift, is indicated.[37]

Against this background, it is not surprising that the European spokesman on competition policies, Pierre Ricard, failed to convince the American hosts about the crucial role of 'commercial accords' in the transition towards integrated markets in Europe.[38] Neither did the latter believe European assurances that cartels were much less frequent than was generally assumed. Occasionally, European participants would voice their frustration and try to push the Americans from their moral high ground. Sir William Rootes, chairman of Rootes Motors and one of the leaders of the British delegation, asked to hear 'from our American friends something in regard to the American enthusiasm for competition when high tariffs are applied to many goods'. This exposure of what must have seemed like American hypocrisy was greeted with 'laughter and applause' by many Europeans.[39]

The debate about the competition issue continued even after the New York conference. *The Economist* of 15 December 1951 reported on the event and quoted extensively from Hoffman's speech, highlighting that much of the less brilliant episodes of American anti-trust legislative history had remained in the dark, namely the fact that American employers had strongly opposed the passage of the Sherman and Clayton acts in 1890 and 1914 respectively. This prompted a response from the American newspaper *Tribune* in Iowa which underlined that both acts had nevertheless become law and were now rigorously enforced.[40]

On most of the other issues the Americans apparently equally failed to convince the European business leaders of the superiority of their model of management. This outcome prompted the following evaluation in the French newspaper *Le Monde* on 9 December 1951:

> Sometimes, the conference left the impression of a dialogue between the deaf: The Americans insisted on their criticism of the outdated and reactionary social practices on the old continent, while the Europeans claimed that it would be impossible to apply the methods of standardisation, specialisation and public relations over night, as much as they seemed desirable in principle.[41]

However, as seen above, the American organisers did not perceive the whole venture as a failure, despite the obvious disagreements and mutual accusations. On the whole, the European delegates appear to have come to similar conclusions. Even the British participants declared that they were 'glad to have been at the Conference', despite putting more into it than getting out of it. From their final report, it becomes clear that one of the major reasons for this relatively positive evaluation was the American hospitality: 'Finally, all members of the British delegation feel the warmest appreciation of a great many kindnesses. They have experienced the stimulation that always comes from the great energy and determination of Americans, and at the same time the friendly naturalness which is so endearing a characteristic of all of them.'[42] Most of the other delegations certainly shared this appreciation. Indeed, during the productivity mission many American industrialists entertained the European visitors at their own homes.

But another factor was even more important in preserving a sense of unity, despite the obvious differences in outlook. The communist threat and the common rearmament effort acted as a sort of 'federator'. Thus, the one-day visit to Washington comprised an afternoon at the Pentagon with detailed information about the war in Korea and the US defence programme. European participants were quick to seize on this American preoccupation and to profess their allegiance to the idea of 'free enterprise'. This was most pronounced in the concluding speech of CEIF president Georges Villiers, who spoke as representative of all the participating European industrial federations. He mentioned the great 'ideological conflict dividing the world' and stressed that all countries of the 'Atlantic Community' shared the same basic values.[43]

In addition, many of the delegations used the interest generated by the conference and the press coverage it received to address their respective domestic audiences. The Americans constituted no exception in this respect. In a luncheon speech, Philip D. Reed of General Electric criticised the US armament programme as 'too large and too sudden'. He highlighted the dangers of inflationary pressure it created for the American economy. His intervention revealed the considerable differences which existed within the United States in general and the Marshall Plan administration in particular on this issue.[44]

The German delegation, on the other hand, used the American insistence on a European contribution to the common defence effort and complaints about the shortage of raw materials to reiterate its often stated demand to reverse the dismantling of German steel works.[45] In the discussion during the session on employee relations, Fritz Berg, the president of the Federation of German Industry, or Bundesverband der Deutschen Industrie (BDI), endorsed the idea of a better understanding between employers and workers. But almost in the same breath, he accused the German Trade Union Federation of aiming to eliminate free enterprise or *unternehmerische Wirtschaft*. Berg also strongly opposed the proposed codetermination in the German iron and steel industry, since it would undermine the exclusive right of managers to manage.[46] Not surprisingly, both of these interventions found an ample echo in the German press, a publicity certainly welcomed by the business representatives.

As seen above, participants from the UK also scored a number of points but, to their own embarrassment, could provide no satisfactory answer 'to the universal criticism levelled at Britain for her failure to produce coal'.[47] The French delegates were quick to seize on everything that was said about excessive government involvement for their own attacks on the alleged *dirigisme* in France. In his concluding speech Villiers vituperated against the welfare state as a socialist effort towards equalisation, almost as much as against communism.[48]

Finally, the business representatives from the six countries which had signed the ECSC treaty issued a carefully worded statement, endorsing the establishment of a common European market but highlighting the need to involve business representatives in its organisation.[49] They also welcomed it as a step towards French–German reconciliation and the creation of a federal Europe. Delegates from France and Germany very ostentatiously demonstrated their new found unity at the New York conference. The close relationship between the employer organisations of both countries benefited from the personal friendship between Berg and Villiers, and had been cemented only a few weeks earlier at a meeting in Düsseldorf with the establishment of a joint committee.[50]

Much of the joint efforts of the French and German employers association in 1950–1 had focused on the negotiations of the ECSC treaty, namely on a weakening of its strict anti-cartel provisions; but with little success. Somewhat ironically, the most important and lasting – though unplanned – contribution of 'Operation Impact' towards the transformation of European business systems may have occurred in this area. The French government scheduled the parliamentary debates about the ECSC treaty in late November/early December 1951, when many of those who opposed the creation of a large and competitive coal and steel market in Western Europe were in the United States. The absence of leading representatives of the steel industry and the top employers' association seems likely to have facilitated the ratification of the treaty.[51]

Thus, with the possible exception of the ECSC treaty ratification in France, 'Operation Impact' seems to have achieved very little. The close encounter between leading European and US industrialists certainly highlighted the significant differences between their outlook on most of the topics discussed, but quite clearly failed to convince the former of the – alleged – superiority of US-style capitalism. Nevertheless, most of the European delegates certainly would have drawn a positive conclusion from their participation in the event. On the one hand, American hospitality created a very positive atmosphere. On the other hand, and more importantly, the common defence efforts and the common enemy could be invoked to bridge the gap between both sides of the Atlantic. However, this 'community of values' did not extend into more mundane areas such as industrial democracy or the benefits of competition.

Conclusion

The American idea to invite a large group of business leaders from Europe certainly appears justified, given their important 'linking role' in the transfer of management know-how. However, there were a number of barriers which prevented the European representatives from adopting the US management model, and sometimes even from considering its merits. One of these was their concern with questions of a political rather than a managerial nature, both at the national and the international level. The insistence of the Americans on the superiority of their model and their failure to acknowledge the large diversity in Europe also appear to have been rather counterproductive.

The overall reaction from the European delegates towards the proposed changes to their management and competitive practices was therefore one of friendly rejection, softened by the appeal to some very general common values. Some variations between the participants from the different European countries could also be observed, with the British appearing most hostile, but they remained smaller than the gap between America and Europe as a whole. At the same time, the business leaders who participated in 'Operation Impact' and their opinions cannot necessarily be considered representative of European industry as a whole. As the debate about the cartel legislation in many European countries and about the anti-trust provision in the ECSC treaty show, there was an outspoken and influential group of industrialists ready to espouse a somewhat stylised US-inspired model of competition. Further studies will be needed to show to what extent they were successful in substance, beyond the mere text of legislation.

Regarding the diffusion process, the analysis of 'Operation Impact' suggests that the original American idea of targeting middle managers, technicians and workers had its merits, at least when considered over the longer term. The same is true for management education, as has been pointed out by recent research. In addition, the actual and potential impact of other 'linking roles', such as consultants, for the US productivity drive should be considered in more detail, in order to examine whether they achieved measurable results in the short term.

Notes

1 From his presentation at the First International Conference of Manufacturers, in the session on production policies; see note 29 below, p. 148.

2 The most extensive treatment of the diffusion process can probably be found in R.G. Havelock *et al.*, *Planning for Innovation: A Comparative Study of the Literature on the Dissemination and Utilization of Scientific Knowledge*, Ann Arbor, University of Michigan, 1969. The author would like to thank Ove Bjarnar for pointing this important reference out to him. See also E. M. Rogers, *Diffusion of Innovations*, 4th edn, New York, The Free Press, 1995; P. Fridenson, 'La circulation internationale des modes manageriales', in J.-P. Bouilloud and B.-P. Lecuyer (eds), *L'invention de la gestion. Histoire et pratiques*, Paris, L'Harmattan, 1994, pp. 81–9; and M.F. Guillén, *Models of Management: Work, Authority, and Organization in a Comparative Perspective*, Chicago, The University of Chicago Press, 1994.

3 There is an abundant literature on 'national management systems' and on the influence of national culture on management. The research about the influence of cultural and social determinants on the *international* transfer of management models is, however, more limited.

4 See, among many others, Guillén, *Models of Management*; J.A. Merkle, *Management and Ideology: The Legacy of the International Scientific Management Movement*, Berkeley, University of California Press, 1980; M. Nolan, *Visions of Modernity: American Business and the Modernisation of Germany*, New York, Oxford University Press, 1994.

5 After an interim meeting in Paris in 1953, the second conference of manufacturers, called 'Operation Reverse Impact', was held in Paris in 1954, followed by the third in New York in 1956 and the fourth and final meeting in London in 1960; their proceedings can be found in the Hagley Museum and Library, Wilmington, DE, Accession 1411, National Association of Manufacturers (hereafter NAM Archives), Boxes 70 and 71.

6 International Cooperation Administration, *European Productivity and Technical Assistance Programs: A Summing Up (1948–1958)*, Paris, 1958. These missions have also been a major focus of the academic literature on the productivity drive; see, for example, A.B. Carew, *Labour under the Marshall Plan: The Politics of Productivity and the Marketing of Management Science*, Manchester, Manchester University Press, 1987; R.F. Kuisel, *Seducing the French: The Dilemma of Americanization*, Berkeley, University of California Press, 1993: pp. 70–102; J. McGlade, *The Illusion of Consensus: American Business, Cold War Aid and the Reconstruction of Western Europe 1948–1958*, unpublished PhD dissertation, Washington, DC, George Washington University, 1995.

7 The rationale of these short plant visits is most explicitly spelt out in a report written at the end of 1948 by James Silberman, Chief of the Productivity and

Technological Branch in the US Bureau of Labor Statistics, *ECA Survey of French Productivity*, United States National Archives and Records Administration, Washington, DC and College Park, MD (hereafter NARA), Record Group (hereafter RG) 469, Office of the Special Representative to Europe (1948–53) (hereafter OSR), Office of the Deputy for Economic Affairs, Productivity and Technical Assistance Division (hereafter PTAD), Country Files 1949–54, Box 8. Incidentally, very recently Silberman helped design a similar programme for visits of managers from Kazakhstan to Germany, organised by the German productivity centre RKW and financed by the World Bank.

8 See for example L. Boltanski, 'America, America . . . Le Plan Marshall et l'importation du «management»', *Actes de la recherche en sciences sociales*, May 1981, no. 38, pp. 19–41.

9 J. McGlade, 'The Big Push: The Export of American Business Education to Western Europe after World War II', in V. Zamagni and L. Engwall (eds), *Management Education in an Historical Perspective*, Manchester, Manchester University Press, forthcoming.

10 NARA, RG 469, OSR, Office of the Deputy for Economic Affairs, PTAD, Subject Files 1950–56, Box 8, *Survey of Technical Assistance Program*, 31 May 1950; for more details about the Mosler report, see M. Kipping and J.-P. Nioche, 'Politique de productivité et formations à la gestion en France (1945–1960): un essai non transformé', *Entreprises et Histoire*, June 1997, no. 14, pp. 65–87.

11 For these efforts and the response in different European countries, see T. Gourvish and N. Tiratsoo (eds), *Missionaries and Managers: United States Technical Assistance and European Management Education, 1945–1960*, Manchester, Manchester University Press, 1998; and, more generally, R.P. Amdam (ed.), *Management, Education and Competitiveness: Europe, Japan and the United States*, London, Routledge, 1996.

12 NARA, RG 469, OSR, Office of the Deputy for Economic Affairs, PTAD, Subject Files 1950–56, Box 24, National Management Council Report on the International Management Productivity Mission, November 19 to December 1, 1951, prepared for the Mutual Security Agency, 7 January 1952 (hereafter quoted as NMC report), Appendix E: Memorandum to the ECA Administrator William C. Foster by his Assistant William H. Joyce, 29 May 1951.

13 NMC report, p. 15.

14 NARA, RG 469, OSR, Office of the Deputy for Economic Affairs, PTAD, Country Files 1949–54, Box 6, confidential telegram from Henry Parkman, ECA Mission to France, to ECA Washington, 29 November 1950.

15 C.S. Maier, 'The Politics of Productivity: Foundations of American International Economic Policy after World War II', *International Organization*, Fall 1977, vol. 31, pp. 607–33; see also M.J. Hogan, *The Marshall Plan: America, Britain, and the Reconstruction of Western Europe, 1947–1952*, Cambridge, Cambridge University Press, 1987, and the contribution of Jacqueline McGlade in this volume (Chapter 2).

16 NARA, RG 469, OSR, Office of the Deputy for Economic Affairs, PTAD, Country Files 1949–54, Box 6, ECA airgram to Paris, 21 December 1950. It is not clear whether the proposed French visit actually went ahead. A small group with reduced objectives might have visited the US in April 1951; ibid., telegram from ECA France to ECA Washington, 13 March 1951.

17 NMC report, Appendix E (see note 12 above).

18 NMC report, p. 1.

19 For the origins of the CEIF, see M. Kipping, *Zwischen Kartellen und Konkurrenz. Der*

Schuman-Plan und die Ursprünge der europäischen Einigung 1944–1952, Berlin, Duncker & Humblot, 1996, pp. 78–9; cf. W. Bührer, 'Wegbereiter der Verständigung. Deutsch-französische Industriellenkontakte 1947–1955', *Revue d'Allemagne*, 1991, vol. 23, pp. 73–86, here pp. 76–8.

20 French National Archives (hereafter AN), 72AS 809, minutes of the CEIF general assembly on 4 July 1951; see also his statements at the general assemblies on 13 December 1949 and 7 January 1950, ibid., 873 and 840 respectively.

21 NARA, RG 469, OSR, Office of the Deputy for Economic Affairs, PTAD, Country Files 1949–54, Box 6, telegram from ECA France to ECA Washington, 23 December 1950.

22 AN, 72AS 809.

23 Regarding the resurgence of cartels in post-1945 Europe, see W. Asbeek-Brusse and R.T. Griffiths, 'L'«European Recovery Program» e i cartelli: una indagine preliminare', *Studi storici*, January–March 1996, vol. 37, no. 1, pp. 41–68; for the almost non-existent government control over the CPS, see Kipping, *Zwischen Kartellen und Konkurrenz*, pp. 65–7.

24 See ibid. for this and the following in more detail; see also M. Kipping, 'Concurrence et compétitivité. Les origines de la législation anti-trust française après 1945', *Etudes et Documents*, 1994, vol. VI, pp. 429–55; and H. A. Schmitt, 'The European Coal and Steel Community: Operations of the First European Antitrust-Law', *Business History Review*, 1964, vol. 38, pp. 102–22.

25 AN, 72AS 874, minutes of the *Comité directeur* meeting on 18 April 1950.

26 See the contribution of Ruggero Ranieri in this volume (Chapter 12); for similar discussions in Germany, see V.R. Berghahn, *The Americanisation of West German Industry 1945–1973*, Cambridge, Cambridge University Press, 1986.

27 Quoted in Conseil Economique, Etudes et travaux, no. 22: *La Communauté européenne du charbon et de l'acier*, Paris, 1952, p. 115.

28 For more detail on this point, see Kipping, *Zwischen Kartellen und Konkurrenz*, especially pp. 350–2.

29 For this and the following, see NMC report; Hagley Museum and Library, *Proceedings of the First International Conference of Manufacturers*, sponsored by the National Association of Manufacturers of the United States of America, New York, December 3, 4, 5, 1951 (hereafter *Proceedings*); Archives of the Bundesverband der Deutschen Industrie or BDI, Cologne, PI 171, Report and Speeches of the British Delegation, undated (hereafter British report).

30 NMC report, pp. 21, 23.

31 Letter of Gordon B. Michler of TWA to the NMC, 26 December 1951, reproduced in the NMC report, pp. 16–8.

32 ibid. The report of the British delegation also highlighted the fact that many of the American hosts and/or participants 'had seldom or never visited Europe'.

33 From the letter of Michler (see note 31 above); emphasis added.

34 NMC report, p. 5.

35 ibid., p. 17, emphasis added; for the critical attitude of many British industrialists towards mass production, see J. Zeitlin, 'Americanization and Its Limits: Theory and Practice in the Reconstruction of Britain's Engineering Industries, 1945–55', *Business and Economic History*, Fall 1995, vol. 24, no. 1, pp. 277–86; for an alternative view, see the contribution of Jim Tomlinson and Nick Tiratsoo in this volume (Chapter 7).

36 British report, p. 5.

37 P.G. Hoffman, 'Productivity – Buttress to Freedom', in *Proceedings*, pp. 39–47, quote p. 43.

38 For his speech and the subsequent discussion, see *Proceedings*, pp. 231–64. The

idea that cartels could act as 'shock absorbers' in the process of European integration has been voiced again and again by French employers in the postwar period and found its way into many projects for an integrated Europe; for details, see Kipping, *Zwischen Kartellen und Konkurrenz*.

39 British report, p. 21.

40 Translated excerpts of both articles are reproduced in BDI (ed.), *Erster Internationaler Industriellen-Kongress, New York, 2.–5. Dezember 1951, Dokumente und Berichte*, Cologne, 1952. Similarly, French advocates of cartels stressed that these had been legal under the New Deal; see Kipping, 'Concurrence et compétitivité'. This fact was actually recognised by Hoffman in his speech, but described as 'short-lived' and a clear exception.

41 Reproduced in BDI (ed.), *Erster Internationaler Industriellen-Kongress*.

42 British report, p. 5. The tone of this statement sounds somewhat condescending.

43 G. Villiers, 'The Atlantic Countries at the Service of Freedom', in *Proceedings*, pp. 315–324. The summary of the German delegation also highlighted this 'community of convictions', BDI (ed.), *Erster Internationaler Industriellen-Kongress*, p. 12.

44 P.D. Reed, 'The Challenge of this Conference', in *Proceedings*, pp. 211–18; for more details on the divisions with the US about American aid objectives, see the contribution of Jacqueline McGlade in this volume (Chapter 2).

45 BDI vice-president W.A. Menne claimed that such an operation would create additional capacity at less than 25 per cent of the cost of new installations; BDI (ed.), *Erster Internationaler Industriellen-Kongress*, pp. 51–2. For the resistance of German industry against dismantling see W. Bührer, *Ruhrstahl und Europa. Die Wirtschaftsvereinigung Eisen- und Stahlindustrie und die Anfänge der europäischen Integration 1945–1952*, Munich, Oldenbourg, 1986.

46 This law foresaw equal representation of worker representatives on the supervisory board and the appointment of a worker director on the executive board of the iron and steel firms. Both had been introduced by the British occupation authorities and were now offered to the unions by Federal Chancellor Adenauer as part of a 'package deal' to ensure the ratification of the ECSC treaty; see for details G. Müller-List, 'Adenauer, Unternehmer und Gewerkschaften. Zur Einigung über die Montanmitbestimmung 1950/51', *Vierteljahreshefte für Zeitgeschichte*, 1985, vol. 33, pp. 288–309.

47 British report, p. 5; on the coal question in general, see R. Perron, *Le marché du charbo: un enjeu entre l' Europe et les Etats-Unis de 1945 à 1958*, Paris, Publications de la Sorbonne, 1996.

48 Villiers, 'The Atlantic Countries'. It should not be forgotten that, at the time, France had the most elaborate welfare system and the highest fringe benefits in Western Europe. On the other hand, French employers tended to level the charge of *dirigisme* against any government intervention in the economy, even when it attempted to address clear market failures; see Kipping, *Zwischen Kartellen und Konkurrenz*.

49 BDI (ed.), *Erster Internationaler Industriellen-Kongress*, pp.11–12.

50 These were part of a more conciliatory – and realistic – policy towards the Schuman Plan adopted by both the French and the German top employer organisations at the time. In preparing the declaration, the business representatives must have remembered their efforts to influence the text of the treaty with a joint statement in January 1951, which led to a public relations disaster. Its repercussions could still be felt at the conference. In reaction to this statement, Jean Monnet carefully orchestrated a campaign accusing them of wanting to resurrect the old

international steel cartel. In light of the above, Villiers cannot have been too pleased with the hostile declaration towards the Schuman Plan given to the press in New York by the president of the trade association of the French steel industry, Jules Aubrun. This *faux pas* might have contributed to the pressure from the CNPF for the replacement of Aubrun after the ratification of the Schuman Plan on 13 December 1951; see Kipping, *Zwischen Kartellen und Konkurrenz*, pp. 231–50 and 311–19.

51 For details, see ibid., pp. 307–11.

5

US-OWNED MANUFACTURING AFFILIATES AND THE TRANSFER OF MANAGERIAL TECHNIQUES

The British case

John H. Dunning

As part of the economic recovery programme after the Second World War, there was intense interest by UK politicians, economists and industrialists in raising the standards of UK industrial productivity, both by increasing the static and dynamic efficiency of individual firms, and by a reallocation of indigenous resources and capabilities towards more productive economic activities. In the late 1940s and early 1950s, there were several pieces of research which showed that, on average, labour productivity in US manufacturing industry was two and one-half times higher than in UK industry.[1] The sixty-six Anglo-American 'productivity missions' that visited the US from 1949 came to similar conclusions.[2]

One of the important questions at the time, which has not lost any of its relevance today, was to what extent US-owned multinationals could help bridge this 'productivity gap' and act as a 'conduit' for the transfer of American managerial know-how. In order to assess, as objectively as possible, the contribution of American financed firms in the British economy to UK industrial development and economic welfare, a major research project was launched under my direction towards the end of 1953.[3] In the course of the following three years, I and my research associates interviewed 160 US affiliates in UK manufacturing industry, and a further 45 provided us with postal information. At the time, we estimated that these 205 firms accounted for between 90 and 95 per cent of the total labour force of all American manufacturing affiliates in the UK. Although the share of UK manufacturing employment by US affiliates was less than 5 per cent in 1955, in some of the – relatively – newer UK industries of

74

the time, such as pharmaceuticals, oil refining, agriculture and office machinery, 'white' electrical goods, motor vehicles and industrial instruments, the proportion was 25 per cent or more.

The results of our research – the first major postwar study of the impact of inbound foreign direct investment or FDI on the economic welfare of a host country – were published in 1958 in a book entitled *American Investment in British Manufacturing Industry*. One part of that volume was directed to identifying the distinctive characteristics of the management style and strategies of US owned affiliates, and the extent to which the managerial practices transferred from the US parents to their UK affiliates (a) needed to be adapted to the cultural business environment of the UK and/or (b) were disseminated, through competition, subcontracting and other forms of commercial interface, to UK indigenous firms. It is the purpose of this chapter to rehearse some of our earlier thoughts and findings on these issues and to assess the extent to which these thoughts and findings have stood the test of time over the last four decades.

Multinationals and the transfer of managerial know-how

Regarding the 'productivity gap' between the US and the UK manufacturing industry, the crucial question was whether these differences were due to the superior and immobile indigenous resources and market conditions of the American economy, that is, those traditionally explained by trade and location theories, or to the superior way in which US managers organised and managed the resources at their disposal. The research project was designed to test the following two hypotheses. If the productivity gap was entirely due to the latter, and US attitudes and techniques were thus transferable across the Atlantic, then American-owned manufacturing subsidiaries in the UK should perform at least as well as their parent companies, and fare considerably better than their UK-owned competitors. This we called the *ownership-specific* effect, as the productivity differences would reflect the country of ownership of the firm. If, however, US subsidiaries in the UK performed no better than their indigenous competitors, and hence much less well than their parent companies, this would be due to the immobile – and hence non-transferable – characteristics of the US economy. This we called the *location-specific* component of any productivity differential.

As might be expected, we discovered that affiliates of US companies were not as productive as their parent companies, but were more productive than their local competitors.[4] *Inter alia*, this suggested that Anglo-American productivity differences, when measured at a *country* level, were partly explainable by location-specific characteristics of the US and UK economies, and partly by ownership-specific characteristics of US and UK enterprises. More particularly, the data we obtained suggested that if they were to adopt the managerial and other techniques of US subsidiaries, then 'it would be possible for British firms in like industries to reach a level of productivity at least within three-quarters of that of their American counterparts'.[5]

Obviously, this figure was an average of that recorded by all the US subsidiaries giving data. Indeed, the productivity differences between US parent firms and their UK affiliates varied considerably across sectors according, for example, to the nature – and degree of fixity – of the production process, the age of the affiliates, the need to adapt US products to meet local market needs, and whether the UK subsidiary was managed by UK nationals or US expatriates.[6] However, the general finding echoed that of the Anglo-American team on management accounting who, after visiting the US in 1950, concluded that 'the most significant factor in America leading to high production at low cost is efficient management'.[7]

Whether or not US managerial practices could be transferred via US FDI depended first of all on the extent and kind of managerial control exercised by US parent companies over their UK subsidiaries, and second, on the actual access of these affiliates to American management methods. The control exercised by the parent companies in the early 1950s varied a great deal. Of the 150 US affiliates that expressed an opinion on this subject, 49 (32.7 per cent) said they were 'strongly controlled' by their US associates, 59 (39.3 per cent) that they were 'partially controlled', and 42 (28.0 per cent) that the control exercised by the parent companies over managerial policy and plant organisation was 'negligible'.[8]

As might be expected, the degree and pattern of US supervision varied according to managerial function, and to other factors, notably the vintage of the affiliate. In short, in functions which the parent firm perceived were part of, or complementary to, its core assets, and in situations where the subsidiary was small, had relatively little operating experience and was not fully embedded in the local economy, there was likely to be rigorous control by the parent company. By contrast, in the case of those functions which required greater adaptation to meet local needs, and in situations of older, larger, and more experienced subsidiaries, more devolution of responsibility was allowed.[9]

Concerning the second point, an overwhelming proportion of US subsidiaries asserted that, independently of the kind and extent of trans-Atlantic influence and control exercised over their managerial decision making, not only were they allowed full and easy access to the managerial expertise and experiences of their parent company, but also, for the most part, they widely adopted the latter's 'top managerial methods and business philosophies':

> In all, however, there is sufficient evidence to suggest that the principles of management adopted by the great majority of US parent and branch plants are substantially the same. By this we imply first, that the top management of the UK manufacturing unit is of a sufficiently

high calibre both to understand and appreciate American production and managerial techniques and is willing to apply them where it is economic to do so, and secondly, that the managing director will himself see that his departmental managers operate their departments on the most efficient lines possible, both by sending them for training or periodic visits to the US associate, and by seeing that they are technically equipped to appreciate literature and ideas made available from that source, whilst having the judicial sense to sort out the applicable from the inapplicable.[10]

As the following section will show, the US parent companies transferred a number of different managerial attitudes, concepts and techniques to their affiliates in Britain, which, in turn influenced their UK competitors, suppliers and customers.

The impact of US managerial techniques on UK productivity

Re-reading and reconsidering the evidence collected more than forty years ago suggests that there are eight different areas where US multinationals had an impact on British management methods and techniques: (1) experience gains, (2) management cultures and practices, (3) financial backing, (4) administrative structures, (5) production control, budgetary planning and costing, (6) personnel management, (7) purchasing, and (8) sales and marketing.

Experience and/or learning gains

In the 1950s, the managerial and organisational experiences of the parent concerns of US subsidiaries invariably extended back many years beyond that of their own. In two-thirds of the 150 firms examined in our research, the US plant had been manufacturing for forty years prior to the establishment of its British outlet, and in 35 per cent of cases, it was more than 75 years older. The advantages which age, knowledge and experience of different cultures confer are self-evident, but, in addition, new working organisational and managerial practices were almost invariably tried out in the US before being implemented in the UK. This meant that the branch plants were able to avoid many of the early mistakes, teething problems and learning costs usually associated with new developments.

In part, these benefits took the form of product and material specifications, organisational charts, management practices, and so on. In part also, they concerned know-how relating to machinery design and layout, waste utilisation and materials handling; the interchange of accumulated personal knowledge and experience; and more general information, such as literature about sales and advertising, the training and payment of labour, office procedures, methods of costing and capital budgeting, work study, inventory control and so on. Certainly it was the rule, rather than the exception, that the design of factories and work layouts of the UK subsidiaries followed closely on the lines of their US parents; and for specialised equipment, managerial talent to be imported from the US to help production get started, or be reconfigured in the case of a merger or acquisition (M&A).

Management: cultures and practices

The extent to which and the speed by which the competitive advantages offered by the US economy can be translated to, and absorbed by, the UK economy is primarily a question of entrepreneurial motivation, management judgement and aptitude, and organisation structure and strategy. We have already indicated that all management techniques utilised by the US parent concerns were freely available to their UK affiliates in the 1950s. By nature, however, these are not easily codifiable or set down in black and white. Partly, at least, the fact that there are such benefits to be derived is yet another aspect of the different environmental conditions facing parent and branch plant. As, in most cases, the US firm was substantially larger, it was possible for it to engage in more specialised management procedures and to attain higher levels of operational efficiency.

This question of decision making itself reflects the will of the decision maker to embark upon a particular organisational or managerial strategy as well as the power to do so. While the latter can be objectively assessed, the former is very much a question of the decision maker's personality, i.e. his or her attitude towards risk, uncertainty and the future which, coupled with an interpretation or assessment of the economic advantages and disadvantages likely to follow from various strategic actions, will determine the final decisions made. This holds true for both the board of directors and line managers.

However, even where the same degree of risk is acknowledged, there is nothing certain as to which course of managerial action will be finally decided upon. If the decision itself is not at variance, then the speed of decision making may be. This is because the valuation of the variables in question, including that of the appropriate timing, may differ in the two countries. The explanatory reasons are complex, but the fact remains, that, in the 1950s, given identical or near identical conditions, the outcome of the final decision often depended on whether a British or US businessman was making it. The fact that many strategic decisions, such as the penetration of a new market or sizeable capital expenditure by the UK subsidiary, had to be referred back to the parent company where they were examined, if not in the light of US circumstances, then certainly from the American perspective towards strategy and risk taking, meant that the pace and direction of development and innovation in the subsidiary was different than if the subsidiary had been under UK ownership. And, as we have seen, in nearly three-quarters of UK affiliates in the 1950s, overall management was 'partially' or 'strongly' influenced by American parent companies. Finally, the continual contact of the branch unit with the US economic environment also tended to make for a greater receptivity of the branch plant to new ideas and practices.

Financial backing

In our 1958 study, we also found that the managerial philosophy and strategies of US subsidiaries in the UK were influenced by the fact that, in the last resort, they could be assured of the financial backing of their parent companies; and indeed, if a major investment seemed particularly desirable, they could obtain additional capital from this source. Again, to a greater or lesser extent, this is an advantage which is enjoyed by all branch plants, irrespective of the nationality of the parent firms. In our analysis, however, the important difference was that a US parent company was likely to be more independent, both as regards its economic prosperity and its ability to raise new capital, than a parent concern of the same nationality as its branch, which had to operate within the same market and tax structure. Psychologically too, the presence of a financially sound parent company considerably larger than its subsidiary must inevitably have a bearing on the latter's financial decisions. For example, the assurance that an additional source of capital is available may well allow US subsidiaries to exploit favourable situations more quickly than their indigenous competitors.

On the other hand, our study revealed that in the 1950s, most US parent companies were unwilling to invest much more money in their UK subsidiaries than the initial start-up capital, except where such investment was used to purchase an additional, already established UK company, or where the loan took the form of machinery, tools or equipment shipped over by the parent concern. In a number of instances, this led to a subsidiary converting itself into a UK public company, and in at least one case, of an American-financed firm selling out its entire interests to a British concern. Generally speaking, however, capital expansion was financed through the undistributed profits earned by the subsidiary, and then only to the extent that the US parent concern was sometimes willing to accept a much lower rate of return from its branch unit in its early period of growth than an independent company; thus this might be considered as an added source of capital.

Administrative structures

In the 1950s, the organisational structure of US affiliates in the UK was primarily a function of their size, both absolutely and relative to that of their parent or associate companies. The great majority of the larger UK subsidiaries adopted American procedures, in that they tended to practice functional specialisation wherever possible and allocated separate responsibility for each of the main products manufactured. By contrast, there was little divisional responsibility for particular geographical markets. Lines of authority and channels of communication were more clearly delineated than was the custom in most UK firms. US affiliates tried to assimilate the methods, or indeed the hierarchical structures, of their parent plants, as their own size did not permit such a division of labour. The only exceptions were that, in almost all cases, the American policy of frequent production meetings and public relations procedures were replicated by subsidiaries irrespective of size.

Production control, budgetary planning and costing

Many of the Anglo-American productivity team reports referred to earlier attached particular importance to the role of production planning and control in explaining the superior US industrial productivity. In the words of the production control specialist team, 'British industry might well follow the lead given by the American industry in this respect, and the Team feels that it cannot over-emphasise the importance of this approach to what is the key to efficient production.'[11]

That it was clearly possible for most of the features associated with US production planning in the 1950s to be economically utilised in the UK at the time was shown by the fact that, more than in any other managerial field and practically without exception, US subsidiaries copied their parent plant's methods in this respect. In fact, 70 per cent of those participating in our study said that they were strongly, and 20 per cent partially, influenced in their methods of financial control and pre-production planning by their American associates, and that they used the same formulae to price their products and processes. Centralised pre-production planning and sales forecasting, detailed scheduling of output, the application of work study, standard costing and budgetary and process control, the proper integration of the various production processes and departmental communications, efficient stock control, and the detailed presentation of balance sheets – all management practices commonly adopted in the US at the time – were both successfully transferred to and widely adopted in the UK, by both large and small subsidiaries, and as such, reflected the American parentage of these concerns.

As was demonstrated in the expanding literature at the time, British firms in the 1950s were beginning to recognise the importance of an efficient system of production planning and budgetary control and, in light of this, were re-examining the structure of their value chains from the sourcing of raw materials and components to the marketing of the finished product. In the 1950s, the adoption of such practices was mainly limited to large UK firms which were already renowned for their dynamic management. In the course of our survey, however, we visited 125 US affiliates employing 750 or fewer workers, and over three-quarters of these stated that it was economic to replicate most of their US parents' production control techniques. In their opinion, the main obstacle to a wider adoption of such techniques was not a question of the high costs of capital and/or energy, but rather the need for careful and systematic thought and a willingness to implement new methods. Notwithstanding the fact that the relative costs of such practices were almost universally greater in the UK than in the US, the majority of subsidiaries agreed that properly organised pre-production planning was an indispensable prerequisite for efficient and profitable manufacturing.

Neither need much be said concerning the comparative accounting and costing procedures adopted. It is sufficient to point out that in most cases, and universally where the US subsidiary was one of a group of overseas companies, the method of accounting was standardised on American lines. While double-entry book-keeping was standard procedure on both sides of the Atlantic, differential costing and the voucher system were more widespread in American parent firms; and in two cases where a British firm had subsequently been taken over by a US company, this latter method replaced double-entry accounting. However, the differences were of minor consequence when compared with best-practice British procedures. In any event, the feature which most impressed us about the accounting techniques of the larger and well-established US subsidiaries was their first-class presentation of very detailed accounts, and the volume of information contained in their balance sheets and related information – which, in most cases, included sales turnover.

Personnel management

This is a wide and complicated field, and one to which our earlier study could do only partial justice. Although the personnel departments of all the US subsidiaries we studied were entirely British-manned, American influence was far from negligible.

First, with regard to the wages system of US subsidiaries in the UK, we could identify no common practice. That there were obvious differences between the American and British methods is illustrated by the fact that when one established British company was taken over by a US concern, it immediately adopted the latter's wages system because it considered this preferable in terms of incentives, plant flexibility and productivity. When another postwar American branch company set up its factory in Britain, US experts were sent over to organise a wages structure entirely on the lines of its parent company. In both instances, the new wage methods were well accepted by the British personnel, but in a third case, the introduction of a variant of the target system – by which each man was provided with a chart of his performance, and though allowed to fall below his set target twice, was dismissed the third time – caused such difficult labour relationships that it had to be withdrawn.

In all, 38 per cent of the US affiliates covered in our survey stated that they assimilated their parent firm's wages policy and procedures in all major respects. A further 22 per cent argued that it was not economically or socially desirable to copy the American system lock, stock and barrel, but its main principles were nevertheless adopted and modified to suit the particular needs of the UK labour market. The remaining two-fifths of the firms either practised a 'when in Rome do as Rome does' wages policy, or were not fully aware of the system adopted in the US but carried out their rate fixing and bonus schemes independently.

We also identified a number of US firms well-known for their pioneering profit incentive schemes. For example, the Dennison Manufacturing Company originated its profit-sharing plan in the form of a non-contributory pension scheme, by which employees were automatically granted shares in the company after a minimum period of employment. The same subsidiary's first managing director was also one of the pioneers of budgetary control in the UK. The holder of this office, at the time of the survey, admitted that he had originally thought of it as a 'waste of time' but now regarded it as an indispensable aid to management. Another US corporation which bought a controlling interest in a British company claimed that, by changing the wages system to that practised in the American plant, labour efficiency was immediately raised by 25 per cent.

A third US affiliate – quite small by British standards – was responsible for pioneering a new system of incentive management in the UK, which later became widely adopted. In this scheme, all workers were paid a basic wage or salary for their job, and also a group production bonus scheme operated on orthodox lines and determined by standard time-study methods. However, in addition, workers also received a lump sum bonus based on the criterion of 'Worker Assessment', which comprised six main components: value of the job, co-operation, quantity, quality, absenteeism and lateness. The total bonus received by any worker was calculated as a percentage of his or her basic wage or salary, the actual percentage being determined by the number of marks the worker received, for each of the components, in the annual assessment.

Concerning the question of industrial relations, only 15 per cent of subsidiaries and Anglo-American firms said their labour was fully unionised and federated. There is little doubt that the above average wages offered by many US branch plants in the 1950s enabled them to maintain an open shop policy, and made work relationships exceptionally congenial. There were, of course, exceptions where the labour techniques adopted by the parent company were not accepted by UK employees and were strongly resisted. High-pressure US incentive schemes were also not always as well received in the UK.

The informal relationships between management and labour, and the tendency for American executives to keep their employees well informed about company policy and developments, were also noted by many subsidiaries and related firms. With respect to promotion policy, there are few unusual features to note, save that there was a tendency among US affiliates to recruit senior personnel from within their own ranks. Although at the time it was unusual for British management to demand that university graduates should start on the factory floor and prove their ability, many subsidiaries said that they were trying to assimilate their US associates' practices in this direction. Labour suggestion schemes were also a very common feature in branch plants, and were usually well organised.

While labour selection and training methods in US subsidiaries tended to follow along the lines of their parent concerns, different economic conditions and, more particularly, the acute labour shortage in the UK in the 1950s, often accompanied by a lack of experience, tended to raise average production costs. Generally speaking, however, very great care was exercised in trying to obtain the best quality of labour. A number of large subsidiaries operated special training schools, and three firms specifically noted that every new employee was shown a film of the production process in the US plant. However, the critical advantage which most branch plants enjoyed over their UK competitors in the 1950s was that they were able to send their senior operatives and staff to America for learning and instruction. In addition, an impressive list of US affiliates operated training schools for their salesmen in the UK. Also noticeable was the attention given by such firms to the question of foreman status, responsibility and training, and the inclination by many of the larger subsidiaries to treat this class of worker as being within the lower strata of management.

To sum up, in the 1950s most of the larger fully-owned subsidiaries tried to assimilate the personnel and wages procedures of US parents wherever possible. At the time, many American affiliates were recognised as being among the most progressive and enlightened employers, both for their willingness to adopt the latest wage and incentive systems, and for their belief that well paid and properly trained labour paid dividends in the long run through improved personnel efficiency and reduced labour turnover. Once again, a scientific approach to personnel management was more widely accepted in the US than in the UK. By a selective application of these principles in this country and the general publicising of ideas, the presence of US manufacturing units had an important stimulating effect on the rest of UK industry.

Purchasing: managerial philosophies and techniques

In our research, we came across no instance of a purchasing department of a US subsidiary being headed by an American national, although in the great majority of cases the operation of these departments was partly, if not strongly, based on current US procedures. Three-quarters of the subsidiaries visited expressed the view that some gain had followed from their trans-Atlantic associations in this respect. The majority of firms, including all those employing more than 1,000 people, operated a central purchasing department assisted by inspection and engineering sections. Since being bought out by US corporations, eight out of twelve UK subsidiaries identified in our study said that they had reconfigured their buying activities along US lines.

The feature which immediately impressed us when talking to the purchasing managers of US affiliates was the attitude they adopted towards their suppliers, and to their sourcing responsibilities. The average fully-owned subsidiary did not just order a particular part or material from a British firm and wait for it to be delivered; it tended to treat its supplier as an integral part of the organisation, recognising the importance of bought-out costs to total costs, and of the quality and consistency of its components and raw materials to its own efficiency and, indirectly, to its share of the market. This interest showed itself in the form of various practices, some of which were commonly adopted in the UK, but the thoroughness with which they were executed was unusual. Almost without exception, the American subsidiary supplied its subcontractor with the most detailed material or part specifications, drawings, blueprints, formulae and so on, and in some cases, prototypes of the part itself, sent over for the purpose by the parent company or its supplier. In the event of a change in techniques or processes in the US, information about these changes was made freely – and in most cases speedily – available to the British supplier, who was also kept up to date about current research and development. Where the production methods involved were unfamiliar to the contractor, and the American company was experienced in producing the component or raw material in question, specialists and work study experts were often sent to the supplier to supervise production in the initial period.

In the course of our study in 1953–4, we obtained data from 150 US subsidiaries and 45 of their UK suppliers. In summarising the impact on UK managerial philosophies and techniques made by US firms investing in the UK, we would make the following points. First, relative to their indigenous competitors, US-affiliated firms were generally stricter in their demands for close tolerances and for adherence to rigid specifications, together with an insistence on very high quality. Second, such subsidiaries also tended to be keener negotiators over price and more thorough in their methods of costing components than were UK firms. Third, the purchasing departments of US firms were more likely than the average UK firm to supply detailed information concerning techniques, formulae, specifications and so on. Fourth, they showed more interest in their subcontractors' production methods, though sometimes business etiquette prevented undue criticism being made. This was not a universal tendency. There was, for example, a distinct difference in the methods adopted by the two largest motor car affiliates, Ford and General Motors. However, where such interest was displayed it was very marked, and there was a definite tendency for US firms to treat their suppliers as 'one of the family'.

At the same time, not all transplanted purchasing philosophies and techniques were welcome. There were three particular causes of dissatisfaction.

First, insufficient allowance was made for differences in and availability of materials and components in the UK and US, and there was sometimes a failure to appreciate the nature of manufacturing conditions in the UK. In particular, US firms were often reluctant to scale down their purchasing demands to meet the UK economic conditions. Second, the latest blueprint specifications and formulae were not always made available to the affiliates, and thus could not always meet US standards. Moreover, it was claimed that information of real value was sometimes held back by the US parent concern for fear it might be made available to competitors of component suppliers. Third, orders tended to be inconsistent, frequently changed and sometimes broken off altogether at very short notice. Too often, the supplier perceived itself to be a stop-gap until its American-financed customers had built up sufficient capacity to manufacture for themselves. In general, such customers expected their suppliers to carry much larger inventory stocks than was accustomed practice, thus increasing storage costs.

Sales and marketing

Perhaps no other function was so obviously influenced by American techniques in the first decade after the Second World War. Over the previous two or three decades, the status of the American salesman and the attention paid to all aspects of marketing and market research led to the function of merchandising being treated as equal in importance to that of manufacturing, or indeed that of research and development. There were many signs of this trend, namely the tremendous growth of advertising expenditure, the attention paid to the training and remuneration of salesmen and the number of sales representatives promoted to senior executives or company directors. The increasingly technical nature of the products also increased the need for expert demonstration and advice on production-related problems and efficient after-sales services, and with this, the need for attractive and informative advertising features which would have far wider appeal in America than in the UK.

It is now generally accepted that the introduction of many of these techniques in the UK was directly hastened by the influx of US branch units. At the same time, because of differences in consumer psychology, tastes and reactions to sales pressures, the slavish transference and adoption of US methods to the UK has not always been successful. Before the Second World War, for example, one consumer goods subsidiary tried to apply the psychology and mass-production methods of US marketing, and almost bankrupted itself as a consequence. Another old established concern, when taken over by an American company in the 1930s, slashed the price of its product by over one-half, thereby aiming to capture the market with its particular product. This policy completely failed to appeal to the UK consumers, who as the subsequent experiences of the company in question were to prove, were less price-conscious and more quality-conscious than their American counterparts.

The class of market served must also be considered. Often in the US in the 1950s, a particular product would be purchased by all income groups, whereas in the UK the same product could only be afforded by the relatively well-off consumers who were wont to prefer high quality goods.

The importance attached by US firms to all aspects of marketing is also shown by the fact that, in our survey, more American nationals were employed in the sales departments of the US subsidiaries than in any other department of these organisations; and by the particular attention paid to the training and status of salesmen. No fewer than 87 per cent of the firms producing consumer goods, and 43 per cent of those supplying capital equipment, said that they assimilated the basic techniques adopted by their parent companies, though some adaptation to the needs of the UK or other non-US markets was often required.

However, in general, and somewhat surprisingly, we could identify few significant differences between the methods of distribution or marketing practised by subsidiaries and comparable British companies in the 1950s. These latter concerns also tended to follow the American pattern, save in the consumer goods field, where there was more direct dealing with retailers. The UK acceptance of resale price maintenance, by which the selling price of a product was fixed by the manufacturer within agreed limits, was less common in the US where it was more usual for wholesalers or retailers to fix their own price. At the same time, and rather paradoxically, the practice of exclusive dealing was being promoted by some US affiliates. For example, in petroleum distribution, the Esso Company imported from America the idea of the 'tied garage' by which garage proprietors, in return for a rebate on sales, agreed to sell only Esso brands of petrol. The Esso example was quickly imitated by other petroleum companies, since when it has become common practice in the UK.

The presence of US affiliates in the UK influenced UK marketing procedures in the 1950s in three other important respects. First, with the increasing knowledge intensity of many products supplied, the significance of expert sales advice and efficient servicing as factors influencing demand also grew. In many cases, where plant and equipment involving new techniques and processes were being installed, the customer either required these to be specifically tailored to the individual factory facilities and layout, or needed advice as to the effect such equipment would have on existing production methods. Sometimes the installation of a particular machine or piece of equipment necessitated an overhaul of the existing production system, either in part or as a whole. Often, American affiliated concerns were among the first to offer a comprehensive consultant service in their particular industry.[12]

Second, an impressive number of US firms provided training facilities for their customers' staff.[13] In the 1950s, this was particularly the case in the more technology intensive and fastest growing industries in the UK, such as office machinery, petroleum engineering, pharmaceuticals and industrial instruments. Third, mention must be made of the attention paid by some US subsidiaries to the efficiency of their distributive outlets. Here the auto industry provides a good example, as the cost and quality of the after-sales servicing of cars and commercial vehicles is such an important determinant of their sales. In this respect, in the 1950s the Ford Motor Company was a 'trail blazer', with its influence being exerted in two main ways. First, with every new car sold, a Ford customer was given a booklet which listed over 500 possible repair or replacement jobs, with their labour cost stipulated. Second, to ensure a high level of service efficiency, Ford operated some twenty training courses, ranging in duration from one week to one month, for employees of Ford dealers, catering to subjects such as transmissions, electrical systems, front axles, steering and braking, as well as instruction in business management and sales promotion.

By the mid 1950s, over 2,500 students were passing through the service school each year, and of these, 90 to 95 per cent passed and obtained a certificate. Advice was also given to main dealers on costing and accounting procedures, and sometimes specialists were sent down by the Ford Motor Company. Regular visits were also paid to ensure that the proper time and motion study methods (e.g. job and stock cards) were applied and used. At the time, no other motor vehicle company in the UK offered such a comprehensive range of service or training facilities, though later such practices became common among all the major UK-based manufacturers.

Like their parent concerns, American-affiliated firms in the UK in the 1950s gave especial attention to all aspects of advertising and market research. The high income and price elasticity of demand for the great majority of consumer goods supplied by such concerns is partly the reason for this. As a proportion of their sales turnover, their advertising expenditures were considerably higher than those of their indigenous competitors. For example, their share of total UK expenditure on press advertising in 1954 was three times their share of total industrial output.

Once again, it should be observed that, at the time, such firms were selling products which were essentially new to the UK consumer. In this, however, they could benefit from the literature sent over by their parent companies in some cases; for example, in the office equipment, foodstuffs and chemical industries, there can be no doubt that the attractiveness and information value of such advertising was first class. New methods to attract consumers' interest were also introduced, such as coupons, free samples and the use of 'test' markets. The modality of advertising was much the same in the two countries in the 1950s, although rather more use was made of cinema and television advertising by US subsidiaries than by their indigenous competitors.

There can be little doubt that in the 1950s, a more virile and professional approach to salesmanship and marketing was injected into many UK industries by the presence of US-financed firms. Through the normal channels of example competition, the attention paid to the status and training of sales representatives helped to raise standards of quality throughout the country, and in this way both firms and consumers benefited. On the other hand, the experiences of several US subsidiaries quite clearly demonstrated that any slavish reproduction of American techniques without regard to the inherent psychological, economic and sociological differences in the two countries might lead to much wasteful and inefficient distribution. As in the area of personnel policy, the extent to which US marketing philosophies and techniques could be deployed to raise UK industrial productivity had to be treated with considerable caution, and applied with great care and discrimination.

Conclusions

While the data set out in the previous section indicate that US affiliates were successful in deploying US style in their managerial practices in the UK in the 1950s, in some cases this was only achieved by a process of trial and error. In our study, we found it was less easy to cite the unsuccessful cases, as they did not receive the same publicity. We did, however, identify some US affiliates which had made frequent changes in their management structures since the time of their initial establishment. Frequently in such cases, we were told that the managerial initiatives were cramped or stifled by excessive parental control or lack of flexibility and insufficient appreciation of specialised conditions. The fact that many managing directors who were also American nationals had little experience of foreign affiliates caused difficulties and misunderstandings to arise. For example, it was usual for subsidiaries which had been manufacturing in the UK for a short while, and which were run by American nationals, to be more critical of the efficiency of their UK suppliers than those which had been operating for several years and were thus in a better position to appreciate the differences between the two countries' economic environments.

The significance of the managerial practices examined in this chapter are brought into relief if we look at the extent and ways in which the managerial practices of some thirty UK firms which, in the period 1927–52, were acquired or invested in by US corporations, were affected by the change of ownership. In the case of eleven of the thirty firms, the major impact took the form of an infusion of new product and process techniques; the impact on managerial and organisation practices was limited to the areas of production, planning and budgetary control and marketing. In nine cases, seven of which were 100 per cent acquisitions, the influence of the acquiring firms was pervasive in all functional areas. In twelve instances, there was a moderate US influence. More details concerning the ways in which the second group of firms have been affected are summarised in Table 5.1.

In conclusion, the evidence strongly suggests that UK industrial productivity in the 1950s was advanced by the implementation of US managerial philosophy and practices, both by the UK affiliates of US firms and by the impact of these affiliates on the strategies and policies of their UK competitors,

Table 5.1 Influence on managerial practice of UK firms invested in by US companies

Managerial practices	Negligible	Partial	Marked
Overall management control	0	12	0
Administration	5	5	2
Production planning and budget control	0	5	7
Sales and marketing	3	5	4
Labour selection and training	6	3	3
Wages system	5	4	3
Purchasing techniques	5	6	1

Source: J.H. Dunning, *American Investment in British Manufacturing Industry*, London, Allen & Unwin, 1958, p. 274.

Note: Selection of twelve firms in which the overall influence was moderate.

suppliers and customers. At the same time, UK management styles and procedures began during this period to take on a distinctive characteristic of their own; and it was a blending of the dynamism and professionalism of US management, together with the latter's unique knowledge of indigenous business cultures, consumer preferences and the innate qualities and aspirations of British workers, that were later to discriminate the successful US affiliates and, indeed, the successful UK firms from their less successful counterparts.

Notes

1 See for example E. Rothbarth, 'Cause of the Superior Efficiency of USA Industry as Compared with British Industry', *The Economic Journal*, September 1946, vol. LVI, pp. 383–90; L. Rostas, 'Comparative Productivity in British and American Industry', *National Institute of Economic and Social Research*, Occasional Papers XIII, Cambridge, Cambridge University Press, 1948; and M. Frankel, *British and American Manufacturing Productivity: A Comparison and Interpretation*, Urbana, University of Illinois, Bureau of Economic and Business Research, 1957.

2 Most of these teams focused on particular manufacturing industries, but some were concerned with specific management related issues. For an overall review of their findings, see G. Hutton, *We Too Can Prosper*, London, Allen & Unwin, 1953.

3 J.H. Dunning, *American Investment in British Manufacturing Industry*, London, Allen & Unwin, 1958 (reprinted by Arno Press, New York), p. 10. The project was financed by a grant from the Board of Trade under the Conditional Aid Scheme for the use of counterpart funds derived from US economic aid.

4 ibid., pp. 113–54.

5 Based on a field study which embraced 128 firms, which between them accounted for about two-thirds of the employment by all US manufacturing affiliates in 1953; ibid., p. 153.

6 Thus, we found that the US affiliates, relative to their parent firms, performed least well in the mass production or capital intensive sectors and in UK-managed

firms, and best in sectors in which there were few opportunities to exploit scale economies, and which were US-managed; see for example, ibid., p. 148, Table 12.

7 British Productivity Council, *Management Accounting*, London, 1951.
8 See for these findings and a detailed description of what is meant by 'strong', 'partial' and 'negligible' control, Dunning, *American Investment*, pp. 107–11.
9 Examples of strongly controlled functions included marketing, capital budgeting and particularly joint ventures and product development. Among those in which subsidiaries were allowed more autonomy in decision making included personnel management and purchasing.
10 Dunning, *American Investment*, p. 122.
11 British Productivity Council, *Production Control*, London, 1950, p. 6.
12 Classic examples include the British United Shoe Machinery Company and the Singer Sewing Machine Company. For further details, see Dunning, *American Investment*, pp. 268ff.
13 Again, for examples see ibid., p. 269.

6

THE REGIONAL DISSEMINATION OF AMERICAN PRODUCTIVITY MODELS IN NORWAY IN THE 1950s AND 1960s

Rolv Petter Amdam and Ove Bjarnar

National productivity organisations made substantial contributions to the diffusion of the productivity message in countries receiving American assistance after the Second World War. Moreover, institutional factors in these countries affected the transformation process.[1] In Norway, for example, the Norwegian Productivity Institute, or NPI, established in 1953, soon developed co-operative relations with institutions and organisations within business, labour unions, government and higher education. As a result of this networking,[2] national and regional institutions influenced and shaped the productivity effort in Norway.

In general, it can no longer be claimed that American productivity models were transferred from the US and imposed on passive receivers in an 'imperialistic' way. The process of Americanisation and its outcome did not only depend upon the strength of American efforts.[3] In other words, the productivity drive was not simply a supply-driven process.[4] On the contrary, scholars like Mauro Guillén have demonstrated how national institutional forces in the receiving countries were an important influence in whether or not models were transmitted and, indeed, how they were translated. In fact, national institutions emerged as active partners in the process and influenced what should be transferred. Nations selected different models matching different institutional arrangements, and the state can be seen as a structured setting for a variety of solutions infused by economic, technological and institutional factors.[5]

Such mechanisms have also been identified in studies of the growth of management education. Rolv Petter Amdam, for example, in his recent study focused on the role of institutional factors in the adoption of foreign models in

91

management education: 'Since imported ideas are absorbed differently in different national contexts, the role of institutional constraints and opportunities within the national system should be examined.'[6] In Amdam's studies, however, this approach was combined with a closer examination of the roles of specific channels and participants, and hence a better understanding of the dynamics of the transfer as a process is offered.[7]

The purpose of this chapter is to develop further the process-orientated study of the diffusion of productivity models. This will be undertaken by a discussion of how the Norwegian national productivity movement was processed through a business networking channel, an educational channel and a public co-operative channel,[8] all of which connected the movement to regional preferences. The development of the Norwegian productivity movement was based on the interaction of American producers of knowledge, agents who transferred that knowledge, and domestic participants. American ideas were reinterpreted by the NPI according to the national industrial policy and industrial structure.[9]

However, to enable the proposed productivity gains to be realised, a wider set of channels was also activated which brought the NPI and the productivity work closer to participants at regional level. Inside the NPI, a growing concern for improved co-operation between businesses and local authorities was matched by a strengthened emphasis on forging links between education and business. At the regional level, bridging gaps between education and business gained priority as a central part of the productivity effort. Accordingly, the scope of the productivity movement was broadened constantly, especially during the 1960s.

The inclusion of the regional level in the productivity movement took place at the same time as the regional perspective was strengthened within general economic, industrial and welfare policy in Norway. It is the contention of this chapter that the productivity drive was increasingly transformed into general productivity-enhancing efforts included in policy areas such as educational and regional policy. This process, while contributing to the strengthening of different aspects of productivity work through the 1950s and 1960s, also made it vulnerable as a distinct productivity movement.

Norway is an interesting case which warrants inclusion in the debate surrounding the Americanisation of European business after the Second World War. The country's industrial structure was characterised by a comprehensive small and medium sized business sector, and thus might be expected to have been unsuitable for a productivity drive based on 'American' ideas about the fortunes of big business and mass production.

The NPI carried out its most comprehensive regional work in the county of Møre and Romsdal on the west coast of Mid-Norway (see Figure 6.1). This region offers an excellent area on which to focus a study of the regional dimension in the national productivity drive. During the 1950s and 1960s the area was dominated by small companies engaged mainly in shipbuilding, textiles

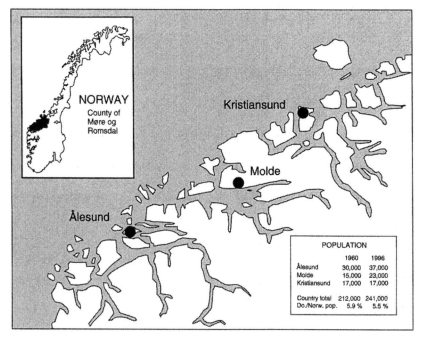

Figure 6.1 The Norwegian county of Møre and Romsdal

Source: Norge Offisielle Statistikk, Statistisk Årbok, 1960 and 1996, Statistisk Sentralbyrå (Central Bureau of Statistics of Norway), Oslo. This map was made for this chapter by Knut Bryn, Møre Research Centre, Molde, Norway.

and furniture production. These small companies were innovative and several types of vertical networks were in operation between independent firms.[10] In fact, Møre and Romsdal is seen as one of the most advanced examples of a successful regional system of innovation in Norway.[11]

The productivity drive and regional policy in Norway

When the US productivity drive reached Norway after the Second World War, the Norwegian Productivity Institute, or NPI, became a key institution for the transfer of American management, organisational ideas and techniques. The Institute was set up in 1953 and was financed jointly by funds from the Norwegian government and from American sources. On a national level, the NPI managed projects initiated and organised by the Technical Assistance Programme, established in 1948 by the Americans. In addition to projects initiated by the NPI itself, the institute also organised projects financed by the European Productivity Agency, or EPA, set up by the OEEC in 1953. Indeed, from 1954 to 1960, almost half of the projects undertaken by the NPI were organised jointly with EPA. As a result, the NPI came to support a wide range of different projects related to the productivity efforts, which were aimed at improving management education, accounting and marketing practices.

The Americans played an active part in setting up the NPI in 1953. In effect, the organisation emerged as a compromise between the Norwegian government and the United States Foreign Operations Administration. Not only was the role of the Americans crucial in launching a productivity drive in Norway, it was also from the outset connected to ideas about the national economic advantage of large scale production and big business.[12] Yet from the start, the efforts of the NPI were influenced by the existing dualistic industrial structure, comprising a few large companies besides a comprehensive small business sector, and a correspondingly dualistic industrial policy. Furthermore, it met with growing concerns for regional development in national economic and welfare policy.

After the Second World War, one of the most characteristic features of the evolution of Norway's welfare state from an international comparative perspective was the effective regional distribution of welfare.[13] This development was stimulated by policies undertaken to promote industrial expansion in the regions. The first major strategy for regional development was the Northern Norway Plan, or *Nord-Norge-Planen*, launched in 1952. From its results, it became evident to both businessmen and politicians that, to some extent, these plans actually achieved their objectives,[14] which in turn encouraged the setting up of other programmes.[15] As a result, regional policy increasingly became an integrated part of Norwegian industrial and welfare policies. Moreover, new measures were introduced during the 1960s in support of the regions. In 1961, for example, the government set up a public fund, the *Distriktenes Utbyggingsfond*, or DU, for regional development. In 1968 the *Statens Industrivekstanlegg*, or SIVA, an institution which provided infrastructure such as buildings and equipment in regional centres, was created and subsequently utilised by industrial enterprises.

The plan for Northern Norway ran until 1960, by which time the programme had accomplished much, but not all, of its purpose. Moreover, demands were increasingly being made by interested parties from other parts of the country for similar programmes to be introduced in their regions.[16] From around 1960, regional development became recognised as a more general national problem where the regions lagged behind the central areas as a result of lack of industrial and economic development and a weak capital market. From the beginning of the 1960s, therefore, a new deal for a policy to encourage regional development can be related to a more strident general industrial policy. Accordingly, there was a change in the supporting regime from stimulating economic activity in the regions to the encouragement and support of industrialisation in the regions in a broader sense. The creation of the first genuine regional policy at the beginning of the 1960s was therefore

94

infused by the hope that industrial expansion could counteract stagnation in regions. This not only required more active state involvement but also meant that co-operation between the state and the business sector was intensified.

Moreover, industrial and regional policies were adapted to meet developments in European market regulations, such as the creation of so-called 'growth poles', for example, which were also set up in Norway.[17] A more comprehensive system for regional long-term planning was introduced, although to what extent the system aimed at genuine regional development or was biased towards a controlled structural rationalisation has been the subject of some debate.[18] Concern for the regions was also found in different policy segments. Revenue policies such as *Distriktsskatteloven* (1969) and *Investeringstilskudd* (1971), localisation of state-owned production, transfer of capital to county and local authorities and support for infrastructure were all influential in regional development. From the evidence, it can be concluded that until the mid-1970s, Norwegian regional policy experienced a steady expansion both as an explicit region-specific policy and as regionally motivated aspects in other policy segments.[19]

These developments placed the productivity drive in an environment of changing institutional factors. While productivity had been seen as a major problem for industrial development in the 1950s, the need for an efficient public sector attracted more attention from the early 1960s. Norway's political and economic stability was widely recognised, and efforts now increasingly focused on the nationwide distribution of welfare.[20] The role of the 'welfare communes', the local municipal political and administrative bodies, expanded greatly in almost all sectors. Indeed, the growth within the public sector was spectacular. In 1939, state and commune spending accounted for 20 per cent of GNP; by 1960 this figure had soared to 50 per cent. Moreover, where 200,000 employees had worked in the public sector in 1950, more than 335,000, between 25 and 30 per cent of the nation's labour force, earned their living in this sector in 1970.[21] Furthermore, during the course of the 1960s, Norway witnessed an important administrative rationalisation when the number of small local communes was substantially reduced and larger local administrative units set up in their place.

Between 1950 and the middle of the 1960s, industrial growth was particularly strong in the central parts of the different regions, that is, the area within a region which contained the larger communes and commune centres.[22] The establishment of larger companies in the regional centres, which were already fairly industrialised, contributed to this expansion. Yet regional industrialisation was further stimulated by a growing number of smaller companies serving local markets. From the mid-1960s, however, this pattern changed as communes which originally had few industrial enterprises experienced a faster growth in industry.[23]

Added together, then, the welfare distribution policy, the expansion of the public sector levels and regional industrialisation required a broader productivity strategy in the 1960s. Businesses at all levels were compelled to cope with more complex external environments. The potential of the NPI to implement new strategies adjusted to these circumstances had, however, become established in a business networking channel which was in operation during the 1950s.

The business networking channel of the 1950s

Small firms have traditionally played a major role in the Norwegian economy, both in terms of number of companies and their contribution to economic development. During the course of the 1930s and 1940s, Norway experienced strong growth within the manufacturing sector. The percentage of the country's total labour force employed in industry increased from 27.5 per cent in 1930 to 36 per cent in 1950.[24] In 1930, 27.2 per cent of all employees in the manufacturing sector worked in small enterprises with less than 50 employees; by 1948, 41.9 per cent of all employees worked in small companies.

The industrial policy of the Norwegian Labour government after the Second World War was intended to encourage the growth of large companies. The Norwegian economy was, however, still dominated by the small business sector during the 1960s, when the percentage of employees working in manufacturing companies with less than 50 employees had fallen only slightly from 41.9 per cent in 1948 to 38.4 per cent in 1963.[25] This prevailing industrial structure affected the country's industrial policy. On the one hand, the idea was advocated that large companies were better suited to take advantage of modern technology than small companies, and subsequently there was a need to increase the average size of Norwegian firms. On the other hand, by the early 1950s the government realised that because of tradition, resistance from owners and resistance from different regional interest groups, radical changes would only be possible in the long term. The government's advice on the productivity question was, therefore, to maximise the potential of the existing industrial structure dominated by smaller businesses. Developing horizontal networks and co-operation between firms in marketing, purchasing, technological development and research activity would thus be an efficient strategy.[26]

The Americans and the Norwegian government shared a common goal, namely 'the greatest possible modernisation and rationalisation of means of production through close collaboration between the unions, industry, and the government' and this approach was maintained throughout the 1950s.[27] On the one hand, the NPI was concerned with the lack of large units within industry, which hampered the use of modern technology. On the other hand, it made substantial efforts to develop co-operation among small firms within areas such as accounting and marketing. Local productivity branches were set up in districts which were dominated by small firms. The first of these branches was established in 1957, and by 1963 thirteen branches, three of which were in the county Møre and Romsdal, were in operation.[28] This represented an important expansion of the national productivity drive, and opened up a new channel of regional business networks.

During the 1950s and early 1960s, different local branches of the NPI were set up in three of the region's small towns, Kristiansund, Molde and Ålesund (see Figure 6.1). In 1959, one of the local branches counted among its membership fifteen different organisations representing almost all of the manufacturing industry, craft-related industry and wholesale trade in the sub-region. Businesses in the region, dominated by small firms and business groups, regarded the NPI as an opportunity to promote their own interests.[29] Since small businesses lacked both R&D capacity and managerial resources, the NPI launched a policy creating substitutes for such institutions. In 1962–3, due to initiatives and financial aid from the NPI and a semi-public consultancy *Statens Teknologiske Institutt* or STI, an 'industrial laboratory' was set up in the town of Ålesund. The establishment of this laboratory had, since 1954, been a matter of high priority within both the NPI and the local branches. The main purpose of the laboratory was to serve local industries, and it was intended that it would act as a stimulant to automation within industry in the region. The NPI also established model enterprises with the intention of encouraging further rationalisation and, in 1957, set up a committee which undertook a thorough study of all mechanised industry within the county in order to introduce the subcontracting system. By 1959, over 160 mechanised enterprises had taken part in a programme specifically designed to increase this system. Clearly, it can be argued that, even at the regional level, at least a vision of the advantages of economies of scale was present and was intermingled with an American-inspired productivity drive.

The industrial structure and industrial policy, however, also demanded a dualistic productivity drive at regional level. Co-operative projects that were clearly intended to promote economies of scale and mass production techniques emerged as networks between independent firms in the Møre and Romsdal region. In the textile industry, for example, both co-operation and specialisation between enterprises was increased so that firms agreed to concentrate production in the ranges at which they were particularly adept, in order to avoid overproduction of clothes that were too similar. In 1962, twelve such companies jointly established a common production unit which enabled each independent firm to specialise in certain products and to achieve a more flexible production. The business networks took various forms. Hans Hauge, one of the central figures of the STI which co-operated extensively with the NPI, described one such project as follows:

> I must also mention a co-operation project in the woodworking industry in this country. One large enterprise has set out the production of parts for kitchen furnishing, office-lockers etc. on a sub-contracting basis to several smaller enterprises. This large enterprise then puts the

parts together and sells the products to a network of dealers who only handle this group's products in kitchen furnishing and office lockers. Partial vertical co-operation need not be partial only because it encompasses some of the links in the chain from the raw material to consumers. It may also be vertical and partial because only part of the participants' production capacity is engaged in the co-operative project.[30]

Hauge also described various forms of horizontal co-operation where 'two or more enterprises co-operate to solve special problems they have in common in one or a number of functional fields.'

A common characteristic of the regional business networks, which have been reconstructed in different industries, was specialisation and division of labour between independent units engaged in networking. It was believed that this networking would enable each firm to engage in a wider delivery of products than could have been carried out on an individual basis.[31] Placed in a structural and institutional context, these techniques emerged as a productivity model based on networking. A number of business networks have been traced in the county within motor production, the furniture industry and the textile industry.[32] Thus, a tendency in the region which was apparent from the 1930s, to create co-operative arrangements between independent firms, was followed up by the NPI.

On a national level, however, networking competed with mergers as the main strategy for developing co-operation between firms. From the mid-1960s the government, jointly with industrial associations, began to promote and support the expansion of a large-scale business sector through mergers and acquisitions, which meant the sacrifice of small companies.[33] By 1974, it became clear that only a few mergers had been achieved during the 1950s and 1960s, and the NPI conceded that in future the SME sector would remain the major target area for their work, including improved management education.[34] According to the NPI's own investigations in the early 1960s, 28 mergers involving 65 enterprises were achieved between 1959 and 1961, while 83 new co-operative agreements, embracing over 284 companies, were entered into during the same period. Documents reveal that at least 141 co-operative contracts were entered into in 'recent years' (i.e. to September 1963).[35] The number of merger contracts, on the other hand, was stagnating.[36] Although these sources are not wholly reliable, they do demonstrate that the majority of the mergers occurred in central parts of Norway, while the co-operative contracting was most often a regional phenomenon. It must be pointed out, however, that these figures highlight the NPI's strategy in regional Norway and we cannot at this stage of our research accurately define the in-depth structural or economic influence of such business networks.

The local co-operative channel of the 1960s

As the general focus on regional development intensified at the beginning of the 1960s, the local branches of the NPI faced new challenges. Business networking was extended to incorporate a local co-operative channel involving business and local authorities. The NPI sources from Møre and Romsdal reveal the ways in which the local branches of the NPI intervened in areas of regional development at this time. There was 'a new vision', according to the local branch in Kristiansund: 'The new vision is that good administration and management constitutes the dynamic element which determines the degree of effectiveness both in business and in public affairs.'[37] Regional policy and its development created new and more complex challenges to local commune administrations, and the relations and interaction between businesses and these authorities became much tighter. One outcome was that the local branch of the NPI proposed that the position of financial officer be created in the town's central administration. The idea was received positively and financial officers were appointed to many of the commune administrations in Norway during the 1960s and 1970s. Moreover, these financial officers came to play an influential role in both local politics and administration.

A financial officer within the local public administration could be an important link between an expanding local administration and business. Furthermore, rationalisation projects carried out in the region involved several industrial organisations, central authorities within the fish industry, and the national public fund for regional development (*Distriktenes Utbyggingsfond*, or DU). A more complex organisation of productivity work required a new kind of expertise. The expanding public administrative sector offered a challenge to the productivity work. Indeed, the 1964 Annual Report of the Kristiansund branch concluded that, 'with a fast, growing need for links between business and local community authorities, a genuine productivity promoting strategy must be to create a better mutual understanding between the sectors.'[38]

One response by the NPI to this problem was the introduction of the *Bedriftsledersamlinger*, regional conferences for SME managers which were seen as 'a new form of local productivity work'. The conferences resulted in more frequent use of consultancies in the regions and also led to 'a substantial increase in the number of applications from local businesses to the DU'.[39] No doubt these conferences were also intended to promote enthusiasm for improved management training and local co-operation. In 1963, the local NPI branches in Møre and Romsdal established regular meetings between politicians, administrators and business representatives in Rindal and Stranda, the latter being the most important centre for the region's furniture industry. Moreover, the local branch in Kristiansund organised co-ordinating conferences between all enterprises within the sub-region's mechanised industry in order to strengthen co-operation within the business sector.[40] Again, in 1964 the Kristiansund and Nordmøre branch of NPI set up four co-ordinating meetings between commune authorities and business managers. The objective of the meetings was to discuss in what ways local authorities could support businesses. They addressed problems such as improved infrastructure, better access to finance capital and loans, and also greater opportunities for continuous education for both workers and managers. That these meetings were a success is reflected in the statement that 'these meetings have attracted great public interest and a lively discussion has taken place, resulting in better mutual understanding across the business–public line'.[41] Further evidence of the NPI's commitment to improved co-operation was the organisation of a 'regional development day' in Molde and Sunndalsøra in August 1964.[42]

A substantial number of *bedriftsanalyser* (analyses of a firm) were carried out up until 1965. During 1966 this work was expanded to include a method of systematic 'learning from each other'. Here, managerial teams from different local enterprises visited and studied each others' firms, and the visits were followed up by conferences that systematically discussed the participating teams' impressions. A spokesman from the NPI declared that 'this method has been met with enthusiasm, and seems to have strengthened each firm as they can learn from each others experiences'.[43] Many firms also used consultancies in order to improve organisational and managerial practice, establish better accounting systems, set up co-operative agreements in order to lower the production costs, and investigate new market and export potentials. The work also included the training of skilled workers and middle managers. All these measures were successful, according to the local branch of the NPI.[44]

It is interesting to note that some company analysis received public financial support, both in the form of local authority grants and from the DU. Another interesting point is that the NPI held a seat on a committee set up by the finance banks and local savings banks in order to develop financial advisory services for businesses in the region.[45] Clearly, regional development required a broader business and organisational networking in order to realise productivity ambitions.[46]

Such mechanisms can be illustrated at company as well as branch level. The NPI launched a comprehensive rationalisation project in the dried cod fish industry in the Møre and Romsdal region, an industry which had been flourishing in the area for over 200 years. Exports by this industry, to southern European markets, Nigeria and South America, to name but a few destinations, were considerable. Although the industry was still a very important one in the district in the 1960s, it faced growing problems. Central members of the NPI ended a visit in 1960 to Berstad Klippfiskanlegg, one of the exporters held to be representative of the industry as a whole, by stating that 'it is evident that this industry is far behind in productivity matters'.[47] Moreover, it was realised that the problems of stagnation and decline within the industry at this time was a wide and complex matter.

In seeking a solution to the industry's problems, the NPI considered rationalisation and improvement of the internal transport system within the production process to be the best immediate strategy. Grytten A/S, one of the larger enterprises in Ålesund, was chosen as a model company, and the Industrial Laboratory A/S was engaged at a later stage. The scope of the project was, however, gradually broadened. On 24 October 1962, local municipality authorities asked the organisation Studieselskapet for Nordmøres næringsliv, which had a close relationship to the NPI, to set up a fast-working expert committee to discover the cause of the decline in the fish industry in the region. The committee was especially requested to examine the possibility that the main difficulties stemmed either from a lack of fresh capital, from increasing problems in relation to the industry's export markets, or from an insufficient supply of raw materials.

A report already published by the consultancy firm Industriforbundets Rasjonaliseringskontor A/S, or IRAS, provided a focal point for discussion in the committee and within the NPI, and also among businesses. The main recommendations of this report were to 'create a more dynamic productivity environment, to implement modern production techniques and technology, to adopt new management principles and to strengthen co-operative relations inside companies.' The need for networking was also emphasised as highly necessary in order to 'promote co-operation in production–technical matters among export licensed firms as well as production firms'.[48] First and foremost, it was argued that producers and export firms should enter into much closer co-operation and networking in the modernisation of production and accounting systems. Moreover, they should engage local banks in this networking. In other words, since some of the firms involved in the fish industry were larger enterprises, the application of networking was not restricted to the SME sector.

In implementing the report's recommendations, a two-day conference on product development was held in 1963, supported by the DU and an extensive number of different organisations. Practically all the export licensed firms participated, as did ten of the industry's production firms. In March 1963, a meeting in Kristiansund, which was open only to the central organisations, concentrated on the future of the fish industry. The conference, comprised of the NPI, the consulting company IRAS, the export enterprises, the local banks in Kristiansund, the central bank of Norway (Norges Bank) and public authorities, decided that now was the time to take action.

The strategy adopted consisted of four measures. In the first place, all export licensed firms should have a 'diagnosis of the firm'. Second, a training programme for the *pakkhusformenn*, foremen responsible for managing materials handling, was required. Third, a supplementary training programme for the *tillitsmenn* or shop stewards within the firms should be implemented. Last, a thorough revision of accounting methods based on different new techniques to measure profitability was required.

With the support of the DU, IRAS, NPI and *Fiskeridirektoratet*, the government's central office for the fish industry, much appears to have been

101

achieved. Within the model company, Jens Grytten A/S, a thorough study of every part of the production process was undertaken. For example, the handling of fish as it was delivered from ships, and how it was washed and cleaned, were studied. New methods for controlling the drying and salting processes were discussed, and improvements in internal transport and storage were essential topics. The main strategy was to make more effective use of existing buildings and equipment through improved management at all levels.[49] Additional sources are needed in order to establish in detail what improvements were actually made. However, Harald J. Jensen, the executive manager of the firm selected to be the model enterprise, writing to the NPI in 1969 stated that he understood 'that this rationalisation project has now come to an end', and continued:

> As chairman of the committee responsible for implementing the project, I would like to thank the NPI for its support. It is not wrong to say that this project, at least in Sunnmøre, has resulted in new business thinking within the dried cod fish industry. It has been possible to monitor and measure the results directly, especially concerning internal transport. However, it is equally important that firms discovered that things could be improved, and that improvements and rationalisation could also be achieved by utilising existing buildings and equipment. The rationalisation project produced new ideas and strategies that many firms have now implemented.[50]

The reconstruction of some aspects of the productivity effort at local community and company level seem to indicate that the more 'technical' approach to productivity was still maintained, and was probably operating quite well even in the latter half of the 1960s. Yet it seems reasonable to conclude that, in the daily work of the local branches at least, a wider approach to productivity and the 'new vision' strengthened the networking of the NPI. It also widened business networks to include a number of banks, public funds for regional development, research institutions and local as well as central public authorities. The development of regional policy and regional economic growth created new challenges as well as possibilities for the NPI.

One essential channel in the productivity effort which infused its character nationally, as well as increasingly on the regional level, remains to be examined: the promotion of business education. In fact, the business networking and practical productivity work could hardly have been conducted without the corresponding educational networking.

Education for productivity

The relationship with different educational and training institutions had been important in the productivity movement during the 1950s. At a regional level the necessity for better management training was advocated and through a series of meetings, earlier referred to as *bedriftsledersamlinger*, the performance of many firms was investigated in some detail. As a result, improvements in management techniques and functional as well as general management practices were suggested.[51] A wide range of short management courses were made available which were intended not only to improve the skills of the top managers within the largest enterprises in the county, but also to train middle managers in a variety of management techniques. The SME sector was, however, an equally important target group for most of these courses.

The courses covered a range of techniques such as accounting, sales, marketing and market analysis. A series of courses and conferences on personnel administration, management development and organisational development were also available. Some of the courses did encourage assembly line production and subcontracting, but mostly they were devoted to problems of management in general and cost effectiveness.[52] Thus from the start, the creation of business networks was energetically supported by management training and education on a small scale. The content of a course entitled 'Education for Rationalisation', for example, concentrated on system analysis, work studies, simplification of operations in production, frequency studies, use of standard data and Method–Time–Measurement or MTM principles. In accounting courses, the setting up of financial accounts plans, directions for job costing and complete cost account systems were all considered to be essential elements. Courses in marketing covered topics in, for example, buyer motives analysis, marketing techniques and product development. Such courses were frequently followed up by private consultancies which critically investigated sales functions and sales methods in many firms, and suggested improvements in such functions.[53] All in all, the productivity effort dealt with translating and implementing a range of different techniques, rather than advocating a grand productivity model based on an 'American' example. It is, however, fair to conclude that the USA played an important role in providing knowledge about these techniques.

From its establishment in 1953, the NPI co-operated closely with several educational institutions.[54] In its first year, the NPI co-organised a report on the Norwegian system of management and technical education with the Ministry of Education and the Ministry of Industry, produced by E. Dunlap Smith, President of the Carnegie Institute of Technology. As a result of this report, the NPI began to support changes in the education system at all levels. Furthermore, the NPI also organised visits by American professors to Norwegian educational institutions, and visits by Norwegian scholars to the USA.[55]

In 1962, the NPI launched an extensive scheme at the national level in order to provide better 'co-operation between education and business'.[56] A problem of increasing complexity was then identified: 'The required qualifications within the labour force as well as within business are fast increasing. Subsequently, the extent of in-house or branch specific training and education has also increased.' This development was the background for a national educational conference organised by the NPI in 1963.

The NPI was able to set up three separate fast-working national educational committees. The first committee was designed to define common goals for a closer co-operation between the sectors. Kjell Eide, a central member of this committee and a senior officer in the Ministry of Church and Education, went on to become one of Norway's most prominent experts on educational policy. The second committee was comprised of leading business executives and representatives from the labour unions and the Ministry of Church and Education. Members were appointed to provide a broad picture of how economic and industrial change would also require changes within the education system, and to then find mechanisms to monitor these developments. The committee was also required to examine the division of labour and responsibility between business and education for modernising the education system. The assignment of the third committee was to study the effectiveness of existing co-operative arrangements between education and business. Among the experts who were appointed to this third committee was Bjartmar Gjerde, the executive leader of Arbeidernes Opplysningsforbund, a central educational and training organisation connected to the labour movement. He later became Minister of Church and Education as well as head of the Ministries for Industry and Oil, and Local Government and Labour Relations.

One of the essential conclusions of the work of these three committees, according to the NPI, was that productivity depended on the general educational level of the labour force and the attitude towards business and productivity created in the education system: 'Business development will depend on the attitude towards business in society in general.'[57] Thus, the NPI placed itself in the very centre of society as a, 'link forger' between education and business:

> This comprehensive committee work has improved the understanding of the importance of these questions, and several institutions have expressed the necessity of following up the work already carried out. As a preliminary arrangement, the NPI will be willing to act as a link forger between the parties in order to set up permanent and institutionalised arrangements at a later stage.[58]

Management education was a matter of great concern. The NPI sought better co-ordination between all institutions dealing with management education and training in different forms. Moreover, engaging the universities in this respect was seen as crucial.[59]

Among educational institutions, a number of establishments were in operation. At the higher level, the NPI's main effort was directed towards the Norwegian School of Economics and Business Administration, or NHH, in Bergen, funding chairs in marketing, for example.[60] From around 1960, the NHH participated in the development of a decentralised system for a shorter business education. In Møre and Romsdal in 1958, the NPI supported the establishment of the *Butikkfagskole*, a school especially designed for employees within retailing, situated in the town of Ålesund and established in co-operation with the *Ålesund Handelsgymnas*, a secondary commercial school in the town. The *Ålesund Handelsgymnas* had been established as the result of joint efforts between local business concerns and voluntary organisations. Businesses were extensively represented on the school board, and practising top managers undertook some of the teaching.[61] In 1958 the NPI also became involved in different joint projects with local Rotary clubs to establish summer seminars in administration and personal management. The institute for work psychology and personnel administration at the NHH were also involved in these projects.

In 1960, leading businessmen along with experts from the banking sector and top officials from within the NHH identified the need to establish what they termed a 'Business Academy' in the Møre and Romsdal region. The thinking behind this concept was expressed in 1961 by Ola Skjåk Bræk, the director of the region's leading bank who went on in the 1970s to become the Minister of Industry: 'Our business sector has made substantial progress when it comes to technical and vocational education and training . . . . There is, however, a lack of education in economics and administration . . . . Just a few executive managers have had the opportunity to get such education.'[62]

Especially the fish industry, he claimed, totally lacked any education that took care of the administrative and economic aspects of business.[63] Bræk was also concerned by the fact that the existing flow of information between enterprises in the district gave each firm much easier access to technical know-how than to administrative and managerial knowledge. The idea was channelled through the NPI, but little came of it. Nevertheless, the initiative serves to illustrate how the NPI used, and was itself used by, different institutions across the national–regional line in order to promote business education in the regions.

In the longer term, however, efforts to influence the development of education were successful. A one-year part-time course in business administration was established in Ålesund in the 1960s, the result of the joint efforts of local voluntary educational institutions and the NHH. A local educational environment had emerged in the 1950s in Ålesund, which later became important for the development of private higher business administration education in the region. The final outcome was two private colleges which were established in the 1970s and 1980s, both of which were later upgraded to regional colleges as part of the Norwegian School of Management's regional network in the 1980s.[64]

The 1960s required a constantly widening educational networking. During the course of the 1950s the NPI had co-operated closely, at both the national and the regional level, with the STI. This organisation possessed intimate and extensive knowledge about most subjects concerning the technological, organisational and managerial aspects of small and medium-sized enterprises. In 1960 it established courses in microeconomics and management for managers in the furniture industry, which was expanded in 1965 to cover other sectors.[65] However, the educational policy of the STI and the NPI was increasingly jointly organised during the early 1960s to create programmes in management training for managers of SMEs.

A great educational reform movement took place in Norway from the mid-1960s. The central Norwegian authorities set up national committees to initiate reforms in the education system. The most important committee was named after the chair, Kristian Ottosen. In the NPI's view, the Ottosen Committee raised some of the questions put forward by the three NPI-appointed committees which were discussed above. Nevertheless, the NPI continued its own reform work. From at least 1966–7, some local branches of the NPI worked actively to establish 'economic colleges' in the regions in alliance with the NSEBA.[66] Two years later, the Ottosen Committee proposed the setting up of regional colleges with a two-year study of business administration as the cornerstone of the curriculum. The creation of these colleges proved to be one of the most innovative moves in educational policy ever launched in post-1945 Norway.

As the vision of the Ottosen Committee came into being, the subject of regional public education reforms became an important consideration within the NPI. The three first regional colleges were established as early as 1969, in Molde and Volda, both in Møre and Romsdal, and in Agder, a county in southern Norway. The NPI sources from Møre and Romsdal reveal that the NPI undertook an extensive programme in the late 1960s and through the 1970s to create permanent co-operative relations between these new colleges and business enterprise.[67] During the 1970s, businesses in the region expressed great expectations of these colleges, mainly in terms of the need for management education.[68] One of the prime objectives of these colleges, from their very beginning in 1969, was to become an engine for regional development by serving businesses in their area.[69]

The NHH, together with the NPI, played an important role in the establishment of links between business and academia.[70] Hence, educational policy became an essential part of regional policy, which emerged as a growing challenge to the practical productivity drive at all levels. At the same time, business networking and educational networking became similarly extensively interrelated.

Conclusion

This chapter has argued that the productivity movement in Norway witnessed a transformation in the two decades following the establishment of the NPI in 1953. Throughout the 1950s and 1960s, the scope of the productivity drive in Norway was constantly broadened. During the 1950s, the NPI worked extensively to promote a more effective business organisation and greater management efficiency. The strategy was adjusted to the dualistic industrial structure and a dualistic industrial policy; the NPI moreover operated flexibly through its use of business networks and its partnerships within education.

During the early 1960s, as the general regional political concerns gained new strength and attention and the regions experienced industrial growth, the NPI widened its approach to productivity work in order to meet these trends. The creation of a broad infrastructure for interaction and co-operation between businesses, educational institutions, organisations for regional development and local as well as central authorities became established as a genuine method of increasing productivity. The networking tradition was therefore further expanded. In the process, the NPI developed communications with a wide range of national and regional institutions within business and education. This contact constantly encouraged the NPI to relate its policy to existing traditions and institutions and the norms and constraints embedded within them, and the scope of the productivity movement broadened during this process. What had started as a process inspired by American ideas on productivity had developed into a national movement with its own peculiarities, central to which was an emphasis on networking, educational policy and regional policy.

At the same time, this process acted to blur the borders between the productivity policy and other policy areas, such as industrial and educational policy. Elements from the productivity movement were included within these other policy areas. Indeed, one reason why the strength of the NPI diminished during the 1970s was the growing transformation of the productivity drive into other policy areas. The story of the decline of the NPI, however, still remains to be written.

Acknowledgements

The writing of this chapter has been supported by the Research Council of Norway, within the Coastal and Rural Development Programme, and the Møre Research Centre in Molde, Norway. Earlier versions were presented at the Reading Marshall Plan conference in December 1996 and at a conference on 'The Americanization of the Western European Economy', held at Isegran, Fredrikstad, in August 1997. We would like to thank participants at both conferences, and especially the discussants, Steven Tolliday and Lars Mjøset, for their critical and very useful comments. We would also like to express our gratitude to Hallgeir Gammelsæter from the Møre Research Centre for his valuable comments and suggestions, to Knut Bryn for providing the illustration and, last but not least, to Ann Prior for language editing. The usual disclaimer applies.

Notes

1 For different approaches to the diffusion process, see for example W. Byrt, 'Management Education in Australia', in W. Byrt (ed.), *Management Education: An International Survey*, London, Routledge, 1989; R. Kuisel, *Seducing the French: The Dilemma of Americanisation*, Berkeley, University of California Press, 1993; M.F. Guillén, *Models of Management: Work, Authority and Organization in a Comparative Perspective*, Chicago, The University of Chicago Press, 1994; G. Yttri, 'From a Norwegian Rationalization Law to an American Productivity Institute', *Scandinavian Journal of History*, 1995, vol. 20, no. 4, p. 231; J. Zeitlin, 'Americanization and its Limits. Theory and Practice in the Reconstruction of British Engineering Industries', *Business and Economic History*, 1995, vol. 24, no. 1, pp. 277–86; R.P. Amdam and O. Bjarnar, 'Regional Business Networks and the Diffusion of American Management and Organisational Models to Norway 1945–65', *Business History*, January 1997, vol. 39, no. 1, pp. 72–90.

2 We apply a broad understanding of the network concept; see for example L. Gelsing, 'Innovation and the Development of Industrial Networks', in B-Å. Lundvall (ed .), *National Systems of Innovation*, London, Pinter, 1992; G. Jones, *The Evolution of International Business*, London, Routledge, 1996; G. Easton, 'Industrial Networks – A Review', in B. Axelsson and G. Easton (eds), *Industrial Networks: A New View of Reality*, London, Routledge, 1992.

3 Byrt, 'Management Education in Australia'.

4 For this concept see P. Lillrank, 'The Transfer of Management Innovations from Japan', *Organization Studies*, 1995, vol. 16, no. 6, pp. 971–89.

5 Guillén, *Models of Management*.

6 R.P. Amdam, 'National Systems versus Foreign Models in Management Education', in R.P. Amdam (ed.), *Management, Education and Competitiveness*, London, Routledge, 1996.

7 See especially R.P. Amdam, *For egen regning. BI og den økonomisk-administrative utdanningen 1943–1993*, Oslo, Universitetsforlaget, 1993.

8 Channels can be seen as connecting participants and institutions in a diffusion process in a way that messages are communicated between them; see E. Rogers, *Diffusion of Innovations*, New York, The Free Press, 1995, p. 5.

9 Amdam and Bjarnar, 'Regional Business Networks'.

10 For more details, see ibid.

11 See for example O. Wicken, *Norsk fiskeriteknologi – politiske mål i møte med regionale kulturer*, Oslo, STEP-group Report 17/94, 1995; and O. Wicken, 'Regionenes industrialisering – et historik perspectiv', in A. Isaksen (ed.), *Innovasjoner, næringsutvilding og regionalpolitikk*, Icristiansand, Høyskole Forlaget, 1997, pp. 80–1.

12 See for example Amdam and Bjarnar, 'Regional Business Networks'.

13 T. Grønlie, 'Tiden etter 1945', in R. Danielsen, S. Dyrvik, T. Grønlie, K. Helle and E. Hovland, *Grunntrekk i Norsk historie*, Oslo, Universitetsforlaget, 1991, p. 340; see also A. Isaksen and O.R. Spilling, *Regional utvikling og små bedrifter*, Kristiansund, Høyskoleforlaget, 1996.

14 Grønlie, 'Tiden etter 1945'. Although the NNP is seen as an initial phase of industrial and economic policy designed specifically for regional development in

Norway; see J. Mønnesland, A. Hervik and K. Dahle, *Bedriftsrettet distriktsstøtte. Evaluering av Distriktenes Utbyggingsfonds virkemidler*, Molde, NIBR, Møreforsking og SNF, 1993. The actual socioeconomic content and consequences of the plan have been subjected to much debate; see O. Brox, *Hva skjer i Nord–Norge?*, Oslo, Pax, 1966; B. Hersoug and D. Leonhardsen, *Bygger de landet?*, Oslo, Pax, 1979; cf. O. Rovde, *Distriktspolitikk som etterkrigshistorisk forskningsfelt*, Bergen, LOS Senter notat 90/22, 1994; and, for an overview, T. Bergh, *Arbeiderbevegelsens historie i Norge Bd 5: Storhetstid*, Oslo, Universitetsforlaget, 1987.

15 Like one for the Trøndelag region or *Trøndelagsplanen* and a public fund for regional development, *Arbeidsløshetstrygdens utbyggingsfond*, both created in 1956.
16 Hersoug and Leonhardsen, *Bygger de landet?*
17 For more background material see T.J. Hanisch and E. Lange, *Veien til velstand*, Oslo, Universitetsforlaget, 1986.
18 Hersoug and Leonhardsen, *Bygger de landet?*; see also Rovde, *Distriktspolitikk*, p. 18.
19 Mønnseland, Hervik and Dahle, *Bedriftsrettet distriktsstøtte*, p. 29.
20 Grønlie, 'Tiden etter 1945', p. 298.
21 ibid., p. 321.
22 For a general overview, see Isaksen and Spilling, *Regional utvikling*.
23 ibid., p. 47.
24 Hanisch and Lange, *Veien til velstand*, pp. 9–10.
25 E. Hope, *Næringsøkonomiske oversikter: Sekundærnæringene*, Oslo, 1972.
26 See Amdam and Bjarnar, 'Regional Business Networks', for further details.
27 Yttri, 'From a Norwegian Rationalization Law'.
28 NPI, *Norsk Produktivitetsinstitutt gjennom de første ti år*, Oslo, 1963.
29 In order to reconstruct the regional work of the NPI, the most important sources have been the NPI's Archives in the Norwegian National Archives, Oslo (hereafter NA/NPI), especially Boxes 261, 271, 279 and 410.
30 See NA/NPI, Box 279, preliminary manuscript on 'Various forms of co-operation between small and medium sized manufacturing enterprises', by Hans Hauge, a central actor at the STI.
31 Amdam and Bjarnar, 'Regional Business Networks'.
32 ibid.
33 Hanisch and Lange, *Veien til velstand*.
34 See NA/NPI, Box 479, L 858, report from a committee set up to establish management education for smaller businesses, April 1974.
35 Some of these agreements also included foreign companies.
36 NA/NPI, Box 279, overview of co-operative agreements 1959–1961, Oslo 1962, and similar overview in 1964, covering the period until 1963.
37 NA/NPI, Box 261, 8L, Annual Report from the local branch in Kristiansund and Nordmøre, 1964.
38 ibid.
39 NA/NPI, Box 421, report from a national conference for the secretaries of the local branches,1964.
40 See NA/NPI, Box 261, Annual Report from the local branch in Kristiansund and Nordmøre, 1964.
41 NA/NPI, Box 261, 8L, presentation of the work of the local branch in the Nordmøre subregion, 1963.
42 NA/NPI, Box 261 8L, Annual Report from the local branch in Kristiansund and Nordmøre, 1964.
43 See NA/NPI, Box 261 8L, Annual Report from the local branch in Kristiansund and Nordmøre, 1966.

44 From 1962 until 1964, at least forty industrial enterprises and eight retail firms got their *bedriftsanalyse* in this subregion only. Furthermore, twenty-two firms in different industries received consultancy reports, in addition an unknown number of enterprises in the fish industry and in processing of stone; see NA/NPI, Box 261, 8L, presentation of the work of the Kristiansund and Nordmøre branch, 1963.

45 See for example NA/NPI, Box 261, 8L, Annual Report from the local branch in Kristiansund and Nordmøre, 1964.

46 The role of local initiative in regional development has been debated in N. Aarsæther, 'Tiltaksplanlegging og samfunnssystem', *Plan og Arbeid,* 1983, no. 4, pp. 264–7, and H. Teigen, ibid., no. 6, pp. 395–7. The NPI was co-operating with the county office for regional planning, Kontoret for Områdeplanlegging i Møre og Romsdal, in setting up courses in marketing; see NA/NPI, Box 421, letter (draft version), 10 July 1964.

47 NA/NPI, Box 261, 8L, letter from the NPI to the local branch in Kristiansund and Nordmøre, 2 May 1960; see also ibid., NPI report of 9 April 1960.

48 NA/NPI, Box 261, 8L, annual report from the local branch in Kristiansund and Nordmøre, 1963; see also Box 376, diverse letters.

49 This process within the fish industry is reconstructed based on different letters, reports and diverse application documents in NA/NPI, Box 261 and Box 376.

50 NA/NPI, Box 376, letter to NPI, Oslo, 30 May 1969.

51 In one of the sub-regions in the county, Nordmøre, forty manufacturing firms were involved during 1962–3, and had their 'diagnosis' done; see Amdam and Bjarnar, 'Regional Business Networks'.

52 For further details, see ibid.

53 See NA/NPI, Box 421 for the marketing example, Box 279, Hauge, 'manuscript' for the accounting example, and NPI, Informasjonsbulletin, 1 December 1962, for the rationalisation example.

54 R.P. Amdam and G. Yttri, 'National Institutions and the Diffusion and Adoption of American Management Ideas: The European Productivity Agency, the Norwegian Productivity Institute, and Management Education', in T. Gourvish and N. Tiratsoo (eds), *Missionaries and Managers: The United States Technical Assistance and European Management Education, 1945–1960,* Manchester, Manchester University Press, 1998.

55 See Amdam, *For egen regning;* Amdam (ed.), *Management, Education.*

56 NA/NPI, Box 424, NPI project 548, measures for promoting co-operation between education and business.

57 NPI-project 548, summary of the proposals from the committees 1965, p. 4.

58 ibid., p. 16.

59 See NA/NPI, Box 421, report from a conference for the secretaries of the local branches, 15 June 1964.

60 Amdam, *Management, Education,* pp. 25–6.

61 O. Bjarnar, *Academic Drift and the Market: Some Historical–Institutional Perspectives on the Growth of Private Higher Education in the Region of Møre and Romsdal 1970–1986,* Molde, Møre Research Centre, Research report 9504, 1995.

62 NA/NPI, Box 261, Pro Memoria to the NPI in Oslo, 11 February 1961.

63 ibid.

64 See Amdam, *For egen regning;* Bjarnar, *Academic Drift.*

65 NA/NPI, Box 479, L 858, Committee Report, 1974, p. 34.

66 See NA/NPI, Informasjonsbulletin, September 1967.

67 See especially NA/NPI, Boxes 271, 261 and 510.
68 Bjarnar, *Academic Drift*.
69 S. Kyvik, *The Norwegian Regional Colleges*, Oslo, NAVF's utredningsinstitutt, 1981.
70 See NA/NPI, Box 267, 8 L.

Part II

THE TRANSFER PROCESS

7

AMERICANISATION BEYOND THE MASS PRODUCTION PARADIGM

The case of British industry

Jim Tomlinson and Nick Tiratsoo

Most discussion of the Americanisation issue assumes there is a clear model which the United States was anxious to supply to Europe. Jonathan Zeitlin, for example, argues that 'to contemporaries on both sides of the Atlantic, Americanization of industry meant above all mass production . . . together with a host of "systematic management" techniques developed for its efficient administration.'[1] Zeitlin argues that this model was rejected by the British because of their attachment to a more 'flexible' system, better adapted to European conditions.

The merit of this argument, based on the burgeoning flexible specialisation literature, is that it dethrones mass production from its role as the universal route to greater efficiency, and opens up very interesting issues about how different production systems deliver efficient outcomes in different circumstances. However, two dangers seem to exist in this approach. First, it sets up an overly simple dichotomy of mass production versus flexible specialisation, which continues to exaggerate the coherence of mass production as a system. Second, it has the danger of re-introducing the complacent conclusions of neo-classical discussion of pre-1913 Britain, with the implication that the British rejected mass production because of a wholly economically rational attachment to a superior flexible alternative.[2] The argument of this chapter is both that what the Americans wanted to supply was not in fact a self-contained and entire 'model' of production, and that the grounds for resistance were not attachment to a demonstrably superior alternative.

A single American model?

Certainly the advocates of Americanisation deployed a number of general

115

nostrums about human relations, the professionalisation of management and the importance of competition to productive efficiency. However, there was general recognition that innovations could not sensibly be advocated without reference to their suitability in a non-American context. During the productivity drive, US 'missionaries' recognised, for example, that European firms and their markets were commonly smaller than American counterparts, and made an effort to advocate applications suitable for that context. In preparing a report on clothing, the US Department of Labour stressed that 'every attempt has been made to understand and take into account the differences between the organisation of the apparel industry in America and that which exists in the industry in most European countries.'[3] Similarly, in seeking to demonstrate to European managers how increased use of motors might help them, the Mutual Security Agency, or MSA, emphasised the use of these techniques by American firms of a very wide range of sizes, including the very small.[4]

Missionaries also accepted that they would face objections to their advocacy, and would have to take these objections seriously. The basic manual for field officers on technical assistance programmes noted that 'objections to standardisation on account of the cost of new or different equipment, or changes in plant layout, is a valid argument and must be weighed against the resultant savings' and, further, that standardisation should be 'kept in its proper place' and made 'subject to review and revision by common consent'.[5]

British agencies connected to the productivity drive reinforced this message: 'The first step towards simplification is to *find the facts*, stressed the British Productivity Council [BPC], and standardisation is inevitably an act of compromise between varying and conflicting interests.'[6] L.H.C. Tippett, one of the foremost British productivity experts, wrote in 1950:

> Long runs, and hence productivity, also depend on prior knowledge of market trends and can be assisted by the market organisation. A powerful aid towards a judicious degree of standardisation . . . would be a better knowledge of manufacturing costs on the part of producers. If producers could correctly reflect in their charges the different costs of making standard and special articles, the economically-desirable degree of standardisation would establish itself more surely and quickly.[7]

This message of caution in the adoption of American methods was widely echoed at the time. An editorial in a trade journal of the engineering industry in 1949 warned that 'it is easy to be captivated by other people's methods and to ask why we do this and that; not by any means so easy to adopt and adjust those methods to entirely different surroundings and entirely different temperamental, social and industrial problems.'[8]

Far from being a crass attempt to export a simple model of 'mass production' or 'Fordism' to Britain, the US productivity drive in Britain should be seen as an attempt to persuade British firms to become more efficient, but to do so in a manner consistent with their actual and potential market circumstances.

The three Ss and the size of the market

The most plausible case for resistance to Americanisation in the 1940s and 1950s was based on the idea that what was being proposed was essentially a system of mass production, the core of which was the three Ss (specialisation, standardisation and simplification), and that their deployment was only possible in a market of American size, in contrast to the fragmented markets available to British producers.[9]

In a typical report of the Anglo-American Council on Productivity, or AACP, that on Valves, the discussion of specialisation, standardisation, and simplification is carefully worded. It makes clear both that this is only part of the American success story, and that, while its deployment may be linked to the size of the American market, that is one aspect of the issue: 'The larger US market gives their manufacturers a production advantage, in that their batch sizes are usually larger than ours. The US is not, however, as far forward in this respect as we had expected, and active work on it by ourselves can help to get us the bigger batches that are desirable.'[10]

In the light of this kind of example, we can suggest that the discussion of the three Ss as a key part of Americanisation has often been pitched at an excessively high level of generality. The three Ss can be seen as constituting the objectives of a piecemeal reform strategy, rather than the essence of a whole new world of production. In the case of standardisation, a programme was pursued by the Attlee government, the most well-known example of which being the Lemon Committee on Standardisation in the engineering industry, which has been discussed by a number of authors.[11] What seems clear from these analyses is that part of the problem with this government attempt to encourage change in industry was that employers were extremely sensitive to anything that might imply an enhanced role for government. In particular, the idea of expanding the role of the British Standards Institute (BSI) – a private body, but which had government support and finance – was anathema to employers.[12] In fact, because of this political problem, some participants preferred to emphasise the term simplification, meaning the reduction of variety, rather than standardisation, which implied some kind of body to establish and perhaps regulate standards.[13]

Of course, employer attitudes to the Lemon Committee and other government efforts, while highly politicised, were linked to the perception that in economic terms, simplification/standardisation carried costs as well as benefits, notably the potential inhibition on changes in design and the potential failure to serve diversified markets.[14] Neither of these points is to be dismissed out of hand. The trade-off between reducing costs by increasing the quantity of output on the one hand, and improving the specifications of that product on the other, is pervasive in manufacturing.[15] Similarly, *if* markets are indeed diversified, this has to be seen as a constraint on variety reduction (the existence of such diversity is returned to below).

However, when one looks at the debate on these issues in the 1940s and 1950s, it seems clear that proponents of the three Ss were aware of these issues, and by no means indifferent to the constraints. The advocates of doing more in this direction generally focused on what was plausibly argued to be *excessive* variety, which had accrued over a long period in *ad hoc* changes to products and processes, and which served no useful purpose but raised costs.[16] As a corollary, such advocates were noticeably restrained in their expectations about what the three Ss could deliver. For example, T. Easterfield, the Board of Trade expert on standardisation, wrote in 1949:

> But it is striking that in a large number of cases, in proceeding from current sizes of batch or run to optimum sizes for current production methods, savings are of the order of from 5 to 10 per cent – large enough to be well worth making an effort for, though not the savings of 25–50 per cent predicted by the thorough-going advocates of standardisation. Such evidence as there is suggests that these larger savings, where obtainable at all, are to be associated with vastly increased sizes of run and heavy capital investment in plant.[17]

This was exactly the scale of benefit suggested by Harold Wilson, President of the Board of Trade, to the Chancellor of the Exchequer Stafford Cripps as available 'by the reduction of variety and without any re-equipment'.[18] The two AACP Reports on Simplification have a similarly realistic approach. These two reports make important points about simplification. First, while they again recognise the inherent benefits of the large domestic American market in making possible a limited range of products, compared with the more export-oriented British market, they emphasise that American producers have not just accepted the market but have actively constructed it. In particular

> it is general practice for sales staff to exercise persistent persuasion upon the consumer to accept products from a simplified range with the accompanying benefit of better delivery and lower price . . . . We also found deliberate discouragement by price differentials of the 'special' order.[19]

By contrast, there was a notable reluctance by British producers to actively discourage demand for excess variety. For example, in the bearings industry, the producers accepted in principle the view of the BSI that they should phase out making bearings with imperial dimensions and concentrate on metric dimensions. However, the idea of raising the price of imperial bearings to encourage a shift in the pattern of demand was rejected, on the grounds that instead the industry should wait *until* demand had dropped so far that imperial types could be regarded as 'non-standard'.[20]

In addition, the advocates of simplification argued that many British producers, because of poor costing methods, effectively cross-subsidised their items with short production runs from larger scale output, so that they underestimated how much this attachment to variety was costing them. 'Many small-run lines are receiving a hidden subsidy from the main products. Cost and selling prices of such main products are thus needlessly increased, with adverse effect on sales and in turn on production.'[21] *The Economist* sought to summarise the problems with the adoption of simplification in the following terms:

> If all these advantages are so evident, why is it that British industry continues to provide so much variety in its output and neglects so valuable a means by which costs can be lowered and production and sales raised? The causes are almost as numerous as the variety itself, but the main ones are fairly clear. Many factories still employ production methods rendered obsolete by the development of mass production techniques, automatic machinery, and modern handling devices. There is still a persistent conviction that profuse variety in a catalogue must of itself ensure high volumes of sales. There is much ignorance of the extent to which reduction in variety can raise output and lower cost and an obstinate conviction lingers that such reduction implies rigidity in production and a fall in quality of product. Co-operation between producer and user to bring about the reduction of excessive variety is all too little developed and there are not enough national standards, particularly for components. *The varied demands of the export market are all too frequently inflated into an excuse for complete inaction.*[22]

What was the nature of this export market? It is important when assessing this type of argument to reiterate the point, as in the AACP Report quoted above, that markets are constructed rather than given. Nevertheless, that construction takes place within constraints, and so we need a sense of the nature of those constraints. The US situation *was* different, with a much larger domestic market and a much lower reliance on exports – approximately 6 per cent of GDP, compared with over 20 per cent in Britain. However, too much can be derived from this disparity. As Rothbarth noted long ago, US productivity substantially exceeded that of Britain by 1870, at a time when the home markets were of comparable size.[23]

But the Anglo-American comparison, while driving a lot of the debate in the postwar years, is in a sense irrelevant. If there is a British failure, it is in comparison with the scale of catch-up in other Western European countries. The question then becomes, does the alleged fragmentation of the British market compare unfavourably with the situation of other European countries? As Table 7.1 shows, at the most aggregate level, it is plain that all these countries had a significantly higher level of export dependence than the USA, though Britain's dependence was greatest.

But was the geographical pattern of British exports more 'fragmented'? This term is commonly used to conjure up a picture of British exporters selling in tiny markets in its far-flung Empire. Certainly Empire markets, though in relative decline, were more important to Britain than to any other European country through the 1940s and 1950s, a contrast clearly registered in the low level of dependence on European markets, which in 1950 took 76 per cent of German and 45 per cent of French exports, but only 33 per cent of British exports.[24] But dependence on Empire, while important for the evolution of British trade in this period, is not of course the same as fragmentation of the market. To look at this issue, it is necessary to look at particular commodities and see how far they were dependent on a very large number of markets. The example used here, chosen largely at random, is motor cars. One similarity is that all the big Western European car producers were heavily dependent on export markets.[25] The question is, who did they sell those exports to? The answer can be found in Table 7.2.

These figures are at best only suggestive, but they at least alert us to the point that Britain's dependence on exports to Empire countries – which was not unimportant for France in 1950 – does not imply dependence on a large number of small countries. In the example below, 70 per cent of Britain's car exports went to only 5 markets, while France achieved a comparable share from 10 markets. Whether this is typical we simply do not know, as no one seems to have looked at the trade figures from this perspective, and ideally we

Table 7.1 Export dependence in Western Europe (exports of goods and services as percentage of GDP)

Country	1950	1960
Britain	26.9	23.0
West Germany	11.6	20.7
France	16.4	15.6
Italy	12.0	15.4

Source: A. Milward, *The European Rescue of the Nation State*, London, Routledge, 1994, p. 129.

Table 7.2 Exports of Western European cars in 1950 (percentage of total sales, in order of rank)

Britain		France	
Canada	30	Belgium-Luxembourg	17
Australia	22	Algeria	10
Sweden	8	Sweden	9
USA	7	Switzerland	7
Belgium	4	Morocco	6
Brazil	2	Australia	5

Sources: Annual Statement of the Trade of the UK 1950, vol. 3; Commerce Extérieur, 1950.

Note: Vehicles up to 2200cc in the British case and up to 2000cc in the French case.

would want a range of commodities over a period of years to reach any firm conclusion. At this stage all that can be said is that the idea of the fragmentation of British markets relative to other European countries remains to be demonstrated.

Materials handling

The package of reforms proffered by the Americans included a number of techniques which cannot be seen as integral to any idea of 'mass production'. One such example of a 'stand alone' innovation is mechanical handling, the significance of which was a common theme of many AACP reports. The importance of materials handling, as an OEEC report noted in 1953, 'has been emphasised not only by the specialised mechanical handling teams which have visited the United States, but by almost all the national teams representing every kind of industry.'[26] The specialised team from Britain defined Materials Handling, or MH, as 'the name given to the art of rationalising handling and movement – reducing it to a minimum', and 'encompassing mechanical handling, building and plant layout, and the design of process machinery'.[27]

The report argued that MH was important to nearly all industries, with 15 to 85 per cent of total costs accounted for in this way. A contemporary calculation suggested that 'for every ton of finished products turned out by the British mechanical engineering industry, up to 59 tons of material may be handled in manufacture'.[28] The same source suggested that currently – in 1950 – 80 per cent of this movement was done by human muscle.

The MH Report argued that 'better materials handling offers a greater opportunity to cut production costs than any other single factor'. This was backed up by a list of seventeen advantages from better handling, which, the

Report emphasised, 'can *all* be obtained by British manufacturers'.[29] These advantages ranged from the reduction of indirect labour costs, better use of existing plant and buildings, less work in process and conservation of skilled labour for productive tasks, through to an improved outlook on the part of workers through reduction in manual labour and the incentive to improve plant and building layout as a result of improved handling.[30]

As with almost all AACP Reports, the authors of MH were very sensitive to the question of the applicability of the American model to the UK. They spelled out their view that the US did not possess techniques which were unknown in Britain, but American practices were different because of the determination of US companies to apply these techniques systematically: 'No new or unknown mechanical device not available on the British market is responsible for this increase in manufacturing efficiency; it comes mainly from an extensive and intensive application of known methods and equipment.'[31] The recommendations of the Team Report focused on the encouragement of industry decision makers to employ existing best practice in their own and other industries. This would require *inter alia* an allocation of responsibility for MH to specific individuals, so that it could be the focus of *continuous* attention. Improvement would also be facilitated by liaison with the American Society of Mechanical Engineers, which had its own Handling Division, and by the expansion of training in this area of expertise in Universities and Technical Colleges.[32]

The context for the application of such recommendations in Britain at the beginning of the 1950s looks favourable. Britain had a sizeable indigenous production of MH products, such as conveyors and forklift trucks, an industry with a turnover of £33 million in 1949.[33] There was an established trade press, with the regular publication of *Mechanical Handling*, and a large annual exhibition at Olympia from 1949. Britain also possessed notable experts in the field, such as Frank Woollard, and in some industries Britain was implementing sophisticated mechanical handling schemes, such as in car factories where transfer machinery was increasingly installed in the early 1950s.[34]

Undoubtedly there was a head of steam behind the MH movement in the early 1950s. OEEC Reports supported the AACP view that significant gains could be made even where new investment was highly restricted: 'It appears to be possible, by applying correct materials handling techniques, to raise productivity by as much as 15 per cent in an average factory without any replacement of existing buildings or equipment.'[35] This stream of propaganda was not without effect. The AACP Report seems to have been well received, *Mechanical Handling* suggesting that it 'undoubtedly . . . did a lot . . . to make executives more conscious of the necessity for more efficient methods', and four years later the same journal suggested that 'there can be few of Britain's leading industrial firms who have not introduced some kind of improved handling facilities within the past few years.'[36]

But while the few took note and changed, the many seem to have been little moved. In 1958 F.R. Ford, Chief Production Planning Engineer for Austin in the Midlands, summarised the results of a series of factory visits which had concentrated on engineering: 'A visit to a number of factories will, I believe, convince many people that on the whole the progress in materials handling lags behind the general level of improvement in the process of manufacture.'[37] The following year, *Mechanical Handling* suggested that 'for every commercial or industrial firm having a vigorous and continuously developing handling policy, there are a dozen or more which have scarcely the haziest notion of the importance of the handling function from the viewpoint of time and cost'.[38]

Such a gloomy conclusion seems to be supported by later investigations. In 1974, the Department of Industry established a Working Party to investigate current MH practice in the UK. This found, from a survey of thirty companies, that:

Storage and materials-handling cost at the median value was found to be 12 per cent of conversion cost . . . . MH appears to cost the companies more than it ought . . . from the sample surveyed there was little evidence to suggest that firms engaged in engineering production in the United Kingdom are aware of their true costs of storage and materials handling.

On the basis of these findings, the Working Party urged UK industry 'to take a new look at manufacture by focusing attention on materials flow as well as on the production process'.[39] In examining the reasons for this limited progress, *Mechanical Handling* argued that part of the problem was a misperception of what was involved:

There still exists the thought in many quarters that only large works can be mechanised, that only large firms can consider better materials handling methods. This of course is entirely wrong. Many small concerns could improve their output, and the working conditions of their operatives with in some cases one item of mechanical handling equipment. Perhaps a hoist, an overhead crane, a fork-truck or pedestrian-controlled truck.[40]

In some cases opposition to change came from workers, one case seemingly being shipyards:

Many shipyards have employed production engineering consultants to advise them on production layouts and programmes, but the implementation of such advice has frequently resulted in labour upsets, which, in a period of full order books, may have made the industry as a whole reluctant to use the results of such investigations.[41]

But in this case, as in others, shipbuilding may be a poor guide to the typical position of labour in relation to efficiency improvements in British industry.[42] First, as *Mechanical Handling* spelled out, the key to successful MH strategies was early consultation with the workers.[43] Second, many workers were well aware of the immediate benefits to themselves of improvements in handling. In response to the question of whether workers or directors were the biggest obstacle to mechanised MH, a member of the Institute of Materials Handling answered:

> There is far too much talk going round that the opposition received from the shopfloor on the introduction of mechanical handling or materials handling equipment. The converse is the case. We get pressed by people who are less fortunate and who do not have good materials handling equipment. They want to know what is to be done to relieve them of the fatigue and the out-of-date methods to which they are subjected.[44]

Other inhibitions were probably more important. First, there was a shortage of production engineering expertise in Britain, and this made the introduction of new MH systems, as well as better production layout, more difficult than where such skills were readily available.[45] But even this may have been a second order problem compared with the obstacles at the top of British industry. A Report from the Institution of Production Engineers in 1953 argued that:

> Too many executives in British industry still think that all that is needed to improve handling efficiency is the purchase of new equipment . . . but there are many factories with ample mechanical equipment in which general handling efficiency is still comparatively low. Good handling is not guaranteed by the presence of suitable equipment – it is also dependent on proper attitude of mind.[46]

Such views seem to chime in with the feedback obtained by the Institute of Materials Handling at conferences held with directors and executives. The Report on these events said:

> Apparently, despite the very considerable amount of educational and publicity work already carried out throughout Britain, there are still considerable numbers of industrialists . . . who have not yet appreciated the fact that tremendous savings and improvements are to be gained by systematic study and rectification of materials handling inefficiencies.

124

The same Report referred to 'amazing misperceptions' still being common-place amongst responsible executives and directors.[47]

In sum, the case of materials handling exemplifies the point that much of what was advocated by the 'Americanisers' in the 1940s and 1950s was not dependent on a wholesale revolution in British industry, nor did it require huge capital investment. Improvements in handling of an incremental nature were relevant to a wide range of industries, of all product types and scales of production. While some of the issues are noted above, there remains a puzzle as to why techniques in this field were so patchily employed.

Quality control

Applicability issues can also be examined through the example of quality control, another of those techniques frequently referred to in discussions of Americanisation in the 1940s and 1950s. Traditionally, quality control was enforced through specification and inspection, which were actions at the beginning and end of the production process. But during the Second World War, under US influence, many firms in the UK engineering sector adopted simple statistical quality control or SQC techniques. The most popular instrument for this procedure was the control chart. The operator would plot variations in a product's dimensions and other characteristics on a chart, and intervene to correct the machine settings when the trend was moving beyond acceptable variances.

The aftermath of the war compelled inspectors to accept for many years a lower standard of workmanship than would have been tolerated before the war, and the reasons for this are not hard to seek. We were faced with a sellers' market, material shortages and a shortage of machine tools, to say nothing of the shortage of skilled labour: many manufacturers had fine fat order books. The net result of all this was inevitably a 'take-it-or leave-it' and 'get-it out-anyhow' attitude.[48]

The AACP inspection team visited twenty-two US plants and talked to leading American QC (quality control) experts. The team reported that US firms utilised inspection, but many also employed SQC techniques, often in quite sophisticated forms. Perhaps the most important message of the Report was that quality was viewed as integral to the whole purpose and functioning of the firm: 'The chief of these (outstanding) impressions was the new and broader conception given to the words *quality control*. In this new conception inspection is only part of the wider function of co-ordinating all the influences on quality. There appears to be continuous cycle of *make–test–adjust*.'[49]

The implication of this is that quality control is seen as a central management concern, not just an issue for isolated inspectors, and something that must necessarily involve the shopfloor. The AACP team emphasised how much publicity on quality in American factories was directed at the workers. As one member of the team explained: 'At the back of this policy of publicity was the realisation that inspection and quality cannot produce the desired results. Quality must ultimately be the responsibility of the production department, of the individual operators: all that inspection can do is to assist by providing the information.'[50]

These points are the essential background to the teams recommendations. They noted that 'the best British practice is not behind the American', the differences being in the scale of applications, the number of firms using the techniques and the enthusiasm displayed for such approaches.[51] One of the team observed: 'Here and there in the UK are to be found firms applying these principles, in part at least, and deriving much benefit. What is missing is the methodical study and enthusiastic application by the younger staff which comes from discussion, lectures, and exchange of experience.'[52] The detailed recommendations of the inspection team report begin with a clear recognition of the importance of:

> well designed quality organisations within industry. These would have far-reaching effects on the economy of the nation: not only is the work of individual operatives rendered more effective, not only does the organisation within the firm run more smoothly, but the nation as consumer is presented with an article more suited for its work, less liable to fault and having a more precisely determined life.[53]

The team recommended that to aid the spread of knowledge about quality control technical qualifications in this discipline should be established. At the same time, they listed the steps that firms can take. The central point here is that 'the management should take a continuing interest in the quality of the products. It is imperative that the planning of inspection and its operations have the same careful attention and facilities as is usually given to production operations.'[54]

This report seems to have triggered a series of institutional changes. The British Productivity Council, or BPC, successor to the AACP, took on responsibility for quality control and co-operated with bodies such as the Institute of Engineering Inspection. The BPC was also responsible for co-ordinating European Productivity Agency sponsored tours by US quality control experts in the mid-1950s. Following an EPA conference on the issue in 1955, the BPC set up an Advisory Committee on Quality Control, with representatives from both sides of industry to promote techniques. In the late 1950s the BPC organised twenty conferences and twenty seminars on quality control, and produced a wide variety of relevant publications.[55] The BPC also provided links to the European Organisation for Quality Control, a continent-wide propaganda and consultancy body set up in 1959. Finally, in 1961 the BPC along with other interested bodies formed the National Council for Quality and Reliability, an umbrella body to provide a focus for quality control issues.[56]

The proliferation of bodies and initiatives probably exaggerates the changes which took place. The BPC remained a marginal body. The National Council was fairly small, with thirty-two organisations affiliated and a newsletter with a circulation of 2,700 in 1963–4. Its first national conference was attended by only 270 people.[57] The evidence clearly suggests that the majority of firms remained wedded to traditional techniques – specification and inspection – and only a minority innovated. In the 1960s in engineering companies, it was quite common to find an inspection force 15 per cent of the size of the direct labour force, rising to a ratio of 1:1.2 workers to inspectors in some precision sectors. The corollary was that innovation in this area – building quality into the organisation, involving the workforce, using SQC – was practised only by the few. Two surveys from as late as the 1980s found that under 40 per cent of companies used SQC in the process stage of manufacturing and that 'less than 30 per cent of industry make some use of the techniques and less than ten per cent extensive use'.[58]

This failure to innovate in quality control was costly to British industry. Inspection is not only an expensive form of quality control, it is also an ineffective one, since inspectors invariably let a proportion of defective products pass. This failure led to high levels of faulty products and resultant consumer dissatisfaction, which was increasingly heard as Britain's fledgling consumer movement started to get established.[59] In 1978 the Department of Prices and Consumer Protection commented: 'The cost of defective quality (i.e. scrap, rework and defective products) and of the attainment of quality (through appraisal and prevention) together commonly known as quality costs (for industry as a whole) ... have been estimated to be about 10 per cent of turnover', i.e. about £10,000 million per year for the whole UK.[60]

Why were firms reluctant to take up these new methods? The first possibility is that the various propagandising bodies were defective in their approach. The organisations involved, such as the BPC and EPA, were no doubt imperfect, but they do seem to have produced material carefully aimed at their target, with clear guides to the techniques and cost/benefit figures. Moreover, they were always careful to make sure that the examples they cited included small firms.[61]

Were the techniques relevant to British industry? Obviously, their relevance varied across sectors, but it is difficult to envisage sectors where quality control is wholly irrelevant. BPC publications in particular demonstrated their relevance over a wide spectrum of industries. Academic research by Lockyer and his collaborators showed that while takeup of SQC was low, 'the majority of production managers in the UK would like to have techniques to control quality at the three stages of manufacture'.[62]

Was the takeup of these techniques slowed by prohibitive costs? As noted already, it was increasingly recognised that traditional approach to quality control was expensive, with specification and inspection leading to high levels of defective products, re-working and scrap. The new techniques would lower all these costs by getting a quick response to problems via SQC, and prevent others arising thanks to shop-floor involvement. Companies that did innovate did find these payoffs were realised. Reporting on its local quality and reliability groups, the BPC noted that 'practical results are already beginning to materialise as a consequence of these local quality and reliability activities. One group alone, within a period of six months of its formation, was able to point to savings within individual companies of between £50 and £500 a week.'[63]

Was the failure to deploy new techniques of quality control a failure of management? One quality evangelist wrote:

> The 'professional' nature of this work (e.g. statistical techniques) was undoubtedly one reason why British industrialists did not adopt it with the enthusiasm of their American and Japanese counterparts. But there may have been another reason – a dimly understood but real suspicion that statistics alone could not be the panacea alone for all the troubles facing British industry.[64]

Over two decades later, Oakland concluded that:

> the most frequently occurring barriers to the acceptance of SQC techniques were either lack of knowledge of quality control and quality assurance or a lack of support for quality from senior management . . . . Lack of support from the senior management was itself often due to a lack of knowledge.[65]

In this sense, quality control, like other innovative techniques, fell into the abyss created by the UK industry's relative failure to employ specialists and develop technical competencies. This problem was compounded by another perennial obstacle to improvement: employer opposition to the creation of powerful, state-sponsored bodies in 'their' areas of concern. In this case it was the British Standards Institute, which could have played a key role in the quality arena but was too underfunded to do so. Its method of working, through consensus, gave full rein to the employers who wished to stall the production of standards. The Committee on Consumer Protection reported in 1962 that:

> Whatever the motive they regard as uppermost, there are many who firmly believe that an obstructive attitude by manufacturing interests, often concealed under a cloak of technicalities which the consumer representatives on BSI's drafting committees are ill-equipped to refute, is mainly responsible for delaying and frustrating attempts to produce consumer goods standards.[66]

In sum, the obstacles to more extensive deployment of American methods of quality control are to be found not in their inapplicability to British circumstances, but in the procedures and calculations of British companies and their management.

Conclusion

The argument of this chapter is that there was a failure by British industry to adapt in the years after 1945. This can be exaggerated because of overstated and over-general notions of decline, which often characterise discussions of British economic history. Understanding this failure, we have suggested, is not helped by the dichotomy of mass production versus flexible specialisation. What was at stake in postwar Britain was not adherence to a 'mode of production', but the adoption of a range of specific techniques adaptable to a variety of economic and production contexts. If one looks at examples such as mechanical handling, or simplification and standardisation, or quality control, there seems to be a strong case for saying that these techniques were adaptable to profitable use in British industry, but in many cases were not taken up.

We do not believe that this is solely explicable in terms of the competitive environment which, while certainly less strenuous than in, for example, the 1970s, after the Kennedy Round and EC entry, was not as 'cosy' as others have argued. We also reject the idea that if we do not go along with that particular approach we have to fall back on irrationality as an explanation.[67] What we would argue is that controllers of companies, like all economic agents, have a variety of rationalities rather than one superordinate, profit-maximising goal. Competitive markets undoubtedly force certain kinds of pressures on such agents, but outside the pages of economics textbooks, the idea of competition forcing one kind of 'rationality' on actors seems to be unhelpful and misleading. The forms of calculation deployed by companies, and the organisational structures in which they are embedded are diverse and need to be taken more seriously if we are to understand company behaviour. This emphatically does *not* mean appealing to some vague notion of 'culture', which so often occurs in accounts of the pathologies of British companies; although when deployed in a more specific way, the term culture may be useful, as in Church's attempt to understand the peculiarities of the decision making in Austin.[68]

This argument then leads us back to the points made about the pathologies of British management we have made elsewhere.[69] These pathologies are not the predetermined outcome of the nature of the competitive environment, but flow from a highly specific set of historical circumstances which predisposed management to both a limited willingness and limited capacity to follow the American example.

Acknowledgements

This chapter is first cousin to N. Tiratsoo and J. Tomlinson, 'Spreading the Gospel of Productivity: US Technical Assistance and British Industry, 1945–1960', *Business History Review*, vol. 71, Spring 1997, pp. 41–81, which includes a discussion of the institutional context of 'Americanisation'; see also T. Gourvish and N. Tiratsoo, '"Making It Like in Detroit": British Managers and American Productivity Methods, 1945–c.1965', *Business and Economic History*, 1996, vol. 25, no. 1, pp. 206–16.

Notes

1 J. Zeitlin, 'Americanization and Its Limits: Theory and Practice in the Reconstruction of Britain's Engineering Industries, 1945–55', *Business and Economic History*, 1995, vol. 24, no. 1, p. 277.

2 C. Sabel and J. Zeitlin, 'Introduction', in C. Sabel and J. Zeitlin (eds), *Worlds of Possibility: Flexibility and Mass Production in Western Industrialization*, Cambridge, Cambridge University Press, 1997, pp. 1–33. For a recent neo-classical view on the reasons of British economic decline in the post-1945 period, see S. Broadberry and N. Crafts, 'British Economic Policy and Performance in the Early Post-War Period', *Business History*, 1996, vol. 38; see for a different interpretation our rejoinder, J. Tomlinson and N. Tiratsoo, '"An Old Story, Freshly Told?": A Comment on Broadberry and Crafts' Approach to Britain's Early Post-war Economic Performance', *Business History*, forthcoming.

3 US Department of Labour, *Cost Savings through Standardization, Simplification, Specialization in the Clothing Industry*, Washington, DC, n.d., p. i.

4 MSA, *Case Study Data on Productivity and Factory Performance . . . of Fractional Horsepower Motors*, Washington, DC, 1953, p. 8.

5 MSA, Productivity and Technical Assistance Division, *Increasing Productivity through Specialization, Standardization and Simplification*, Washington, DC, n.d., pp. 75–6.

6 BPC, *Simplification in Practice*, London, 1954, p. 1; BPC, *Standards: An Aid to Productivity*, London, 1955, p. 10.

7 L.H.C. Tippett, 'The Essentials for Increasing Productivity', *Three Banks Review*, 1950, vol. 8, p. 18.

8 'Editorial', *BEAMA Journal*, 1949, vol. 56, p. 259.

9 J. Jewkes, 'Note by Professor Jewkes', in Board of Trade, *Working Party on Cotton*, London, 1946.

10 AACP, Team Report *Valves*, London, 1950, p. 4.

11 *Report of the Committee on Standardisation in the Engineering Industry*, London, HMSO, 1949; Zeitlin, 'Americanization and Its Limits', pp. 277–86; N. Tiratsoo and J. Tomlinson, *Industrial Efficiency and State Intervention: Labour 1939–51*, London, Routledge, 1993, chap. 7.

12 Public Record Office, Kew (hereafter PRO), SUPP14/141, 'Comments by Employer Members of the Engineering Advisory Council on the Report of the Lemon Committee on Standardisation of Engineering Products', 24 January 1950.

13 PRO, BT64/2399, *Standardisation*, 1949; ibid., BT195/1, T. Elliott to A. King, 29 June 1950.

14 Zeitlin, 'Americanization and Its Limits'.

15 J. Zeitlin, 'Flexibility and Mass Production at War: Aircraft Manufacturing in

Britain, the USA and Germany 1939–45', *Technology and Culture*, 1995, vol. 36, pp. 46–79.

16 For examples of industries and the issue of standardisation, see PRO, SUPP14/141, BSI statements and discussions.

17 PRO, BT64/2314, 'Standardisation as an Aid to Increased Productivity', 1949.

18 ibid., Wilson to Cripps, 20 February 1948.

19 AACP, *Simplification in Industry*, London, 1949, p. 9.

20 PRO, SUPP14/141, BSI statement and discussions on bearings, n.d., but probably 1949/50.

21 AACP, *Simplification in British Industry*, London, 1950, p. 5.

22 'The Cost of Variety', *The Economist*, 29 December 1951, vol. 141, p. 1594; emphasis added.

23 E. Rothbarth, 'Causes of the Superior Efficiency of USA Industry as Compared with British Industry', *The Economic Journal*, 1946, vol. 56, pp. 383–90.

24 OEEC, *Foreign Trade Statistical Bulletin 1937–51*, Paris, 1952.

25 J. Laux, *The European Automobile Industry*, New York, The Free Press, 1992, pp. 184–5 and 193–4.

26 OEEC, *Materials Handling Equipment and Methods in the USA*, Paris, 1953, p. 125.

27 PRO, T237/52, *European Technical Assistance*, W.A. Kimbel to T. Hutton, 8 July 1949; AACP, Team Report *Materials Handling in Industry*, London, 1950, pp. 5–6.

28 *Statist*, 17 June 1950.

29 AACP, *Materials Handling*, p. 9.

30 ibid., p. 7.

31 ibid., p. 9.

32 ibid., p. 11.

33 *Statist*, 17 June 1950.

34 K. Williams, C. Haslam, S. Johal and J. Williams, *Cars: Analysis, History, Cases*, Oxford, Berg, 1994, pp. 137–40.

35 OEEC, *Materials*, p. 123.

36 *Mechanical Handling*, November 1955, vol. 42, no. 11, p. 619.

37 F.R. Ford, 'Some Handling Problems in the Motor Industry', *Mechanical Handling*, July 1958, vol. 45, no. 7, p. 487.

38 *Mechanical Handling*, April 1959, vol. 46, no. 4, p. 187.

39 Department of Industry, Committee for Materials Handling (Management and Technology), Working Party on Materials Handling Costs, *Materials-Handling Costs: A New Look at Manufacturing*, London, 1976, p. 4.

40 *Mechanical Handling*, October 1953, vol. 40, no. 10, p. 467; see also the editorial 'Mechanising the Small Firm', *Mechanical Handling*, March 1956, vol. 43, no. 3, p. 133.

41 DSIR, *Research and Development Requirements for the Shipbuilding and Marine Engineering Industry*, London, 1960, p. 11.

42 N. Tiratsoo and J. Tomlinson, 'Restrictive Practices on the Shopfloor in Britain, 1945–60: Myth and Reality', *Business History*, 1994, vol. 36, no. 2, pp. 65–84.

43 L.F. Hoefkens (Lockheed Hydraulic Brake Company), 'The Technique of Introducing a New Mechanical Handling Method', *Mechanical Handling*, November 1951, vol. 38, no. 11, pp. 433–5.

44 'Institute of Materials Handling', *Mechanical Handling*, December 1952, vol. 39, no. 12, p. 588.

45 Gourvish and Tiratsoo, '"Making It Like in Detroit"'.

46 Institution of Production Engineers, *A Review of Materials Handling in British Manufacturing Industry*, London, 1953, p. 8.

47 'Institute of Materials Handling', *Mechanical Handling*, July 1955, vol. 42, no. 7, p. 421.
48 F. Nixon, *Managing to Achieve Quality and Reliability*, London, Institute of Materials, 1971, pp. 26–32; L.H.C. Tippett, 'A View of Quality Control in the UK', *Industrial Quality Control*, September 1962, pp. 15–17; G.C. Richardson, 'Customers Inspection of Engineering Products and Its Value to Industry', *Engineering Inspection*, 1954, vol. XVIII, pp. 50–1.
49 AACP, *Inspection in Industry*, London, 1953, pp. 3–5 and 7.
50 E.D. van Rest, 'Quality Control in the USA', *Applied Statistics*, 1953, vol. II, p. 149.
51 AACP, *Inspection*, p. 6.
52 van Rest, 'Quality Control', p. 151.
53 AACP, *Inspection*, p. 8.
54 ibid., p. 9.
55 BPC Action Pamphlet no. 9: *Quality Control*, London, 1957 on methods; Action Pamphlet no. 3: *Quality Control*, London, 1957 on case studies.
56 *Inspection Engineer*, 1956, vol. XX, p. 3; *Inspection Engineer*, 1957, vol. XXI, p. 1; F. Nixon, 'Control of Product Quality', *FBI Review*, 1960, vol. 116, p. 46; *Inspection Engineer*, 1959, vol. XXIII, p. 57; B.G. Ralfs, 'Quality and Reliability', *Quality Engineer*, 1964, vol. 28, p. 83.
57 National Council for Quality and Reliability, *Third Annual Report 1963/4*, London, 1964, pp. 4–7.
58 K.G. Lockyer, J.S. Oakland and C.H. Dupry, 'Quality Control in British Manufacturing: A Study', *Quality Assurance*, 1982, vol. 8, p. 41; J.S. Oakland, 'Research into Quality Control in British Manufacturing Industry', *Business Graduate Journal*, 1986, vol. 16, p. 41.
59 N. Tiratsoo and J. Tomlinson, *Thirteen Wasted Years? The Conservatives and Industrial Efficiency, 1951–64*, London, Routledge, forthcoming.
60 Department of Prices and Consumer Protection, *A National Strategy for Quality*, London, 1978, p. 3.
61 See note 55 above.
62 Lockyer *et al.*, 'Quality Control', p. 43.
63 B.G. Ralfs *et al.*, 'Quality and Reliability', *Quality Engineer*, 1964, vol. 28, pp. 87–8.
64 F. Nixon, 'Spending to Save. Product Quality and Reliability', *Times Review of Industry and Trade*, 1964, vol. 2, p. 18.
65 Oakland, 'Research into Quality Control', p. 33.
66 Cmnd. 1781, *Final Report of the Committee on Consumer Protection*, Parliamentary Papers 1961/2, vol. XII, p. 23.
67 Broadberry and Crafts, 'British Economic Policy and Performance', p. 86.
68 R. Church, 'Deconstructing Nuffield: The Evolution of Managerial Culture in the British Motor Industry', *Economic History Review*, 1996, vol. 49, pp. 561–83.
69 Tiratsoo and Tomlinson, 'Spreading the Gospel of Productivity'.

8

AMERICANISATION AND THE 'SWEDISH MODEL' OF INDUSTRIAL RELATIONS

The introduction of the MTM system at Volvo in the postwar period

Henrik Glimstedt

Internal adaptation to external competitive pressures has been an enduring theme in the history of the automobile industry. In considering the history of American influences on the Swedish automobile industry, it is often suggested that the history of technology and organisation in Sweden's auto industry has been one of internal adaptation to external pressures from large-scale competition since the 1930s. What started as small scale and craft-based production of advanced trucks was therefore followed, first by mechanised mass production during the postwar period, and then by the widely discussed shift to sociotechnical experiments from the early 1970s onwards.

Hence, no image of the development of Sweden's auto industry looms larger than the struggle to establish new levels of efficiency based on distinct sets of principles, or paradigms, of production. The standard narrative on Volvo's adoption of new organisational models and production strategy in the postwar era appears to be one of fully-fledged Americanisation in the 1950s and early 1960s.[1] Several arguments have been put forward in support of this viewpoint, the first of which is concerned with product standardisation. Given the liberalisation of trade that opened the international market, in conjunction with soaring domestic demand after the mid-1950s, Volvo embarked upon a Fordist trajectory. In essence, most new investment in passenger cars was channelled into the production of a single standardised car, the P444, designed during the war. This new car was a sturdy design that would prove to be a successful competitor in the medium-size market segment. Subsequent designs, the Amazon and the 140, introduced in 1958 and 1968 respectively, shared this same basic quality.

In the second place, there is the question of volume and process. As production runs multiplied, from the few thousand cars typical of the interwar years and the late immediate postwar years, to more than 50,000 units by the mid 1950s, Volvo introduced mechanised moving assembly lines. At the same time, the concept of team work and collective piece rate payments to teams was abandoned and the famous American Method–Time–Measurement or MTM system was adopted. As a result, work became individualised and average work cycle times fell drastically.

In the third place, it is suggested that automation played a significant role. Until the late 1950s the trimming of surplus steel from the pressed body parts, for example, was still carried out by hand. Moreover, the assembly of these body parts remained basically a hand-welding process. By the mid-1960s, however, automatic welding and transfer machines were in operation, allowing impressive productivity gains to be made in both the steel pressing and welding processes of body manufacture. In addition, dedicated machinery and standardised methods of production were gradually developed in the manufacture of engines, gear boxes and chassis, which also resulted in higher levels of productivity.

Emphasis has also been placed on the importance of vertical integration and centralisation. Certainly, centralisation of individual engineering departments was a characteristic of the mid-1950s. Relations with subcontractors were also transformed, in that they were tied closer to Volvo through ownership and joint strategic planning. Thus Volvo became the majority shareholder in a number of businesses who were its key suppliers.

Finally, the relationship between this expansion and workers reactions has been highlighted. The accumulated effects of rationalisation drove down costs and speeded up production. In the years between 1955 and 1965, productivity levels soared from 1.8 cars to 6.5 cars per employed worker. Naturally, such a dramatic rise in productivity was accompanied by increasing volumes of vehicles manufactured and increased employment. In assembly, for example, the number of workers employed increased from around 1,000 in 1950 to about 2,500 in the early 1960s, swelling to roughly 6,500 by the end of the 1960s.

Given the radical changes in working conditions outlined above, it is hardly surprising that the union's and workers' reactions towards these changes has been a key issue in the previous discussion on the Swedish automobile industry. Much of the literature assumes that the Americanisation proceeded rapidly and smoothly during the postwar period. It is, furthermore, widely held that Americanisation at Volvo has to be seen in terms of a larger social and institutional context, the so-called 'Swedish model'. The basic upshot of this literature is that workers were in agreement that they had to accept rationalisation on the shop floor to gain the advantages of the advanced welfare state and, hence, facilitated the implementation of process rationalisation between the mid-1950s and the late 1960s.[2] In addition, it is also widely accepted that the general social unrest and wildcat strikes at Volvo in December 1969 indicated serious discontent among Volvo workers, although it was only after direct intervention from Volvo's new president, P.G. Gyllenhammar, in the early 1970s that Volvo finally departed from the mechanised assembly line as a general paradigm for efficient auto production.[3]

This standard line of argument, however, raises a number of questions. Those central to this chapter concern how deeply Americanisation actually went during the 1950s and 1960s. Indeed, it is the contention of this chapter that the drive for Fordism in the Swedish automobile industry in the 1950s and 1960s was not determined by the conscious political support of domestic volume production to build up the international standing of Swedish industry, and neither was the implementation of American production principles frictionless. Rather, Americanisation was an expression of the managers' strategic response to the complexity of the prevailing economic and institutional environment. The outcome of this process, which eventually led to the recognition of the American MTM system by the Swedish labour market organisations, was open-ended.

An examination of the transfer and transformation process, including the adaptation of the MTM system, reveals that beyond the apparent Americanisation, the US inspiration was combined with the co-operative traditions of Swedish industrial relations. Once the MTM system was established, Volvo's top management departed from the hard-core strategy, involving early efforts to establish pragmatic, high-trust union relations. Even in the heyday of Swedish Fordism during the 1960s, key individuals actively involved at various levels defined some of the elementary principles that years later carried the socio-technical transformation. This transformation comprised pragmatic union–company collaboration and strategies for creating individual incentive structures based on notions of skilled work, and the concept of work groups.

Volvo and the MTM system

Postwar Americanisation at Volvo should also be examined in the broader international context of the indirect social effects of market regulations and trade policy. In postwar Europe, the automobile industry faced surging demand for both passenger cars and commercial vehicles. Moreover, postwar governments in the chief automobile producing countries, eager to exploit the industry's growth potential, were prime movers in the adoption of mass production of automobiles in Europe. However, the political motives that propelled the European drive towards mass production varied across Europe.

Unlike the British or the French, the Swedish government saw the Swedish automobile industry neither as a key to future technical or economic development, nor as a potential export commodity to be exploited. On the contrary, the postwar policies implied slower postwar growth of the car and truck production than could have been expected.[4] As Volvo's managing director, Assar Gabrielsson, concluded on the subject, 'the demand for trucks is what we under normal circumstances would call very weak, but since foreign competition is limited by the import barriers we will get a barely satisfactory share of the market anyway'.[5] Evidently, Volvo's management saw no direct threats against the home market position in trucks, and they were confident that other sectors of the automotive industry would grow at a faster rate. In essence, Volvo sought a long-term solution to their problem by exploring the business opportunities present in the potentially expanding car market.

The transition from flexible to volume production was not without major problems for Volvo. The firm's prewar production of passenger cars can best be characterised as marginal, although the company successfully manufactured commercial vehicles, mainly taxicabs, in batches of a few thousand on a yearly basis. Yet wartime production had emphasised Volvo's heavy vehicle image so that, as Volvo emerged from the Second World War, its passenger car capacity was limited. Given that its car production was still almost negligible in 1948, at less than 3,000 units, Volvo had to develop an industrial strategy and structure which would revolutionise the volume of production in the space of a few years if they were to survive in the market. A target of 50,000 units was, therefore, set for 1952.

The search for a new labour market agreement

Per Söderström, managing director of Volvo Penta and responsible for the supply of engines, was among the first to address seriously the issues involved in the transition to volume production. Söderström, who was later hailed as perhaps the most progressive figure behind the introduction of American work methods in Swedish engineering, identified the piece rate system as the key to future productivity levels.

In a memo of 1947, Söderström outlined his views on how to achieve new productivity levels.[6] In the first place, he stated that central wage agreements allowed for a wage increase of around 15 per cent between 1938 and 1946, whereas, because of local wage drift, the actual wages paid in industry had soared far beyond that level. According to Söderström's estimates, there was a gap of almost 30 per cent between that centrally agreed and actual hourly wages paid in this period, a 44 per cent rise on average. Söderström's explanation for this difference was centred on the piece-rate system. Put simply, the actual wages paid resulted not so much from local agreements on high hourly wages, but rather from an over-generous piece-rate system. Söderström's conclusion was based on the fact that 'general rationalisation of production was hardly ever followed up by a corresponding piece-rate reduction to reflect the new organisational or technical preconditions in production'.

This pattern had emerged in the 1920s and had been reinforced by the war efforts during the Second World War. To Söderström, the situation represented a collective mismanagement of the piece rate system, involving a deep-seated distrust between management and the shop-floor workers. Whatever the cause, the achievement of new productivity levels and volume production required a revision of the piece-rate system. The upshot was to maintain the local flat piece-work contract, but to scrap the old piece-rate standards established through decades of local bargaining and to substitute a new trade-off between wages and labour productivity at a higher level. In short, Söderström's vision of the late 1940s revolved around a new deal with the union to ensure high productivity and high wage levels.

Hence, Söderström drafted an agreement that, basically, was comprised of two sections.[7] Paragraphs 1–5 specified how elimination of the workers' restrictive practices in production would result in improved productivity. Workers had also to assume responsibility for throughput and the achievement of effective work methods. At the same time, the company should assume full responsibility for conditions which were outside the workers' control, such as internal logistics and the supply of materials. The second section protected the workers against unfair reductions in their piece rates and also established a 'floor' in the future local wage negotiations which guaranteed the workers a minimum wage 20 per cent above the central agreement for 1947.

Both the local union and the employers' association reacted promptly. While the local union approved the proposed agreement, the Swedish Engineering Employers' Association, or SEEA, – in a less than friendly tone – refused to accept it on the grounds that the agreement was in violation of the national agreement in terms of both wage levels and the extension of employers' responsibilities. The chairman of the SEEA wrote that 'the local agreement goes far beyond the national agreement . . . . Therefore, we are surprised that you did not, according to § 23 of our statutory, submit the outline of the agreement to us before turning it over to the workers.'[8] In the judgement of the SEEA, the local agreement, drafted by Söderström and anchored among the workers' local union representatives, lacked legitimacy.

The initial, hostile reaction to the MTM system

It was against this background that Volvo's management began, in the late 1940s and early 1950s, to look for an alternative to the blocked local agreement. In an effort to alter the traditional piece-rate system, an American firm, Method Engineering Council, was contracted to implement a new piece-rate system, the so called Method–Time–Measurement or MTM system.[9]

While the MTM system is complex and highly technical in nature, its basic principles are not difficult to illustrate. The basic idea is that engineers shall, under laboratory conditions, discover the most efficient way to carry out a specific task. Once this has been established, the job is next divided into several stages. A simple routine, by way of example, would go something like this: look to the left, look at the screwdriver, move hand, grip the screwdriver, look to the right, look at the screw, move arm, point screwdriver at screw, insert screwdriver, et cetera. Attached to each and every one of these physical movements are standardised times, Time Measurement Units or TMUs, which allows the production engineer to calculate the standard time or MTM 100 per cent needed for a specific job. To express the rate for a specific job, the TMUs are multiplied by their pay factor, resulting in an hourly wage. Actual pay then depends on an agreed pace of work. Should an assembly line move faster or slower than the MTM 100 per cent, then actual pay will depend on the outcome of the central negotiations on the pay factor.

Compared to the traditional collective piece-rate system which had dominated production before the 1950s, the MTM system threatened the workers' discretion in their work in several ways. In 1952, efforts to implement the MTM system in the assembly lines at Gothenburg met, in the initial stages, with severe unrest and a series of wildcat strikes as the company tried to carry through an analysis of the work process to establish the actual labour intensity through a statistical lost work time study. Faced by these unexpected wildcat strikes, the management reacted in a rather heavy-handed way by giving notice to seven workers and suspending no less than 25 per cent of the rest of the work force.[10].

Again, the SEEA became involved in order to establish whether or not the strikes were organised by an isolated clique of communist workers as the Volvo management had claimed. What the SEEA representative Gustaf Toller concluded, however, was that the unrest was not so much a matter of successful communist agitation but was more a case of a severe conflict in which both the local union and the company were in breach of the national labour market agreement. As a result, Toller recommended to both parties that the conflict should be referred to the newly formed Time and Motion Study Committee, a committee established by the central labour market organisations to explore and regulate future uses of time and motion studies in the wake of the 1945 metal workers' strike.[11]

Since the MTM system, and the statistical lost time analysis which had constituted the preliminary phase of its introduction, were virtually unknown to the representatives of both the Metal Workers' Union and the employers, the early findings of the Time and Motion Study Committee, or TMSC, were ambiguous. Volvo were instructed on the one hand to end the suspensions and re-hire those workers previously fired. On the other hand, however, the company was permitted to continue with its work studies for two weeks so that representatives of the TMSC could become familiar with hitherto unknown methods.

Unsurprisingly, the Swedish Workers' Union was pressed hard to convince their opposite numbers in the TMSC that the practice was unjust and highly unreliable. Although the employers' representative on the committee, Oscar Werne, seemed to be in agreement with the rationale of the MTM system in a limited sense, i.e. strictly for assembly work only, he quickly reverted to a more loyal conclusion. His problem, it appears, was not whether the system would work in a technical sense, but rather that he saw a mismatch between what he conceived to be good Swedish engineering practices and Americanisation. Conspicuously enough, in the subsequent negotiations, both organisations arrived at the same conclusion, namely that the Swedish engineering sector should avoid the new methods.

In his report to the SEEA, Werne described a meeting with Erland Fägerskjöld, Volvo's leading production engineer who was at the time heading the implementation of the new system, in the following terms: 'I gave him [Fägerskjöld] some examples of the unrest and confusion that US experts and their systems had already caused in the Swedish labour market, for instance the strike caused by the implementation of the Bedaux-system at Alm's shoe factory in Gothenburg in 1936.'[12] In subsequent communications Werne was even more explicit, allowing continued experiments by which he aimed to convince Volvo, as well as other employers, of the system's unreliability. His counterpart in the negotiations, Lennart Eckerström, was equally frank in his report to the Swedish Metal Workers' Union, or SMWU. 'I came to the conclusion that everything should be done to impede the application of this system in the automobile sector as well as in industry more generally.'[13] Meanwhile, the views held by respective organisations did not influence Volvo in the introduction of the MTM system to the Swedish labour market in the course of the 1950s.

Volvo persists and prevails

While both the union and the employers' association were doubtful about 'radical' Americanisation, Volvo remained committed to the introduction of the MTM system. Indeed, by 1953 Volvo had increased its efforts to implement the new system, although it clearly flew in the face of Sweden's organised labour market. At Volvo's engine plant, located in Skövde Pentaverken, the implantation of the system continued. Time formulas for specific work operations were developed between 1953 and 1955, beginning with toolmakers and advanced machinists. For the first time, engineers integrated the planning of factory layout, construction of machinery and tooling as well as maintenance practices with pre-designed work sequences and time analysis. Early experiments in the tool room were followed by a threefold major expansion, in the foundry and in the assembly of engines at Skövde and in the assembly of trucks at Gothenburg.[14]

These initial introductions of the MTM system owed, however, a peculiarly temporary and experimental character to the fact that the system was operated within the boundaries of the central piece-work agreement of the engineering industry. Any permanent piece-work system under Swedish labour market regulations was required to be integrated into § 4 of the national labour market agreement, which specified the rules for the setting of piece rates. Adopting MTM as a permanent basis for piece work presupposed a revision of the current agreement. Although the wildcat strike of 1952 was not repeated, many of the early experiments were accompanied by heated debates within the local unions at Skövde and in Gothenburg. The membership protested because workers identified the lack of recognition of MTM in the national agreement as a possible way to block the spread of the system.[15]

Workers and, in particular, the communist leadership of the local unions at Volvo in Gothenburg and Skövde, protested against the experiments on numerous occasions. The overriding question was whether or not, as the workers suspected deeply, the new system would lead to more work for less pay. In the event, the results of small-scale experiments conducted in Gothenburg in 1954, which compared MTM-based work and conventional piece-rate setting for sixty assembly-line workers, indicated that the workers' concern for a balance between intensity of work and pay was not unwarranted.

The emerging pattern was quite clear. While the communist majority of workers – encouraged by their recent hands-down victory over management – wanted the SMWU to take firm action against the experiments, the national union itself was more ambivalent. By and large, this was a matter of difference between those who wanted a radical effort to abolish the MTM system all together and those who were convinced that the employers were determined to implement the system come what may. The latter group preferred to allow the incorporation of the system within the collective labour market agreement so that influence could be brought to bear in the future working out of the system. By October 1952, the national leadership had already indicated a more pragmatic view to the membership. When Bertil Steen of the SMWU attended a meeting at Volvo in October to discuss the future of MTM with the members of the local union, he agreed in general with the workers that they faced an inhuman way of setting piece rates; it reduced men to robots, hindered local wage drift and thus reduced the scope for better living standards. More important, however, were his reflections on the future of the system:

> We agree that a system of this kind is undesirable. Therefore, we should try to do what is in our power to avoid it. But if this cannot be achieved, and Volvo still continues to introduce the new type of work studies, we would subscribe to the notion that we should try to influence the realisation of the system within the legal framework of the organised labour market.[16]

An earlier union discussion in 1951, to decide the long-term union strategy in the event that the automobile industry continued to press for the introduction of the MTM system, served as the guideline for Steen's statement. Past experience had taught that radical opposition to new methods and work organisation often proved wrong:

We have learned from experience, that we shall not take the same stance towards the MTM system as the labour movement did in relation to time and motion studies in the 1930s. At the time, we rejected the whole idea of time and motion studies only to discover how hard we have had to fight for collective agreements that allowed us to exercise control over time and motion studies.[17]

Where the SMWU had hesitated in 1952, a few years later it saw no alternative but to accept the system. In the preliminary negotiations before the 1954–5 round of collective bargaining, the union faced demands from the employers' association that they revised the paragraphs in the national agreement concerned with piece-work and -rate setting. The employers argued that the introduction of the MTM system called for a total revision of these paragraphs, however, they did modify their demands so that the revisions were less radical. Nevertheless, the adjustments paved the way for the future use of the MTM system.

Given the cautious and negative attitudes displayed towards the American system of piece work in the disputes during the initial phases of the implementation of the MTM system in the early 1950s, it can be said that the union, at least by the mid-1950s, was in the process of redefining its strategy. The suggestion here is that Volvo stands out as the radical innovator, acting to solve the strategic dilemmas in truck production caused by a complex political process. This process involved the political construction of the market combined with short-term goals, since the state and the organised labour market were still in the process of defining a conceptual framework for the industrial structure of the postwar era. There is no evidence in support of the idea that the Swedish state, or the national labour market organisations, were in the 1940s and early 1950s already committed to a Fordist evolution within the Swedish automobile sector.

Product quality and management choices for the 1960s

Quality and industrial relations: towards union pragmatism

Although Volvo relied on a quite simple and somewhat rugged design in the successful 444/544 model, the company carved out a market niche in 'safe and reliable quality cars'. To become an early mover in safety, Volvo initiated close collaboration in particular with Professor Bertil Aldman of the Chalmers Institute of Technology, the inventor of the modern safety belt and other safety devices successfully commercialised by Volvo. To realise its potentially high value-added, however, Volvo had to focus on quality. To put it another way, the more Volvo presented itself as a high value-added product, the more customers expected from Volvo in terms of high quality.

While Volvo successfully explored the market for safe quality cars, the company was less successful in achieving the necessary production quality. It is quite clear that throughout the 1950s and 1960s, production quality deteriorated. Moreover, numerous sources have suggested that because the adjustments made to cars at all stages of production slowed down the flow, Volvo was unable to keep up with demand.[18] According to a former Volvo production engineer:

> Quality was not something that we achieved on the assembly lines. It was something that we really achieved through adjustments. Yes, I would go so far as to say that the outgoing quality was determined by the level of post-production adjustment. A very expensive business, too.[19]

A series of wildcat strikes from the mid-1950s onwards demonstrated that there was a closely-linked nexus of problems at Volvo. While quality could be reduced to technical and logistical processes, managers began to realise that pay and working conditions, including the local industrial relations system, also played a role. Protesting workers and illegal strikes in the paint shop in the winter of 1955–6 illustrated these connections.[20] This actually turned out to be a vicious circle. Technological problems and lack of co-ordination in the production flow caused repeated stoppages in production. Problems in the body shop in particular caused stoppages in the subsequent production sequences, since bodies accumulated in, for example, the body adjustment or the paint section due to poor incoming quality from the body shop.[21]

Under the MTM system, workers benefited from high projected wages, but when the production flow stopped, workers were paid only a low hourly wage in compensation. This discrepancy between projected and actual wages caused numerous wildcat strikes and general unrest among the workers. In turn, these wildcat strikes aggravated the problems of technical co-ordination and quality, since the production flow became overstrained on these occasions. Moreover, it is highly probable that the frustration caused by the stressed production situation and the uncertain earnings position which resulted can hardly have contributed to an improved standard of work. It soon became apparent to the management that the system of industrial relations under MTM lacked the capacity to deal with this situation. Although quantitative estimates of the actual causes and number of these types of conflict are beyond the scope of this chapter, it suffices to say that the evidence derived from the negotiation minutes suggests a bureaucratisation of the relationship between workers and management.[22]

Not much change in the situation can be detected during the first half of the 1960s. When looking back over the period from the mid-1950s to the early 1960s, Volvo managers started to reflect upon the fact that conflicts ending in wildcat strikes more or less typified the situation in car production. When faced with a new crop of illegal strikes in 1963–4, management again requested central negotiations between the SMWU and the SEEA. The records from that meeting reveal that the management argued that, although 'there was no need to dig deeply into the details of the past, we do need to find guidelines to prevent illegal strikes in the future'.[23]

Holger Olson, the ombudsman representing the SMWU at this meeting, suggested two basic solutions, which in a way also clearly defined the problems. First, Olson asserted that the difference between hourly wages paid during stoppages in production due to technical holdups or quality problems, and the MTM wages should be narrowed by an increase in the hourly wage. Thus the basic problem, and the actual cause, of wildcat strikes could be tackled. Second, Olson expressed the hope that Volvo would become 'more generous in its economic contributions to the local union to enable it to become more efficient in its undertakings'. Among other things, Olson concluded that the 'management should pay the total wages bill of the local union president and some of the local officials'.

Confronted with this proposition from the SMWU, both the chairman of the local union and Volvo's management representative withdrew from the meeting for a personal consultation. Their deliberations resulted in an agreement on the general guidelines for closing the gap between projected and actual earnings as well as an acknowledgement of the union's need for economic support. Svante Simonsson, one of Volvo's most experienced managers and director of the negotiation office, recalled that:

> We tried to establish a continuous, professional and pragmatic relationship with the local union representatives, which means that we tried to formulate common policy goals through centralised management–union relations rather than simply responding to conflicts as they arose.[24]

Beyond union pragmatism

In their search for strategies to solve the emerging nexus of industrial relations problems, Volvo's management attempted to build a pragmatic alliance with the local union. The outcome of the agreement of 1964 in conjunction with the practices of the MTM system, suggests, however, that the local system of industrial relations was pushed towards bureaucratisation. While the number of formal local union negotiations, for example, fell by about 15 per cent in absolute terms between the late 1940s and the late 1960s, the number of workers soared from about 1,200 to about 3,200 during the same period, suggesting a far more dramatic change in relative terms. Also, the issues that were dealt with in local negotiations changed from complicated arguments concerning the actual balance between pay and effort to more formal issues concerning breaks and manning policy.[25]

Experienced production managers were motivated to go beyond the formula for union pragmatism. They did so because poor quality remained very much the Achilles heel of production throughout the 1960s. For example, a consultancy report on Volvo's reputation and customer satisfaction, commissioned by the company's management, showed that Volvo enjoyed a far worse reputation for production quality than its competitors in the important US market.[26] For a reconciliation of efficiency and quality, the company and the union jointly established a new set of internal institutions to analyse and develop new manning policies during the mid-1960s and onwards. These were, in particular, the *Frånvarogruppen*, a joint consultation group formed to develop a policy to reduce labour turnover and absenteeism, and the *Personalkommitén*, a joint consultation group on general staffing policy.

It was not until 1969, however, that management tried to mould these ideas into a more general framework of craft based production principles for the automobile industry. By then, the familiar wildcat strikes over work load and pay had forced managers at the Torslanda plant to take a more active stance. In essence, managers worried not so much about the strike itself as about how the highly mobile workforce would act if the strike lasted for longer than a week. Svante Simsonson's report to top management on the strike negotiations indicated the nature of the real threat:

> The resulting settlement has to be seen against the background of the nature of the illegal conflicts and the nature of the particular prevailing manning situation at Volvo in Gothenburg, with 53 per cent immigrant workers. I estimate that a prolonged conflict would most likely have implied that only about 60 per cent of the work force would have returned to work after the conflict was over.[27]

Against this background, it is hardly surprising to find that ideas of craftsmanship and individual commitment, together with union pragmatism, paved the way for new formulations of production paradigms. It is often argued that it was in fact the wildcat strikes of 1969 and 1970 which were the motivating force behind the decision by Volvo managers to go beyond Fordism. However, it should be noted that internal management reports on alternative production strategies were already advanced and circulating among top managers by the autumn of 1969. By this time production engineers had already formulated their strategy as a 'Programme for Industrial Democracy'. This strategy was based on the work of Louis Davids on job redesign, which he developed from experience in production during the Second World War.[28]

It is also clear from deliberations within Volvo's top management that they themselves doubted their ability to deal competently with the new requirements. Erik Quistgaard, managing director of the Torslanda plant, for example, commissioned younger colleagues to draft reports on alternative production strategies and also hired experts on socio-technical strategies.[29] Judging by internal reports, which emphasised the need for autonomous work groups, quality of working life, job rotation and industrial democracy, it was the individual's motivation that first drew attention. Efforts to formulate a basic company policy in this area favoured concepts like motivation and job satisfaction, but the ideas were still rather crude. A committee on job redesign and industrial democracy, chaired by Quistgaard, concluded in a confidential report that 'the initial goal should be to achieve increased individual stimulation in parallel with increased efficiency – that is industrial democracy'.[30]

At this point, the deliberations within management circles re-integrated the union pragmatism of the 1960s with strategies for socio-technical job redesign. One of the early strategy documents from this period pinpoints the idea of autonomous work groups as the key to craft-based production principles.[31] What was required was a trade-off between quality, productivity and the individual worker's need for meaningful job tasks or job enlargement. In particular, the document stated that Volvo needed to deploy policies rapidly to 'develop procedures for consultation between management and the workforce concerning day-to-day co-operation on the shop floor', and to 'study and design a work organisation that would satisfy the individual worker's job requirements'.

In exploring the institutional grounds for the implementation of neo-craft-based production principles, the same document referred back to the pragmatic union relations and to the various committees and procedures for union consultation developed from the mid-1960s. In addition, it conveys the general argument that management–union relations at Volvo developed into relatively advanced institutional forms in the 1960s. At least two different bodies for union consultations – *Frånvarogruppen* and *Personalkommitén* – could, according to the report, directly contribute to the formation of the institutional basis for the development of new production strategies.

By the early 1970s, as has been widely recognised by many scholars, the search process for a new factory regime gained momentum after Volvo's charismatic new leader, P.G. Gyllenhammar, entered the stage in 1971. One of the first large reports on the working condition problems commissioned by Gyllenhammar, *Volvo Socialkalkyl*, arrived at the same conclusions as the reports mentioned above.[32] Although the importance of immigrant workers was played down, the general conclusion was that Volvo's main problems arose from the worker's low commitment to work, high absenteeism and high labour turnover. In those respects, Volvo's situation was far worse than the average Swedish engineering firm. In summary:

> Worse working conditions at Volvo than in the Swedish industry in general are believed to explain the differences in labour turn over between Volvo and the Swedish industry in general . . . . The interviews showed that psychological effects, like suffering from repetitive

work, lack of freedom in work and heavy work load are the main reasons why Volvo's workers tend to quit.[33]

Poor quality could hence in turn be attributed to the negative effects of the repetitive work on the assembly line. Thus, the consultants' reports to management on the quality problem echoed the insights already gained in the 1960s, although they conveyed increasingly advanced arguments concerning the advantages of socio-technical based production strategies, implying radical departures from the moving assembly line.

Conclusion

From a detailed analysis of the transfer process involved in the adaptation of American-inspired models at Volvo, it is evident that introducing the MTM system challenged existing company-specific industrial relations as well as relations within a broader segment of labour market organisations.

Convergence on a Fordist raw model hinged as much on international pressure as it did on the structure of the internal market. A series of uncoordinated, political decisions channelled Volvo towards Fordism in the 1950s. The direct social effects linked to the collective bargaining system's acceptance of the MTM system should be characterised more as uncoordinated responses to an unexpected path of development, rather than as a planned transformation to mass production. Even if Volvo's commitment to the MTM system and standardisation of the production of cars cannot be denied, Volvo did recognise the incompatibility between Fordism and the need for quality in production.

It was in this process that Volvo, both practically and discursively, established the key elements of a socio-technical transformation in the heyday of Swedish Fordism during the 1960s. This socio-technical transformation emphasised close union–company collaboration and strategies for creating individual incentive structures based on notions of skilled work.

Acknowledgements

A first version of this chapter was presented at the 1995 Business History Conference in Ft. Lauderdale. A more detailed version was laid out at the conference on 'Americanization and its Limits' in Madison, Wisconsin in March 1997, which will appear in Gary Herrigel and Jonathan Zeitlin (eds), *Americanisation and its Limits: Responses to US Technology in Postwar Europe and Japan*, forthcoming. I would like to thank the following for longstanding encouragement and useful advice: Patrick Fridenson, Gary Herrigel, Steven Tolliday, and, in particular, Jonathan Zeitlin. I equally owe thanks for comments on an earlier version to Steve Casper, Tomas Engström, Takahiro Fujimoto, Bob Hancké, Alf Johansson, Dan Raff and David Soskice. I am also very much indebted to the editors of the present volume for their helpful suggestions and their outstanding patience. The usual disclaimers apply.

Notes

1 See in particular, K. Ellergård, *Bilder av ett produktionssystem*, Göteborg, Kulturgeografiska institutionen, Göteborgs universitet, 1982; and P. Sundgren, 'Införandet av MTM-metoden i svensk verkstadsindustri 1950–1956', 1978, vols 13–14.

2 See in particular B. Stråth, 'Metallklubbarna vid Volvo och Saab: facklig politik i två företagskulturer', in B. Öhngren (ed.), *Metall 100 år: fem uppsatser*, Stockholm, Metall, 1988. For the general argument see, for example, A.L. Johansson, *Tillväxt och klassamarbete*, Stockholm, Tidens förlag, 1989, or his working paper 'Technological Optimism and the Swedish Model', Swedish Centre for Working Life Studies, 1984.

3 T. Sandberg, 'Volvo Kalmar – twice a pioneer', in Å. Sandberg (ed.), *Enriching Production: Perspectives on Volvo's Uddevalla Plant as an Alternative to Lean Production*, Aldershot, Avebury, 1995.

4 For a more detailed analysis of postwar trade policy and the automobile industry, see H. Glimstedt, *Mellan teknik och samhälle. Stat, marknad och produktion i svensk bilindustri 1930–1960* no.5. Avhandlingar från Historiska institutionen i Göteborg, University of Gothenburg, 1993, chapter 8.

5 Göteborgs Stadsarkiv, Gothenburg, AB Volvos historiska arkiv, Företagsnämndens protokoll, 23 March 1949.

6 Verkstadsföreningens Historiska Arkiv, AB Volvo, Rapport av den 23 December 1947 by P. Söderström.

7 The details of this draft agreement are described in the subsequent exchange between Söderström and the Swedish Engineering Employer's Association; Verkstadsföreningens Arkiv, AB Volvo, 22 March 1948.

8 ibid.

9 See G. Luthman, H. Bolin and A. Viklund (eds), *MTM i Sverige 1959–1990*, Stockholm, Sveriges Rationaliseringsförbund, 1990; and Sundgren, 'Införandet av MTM-metoden'.

10 The following account of the conflicts in 1952 is, unless otherwise stated, based on Glimstedt, *Mellan teknik och samhälle*, chapter 8.

11 For the Time and Motion Study Committee, see A.L. Johansson, *Tillväxt och klassamarbete*.

12 Verkstadsföreningens Arkiv, AB Volvo, Rapport, 29 October – 8 November 1952, by O. Werne.

13 Svenska Metallindustriarbetareförbundets historiska arkiv, AB Volvo, Rapport till styrelsen, 8 December 1952, by L. Eckerström.

14 Luthman *et al.* (eds), *MTM i Sverige 1959–1990*.

15 For the union debates on MTM in 1952–55, see Sundgren, 'Införandet av MTM-metoden'; also B. Stråth, 'Metallklubbarna vid Volvo och Saab: facklig politik i två företagskulturer', in B. Öhngren (ed.), *Metall 100 år: fem uppsatser*, Stockholm, Metall, 1988.

16 Quoted in Sundgren, 'Införandet av MTM-metoden', p. 8.

17 ibid., p. 18.

18 In particular, Volvo's many requests for increased overtime work mirrors quality problems in production. Failing production, lost bodies due to insufficient painting assembly are frequently cited as causes of overtime; see Svenska

Metallindustriarbetareförbundets historiska arkiv, AB Volvo, ansökningar om utökad övertid.

19 Interview with Bertil Andersson, May 1997. More dramatic glimpses of the arising quality problem are obtainable from quality reports issued in the early 1970s; see AB Volvo's archives, Kvalitetssituationen. Konfidentiell PM utfärdad av P.Å. Sörensson och tillställd Bengt Darnfors, 11 December 1973.

20 The interpretation of this situation is based on the correspondence between the SMWU and the SEEA in connection with the illegal conflicts in 1955–56; Svenska Metallindustriarbetareförbundets historiska arkiv, AB Volvo, rapport från centrala förhandlingar, 8 February 1956.

21 The records indicate that about 15 per cent of the bodies were rejected due to poor quality.

22 Minutes of the local negotiations between 1948 and 1968 were kindly made available to the author by Svante Simonsson, director of Volvo's negotiation office.

23 For this and the subsequent quotations from this meeting, see Svenska Metallindustriarbetareförbundets historiska arkiv, AB Volvo, rapport från centrala förhandlingar, 29 September 1964.

24 Interview with Svante Simonsson, director of Volvo's negotiation office, May 1985.

25 These estimates and the analysis of the content are based on the record of proceedings of local negotiations 1948–68 and on interviews with Svante Simonsson in May 1985. The reports of the proceedings were made available to the author by Svante Simonsson.

26 'Kvalitetssituationen'; see note 20 above.

27 AB Volvo, Produktionstekniska huvudkommitten, 19 December 1969.

28 AB Volvo, Reg. no. 71000–204, 'Programförslag för ökad industriell demokrati inom Volvo Göteborgsverken', Utfärdat av H Lenerius och tillställt B Danfors och E Quistgaard, 10 November 1996.

29 For example Berth Jönsson, a US-trained social scientist with a background in industrial sociology and psychology, who later emerged as one of P. G. Gyllenhammar's most trusted co-thinkers in this area.

30 Confidential report of the proceedings of the reference group on forms of union consultation and work organisation, dated 15 January 1970. The author would like to thank director Torsten Hagenblad of AB Volvo for making this document available to him.

31 AB Volvo, "Programförslag"; see note 29 above.

32 This project was monitored by a reference group appointed by Olof Palme.

33 AB Volvo, Volvo Socialkalkyl. Delrapport IV. Försök till helhetssyn, 1973, p. 72.

9

THE LIMITS OF AMERICANISATION AND THE EMERGENCE OF AN ALTERNATIVE MODEL

The Marshall Plan in Emilia–Romagna

David W. Ellwood

In ever-increasing numbers, today's economic historians demonstrate how restricted was the impact of the Marshall Plan in the various national economies and industrial sectors to which they have turned their attention.[1] Emilia–Romagna's experience seems to offer yet another confirmation of this trend. The region's post-Second World War 'take-off' began over three years after the ERP had ended and bore no relation in its forms or directions to the 'be-like-us' modernising recipes handed out from Washington. Coinciding with the worst years of Emilia's postwar adjustment crisis, the Marshall Plan's mission in Rome can claim little credit for relieving or even showing any particular awareness of the crisis. It was at best disingenuous of the mission's head James Zellerbach to claim to his friends in industry and business, when back home in San Francisco, that Emilia–Romagna showed how Communism could be rolled back with the aid of the ERP.[2]

However, as soon as the region is inserted into the national picture of economic transformation in the second half of the 1950s, the equations begin to change. Emilia's spontaneously chosen path of adaptation was neither autarchic nor isolationist. For every long-established artisan workshop providing for a local clientele, there was another which succeeded in tying itself in to a national market, or to the nationwide production chain of some larger firm. Subcontracting became widespread and took a myriad different forms. The roots of the very largest national firms, such as FIAT, spread up and down the peninsula and, as key beneficiaries of the Marshall Plan, their success spread the Plan's benefits indirectly to all their suppliers and customers. With the liberalisation and expansion of intra-European and international trade after 1957–8, in fulfilment of a key Marshall Plan objective, so these trends spread upwards and outwards, opening the way for the region's remarkable success in export markets from the 1960s onwards.

The region and its immediate postwar history

Emilia–Romagna is a large area of northeastern Italy bounded to the north by the Po river, to the east by the Adriatic coast and to the south by the steeply rising Apennines, which fall away from northwest to southeast. The regional capital, Bologna, governs the crossing point where the old Via Emilia, from Milan to the Adriatic running along the base of the Apennines, encounters the principal routes linking Florence to Venice and Austria, and to Verona and the Brenner pass. Historically, Bologna was the meeting point of the hill folk with the peasants who cultivated the vast, rich flat lands of the Po Valley. It was the hub of the long strip development which accompanied the evolution of the Via Emilia. Today the capital of one of the richest regions in the European Union, in 1945 Bologna lay half ruined, surrounded by lands which had seen some of the worst fighting in the Italian campaign, and on which the front between the two armies had stayed and stagnated more than anywhere else.

Emilia–Romagna came out of the war with a higher rate of damage to its bridges, roads, railways and houses than any other region in the country.[3] Unlike Piedmont and Lombardy, the substantial Resistance movement in the area had not been able to prevent the deliberate destruction of bridges, factories and power stations by the retreating Nazi armies. Attacked as a railway hub, Bologna's station and surrounding network of lines and marshalling yards were a mass of rubble: no bridge stood in any direction for a distance of 50–70km.[4]

Reconstruction then was first of all a physical and social task involving the supply of order, work, shelter and food. It was the first great challenge faced by the new political forces governing the region. The part of Italy which had given birth to Mussolini himself and his Fascist movement saw the growth of a substantial anti-Fascist resistance during the years of German occupation. The dominant force in the Resistance campaign, the Italian Communist Party or PCI, now set about offering a radical alternative to the solid regime which Fascism had constructed in the region, based on the landowners, the small moneyed class and the petite bourgeoisie.

Firmly installed in the seats of local power, the party sought to build a synthesis combining its own idea of participatory democracy, faithful dedication to the national and international party line, and the realisation of concrete results as quickly as possible. In a political context which degenerated rapidly from the spring of 1947 onwards, aggravated by the partial collapse of the local economy, the party's local leaders nevertheless showed themselves capable of addressing the fundamental needs of the populations under their control. Such was their effectiveness that the hegemony they constructed in those years remains in diluted form to this day.

Although profoundly convinced that capitalism in Italy was bankrupt and had no future, in the short term the policy choices of the PCI did not imply radical designs for social or economic innovation. At the national level, the party leader Palmiro Togliatti, founder and guarantor of the PCI's distinctiveness – much of which would eventually be identified with the Emilia–Romagna experience – explicitly ruled out the possibility of constructing any sort of national economic plan of reconstruction.[5]

The result was that the forces running the cities and towns of the region were left very much on their own when it came to rebuilding. The national governments of the day were far too concerned with their own political survival, and with re-establishing the fundamentals of institutional, financial and legal order, to be able to provide a lead in the daily effort of reconstruction. So, with no trace of a concerted vision of reconversion from war to peace, the energies of individual initiative and the market, more or less stimulated by local government, were left to do the work as best they could according to their own capacities and priorities. The spontaneous processes of adaptation thereby set in motion were eventually, after years of suffering and dislocation, to produce a model of development which was unique in its social and economic structure, its popular participation and its effectiveness.

The economic situation in Emilia–Romagna at the start of the Marshall Plan

Although a largely agricultural region – 42.7 per cent of its active population had been directly employed in agriculture in 1938 – Emilia–Romagna was by no means underdeveloped. Roughly another 25 per cent had been employed in food processing industries at that time, while just under 20 per cent worked in engineering, a sector involving a handful of substantial firms and a number of small and medium-sized companies, many of which expanded very rapidly in Mussolini's wartime economy.[6] It was this latter range of concerns which felt most intensely the collapse of the Fascist productive system, and the new national government's inability or unwillingness to organise reconversion.

After the drastic credit squeeze of 1947, which finally halted the inflationary spiral of wartime but plunged the enfeebled country into severe depression, Emilia–Romagna's industries entered a period of intense crisis which lasted until 1954, well after the rest of the north had started on the road to recovery. With no prospect of new orders from Rome, the large firms dependent on war production collapsed. The small and medium-sized producers related to them met the same fate, and as general demand dwindled, the mass of small artisan workshops linking town and country across the region also faced extinction. Redundancies and closures came in waves, forcing unemployment up to historically unprecedented levels. The figures in Table 9.1 speak clearly.

From 1948 onwards, in fact, a progressive de-industrialisation struck the

151

Table 9.1 Employees in metal-working industries in the Province of Bologna

Year	Number of employees
Wartime maximum	c.30,000
1945 (year end)	9,800
1947 (mid-year)	19,705
1949	18,400
1950	17,587
1952	16,124

Source: Proceedings of the IVth Congress of the Confederal Chamber of Labour, Bologna, 26–8 September 1952, p. 32.

Note: 1947 was the postwar maximum.

entire region. In December 1949, in its first number, the economic journal *Emilia* published a list – 'certainly not complete' – of this process as it developed, citing sixteen cases of factory closures in Bologna, four in Reggio Emilia, six in Ferrara and two in Forlì.[7]

In agriculture, the relationship between structural crisis – the persistence of antiquated techniques, oligopolistic ownership, sharecropping – and the misfortunes of the moment was more clear than in industry. However, Emilian commentators pressing for agrarian reform were much more likely to attribute the post-1949 difficulties in the sector to the government's deflationary policies, and the consequent effects of these on the spending power of the urban masses. They emphasised too that the crisis was made worse 'by the absolute lack of any sort of general plan, either from the land-owners or the state, which might reorient business and reorient the export trade'.[8]

The political consequences of these trauma were immediately visible. In 1980, the economic historian Bellettini recalled:

> The political climate in which all this took place was as bitter as could be. The furious struggle of the workers against factory closures and redundancies clashed with the openly confessed determination of the industrialists to use the situation to break down working-class resistance, to strike at class solidarity and bring about the collapse of the workers' parties and unions. Selective redundancies was the main weapon used.[9]

Social tensions in the countryside were just as high as in the towns. All in all, the region in these years was one where, in Bellettini's words, 'the class struggle reached some of its fiercest levels'.[10]

Commentators to this day suspect that the government's relative indifference to the plight of the region in this period was not casual. 'The fundamental choices in economic policy', wrote the labour historian Anderlini, 'ended up by being either explicitly *against* it – the refusal to convert and consequent dismantling of war industries – or *outside* it, in order to favour the monopolistic development of the big industrial groups of the North.'[11] When the state eventually came to invest in the region in the 1950s, it chose capital-intensive projects even in areas of the highest unemployment, such as chemical industries in Ravenna.[12] In the meantime, say writers such as Anderlini, the same message was clearly spelled out by the national government's choices in its use of Marshall Plan funds.

The national economic and political context

Estimating the impact of the Marshall Plan on the Italian economy has always been a difficult task. On the strictly financial level, it is worth noting that the millions of dollars which arrived as grants and loans in these years, that is until the end of 1951 – $1.575 billion to be precise – add up to a total which is slightly *less* than those provided under the first aid programmes going back to the wartime period – $1.597 billion. The ERP's loans to industries totalled less than the cash obtained from the sales of war surplus, and the entire figure awarded in loans – $435 million – was less than that spent by the US between 1944 and 1954 on off-shore procurements in the country – $490 million. In other words, neither the dimensions nor the originality of the ERP's role in Italy's postwar recovery should be overemphasised.[13]

At the policy level, the infamous deflationary strategy imposed by the Liberal treasury minister Luigi Einaudi had already begun before the ERP's experts began to make their weight felt, and it is by now clear that the government saw the Plan as a gift horse which could be exploited for its own immediate and direct benefit, whatever the more ambitious ideas of the Americans. (One of the few specific government criteria for approving a grant application involved banning the importation of any machinery which might result in increased competition for established domestic producers.[14]) The ERP provided the equivalent of about 2.6 per cent of Italian GNP at its height, a figure whose impact was hotly debated at the start – though much less so by 1949 – and which today's economic historians see as being of direct significance only in a few key sectors such as electricity generation, steel, petroleum refining, cars and the rebuilding of infrastructure.

On paper, there could be no doubt: stimulating investment in production facilities was the supreme task according to all the instructions, exhortations and official declarations of the ERP administrators in Rome, Paris and Washington. In April 1949 Roberto Tremelloni, vice-president of the Interministerial Reconstruction Committee, or CIR, the co-ordinating committee linking the government to the ERP, explained that this did not mean direct aid to firms but improving the environment for investment, 'i.e. creating better general conditions . . . especially in terms of public goods'. Hence 33.6 per cent of the counterpart funds for 1948–9 would go to rail transport, 28 per cent to agriculture – especially labour-intensive land reclamation – and 22 per cent to public works. Because of the special needs of the so-called 'depressed areas', about two-thirds of the entire counterpart fund would go to the South, although the southern part of the Po delta area in Romagna was also officially designated as a 'depressed area'.[15]

Official Marshall Plan policy for the country's economic future – which did not distinguish between regions, except for the special case of 'the South' – accepted the need for special short-term measures to absorb unemployment, but was strategic in its thrust, suggesting how to reduce the long-term need for basic imports, improve the country's international competitiveness and provide structural responses to the employment crisis. This was seen as being due to overpopulation as much as to the inadequacies of the labour market.[16] In the second of its famously controversial country studies, dated February 1949, a vision emerged of a full-scale industrial reconversion in Italy, with industrial expansion and modernisation as the keynote, in a context of increased competition and urbanisation. The government view, as expressed by Tremelloni and others, was much more cautious. While the country study expressed concern that half the population 'still depended on agriculture', Tremelloni seemed to see this as an immutable feature of national life. Agreeing that increased output was essential, the CIR representative insisted that it should however be obtained only by means 'consistent with the nature of the country and the character of its inhabitants'.[17]

However, a distorted but true development pattern did emerge gradually at the national level during the ERP years. A variety of sector plans was accompanied by an ever-growing drizzle of public works to 'compensate' the weaker sectors of the economy for the success of the others. A pattern developed by compromise and improvisation, sometimes with the approval of the Americans, most often without it, which was destined not just to endure but to prosper.[18]

In political terms, the development of the ERP is associated in Italy with the expulsion of the Communist–Socialist left from the national government in May 1947 – a moment of extreme political and social tension – and with the violent electoral campaign of April 1948, which precipitated an unprecedented investment of American men, money and propaganda methods in order to ensure a conservative victory.[19] Partly as a result of this experience, and the awareness that the Italian Communist Party retained the potential to come to power by legitimate means, the ERP was accompanied by a massive effort of education and information when it began its operations in Italy after June 1948. This campaign was designed to get the Plan as close as possible to the people it was supposed to benefit, in order to channel attitudes, mentalities and expectations in favour of America's ideas of prosperity, free enterprise, productivity and integration, or in other words, in the direction Americans understood as modernity: mass production for mass consumption.[20]

Ignoring all this, the Left's economists complained that the division of Europe brought about by the Plan penalised Italy in particular, since large portions of its foreign trade had traditionally been carried on with the central and eastern parts of the Continent. In addition, a new division of labour was predictable within western Europe itself, with the Mediterranean countries doomed to suffer the fate of the southern regions of Italy after national unification.[21] The counterpart funds provoked particular suspicion, characterised as 'a permanent threat to our independence; in practice a large monetary mass available for manipulation, by means of which the State Department intervenes in our industrial output'.[22]

While the Communist Party's economists tried to predict the positive as well as the negative results of the Plan, and took part in a rather sophisticated debate on its meaning which included government experts, the PCI propaganda machine was not so scrupulous. The 1949 pamphlet entitled *The Marshall Plan and the Communists*, written for a wide party readership, compared the world economic hierarchy implied in America's designs with the benefits of egalitarian participation in the 'Assistance Committee' run under the auspices of the Soviet Union and its allies. With the North Atlantic Treaty confirming the warlike nature of true US intentions, the whole scheme could now be seen in its malevolent entirety, promising nothing but 'misery and hunger for the workers'.[23]

The situation in Emilia–Romagna as seen by the governing forces of the Left

Whatever ideological approach is applied to the condition of the region in these years, no analysis can escape the strident contrast between, on the one hand, the declared intentions of the ERP managers in Rome and their government allies, and on the other, the actual situation of economic degradation on the ground as reported by local government and trade union sources.

Seen from this point of view, the Marshall Plan had none of the characteristics of a reconstruction programme but was just one more cause among many for the difficulties of the period. For instance, the fall-off in the production of materials based on hemp, a traditional local industry, was seen as entirely due to the ERP, 'which while limiting our exports to the West, puts serious obstacles in the way of our trade with the East, the USSR in particular'.[24]

This was one of the commonest complaints of the time. It was at the head of the list of motives for protest against the ERP supplied to PCI militants in Emilia–Romagna by the review *Propaganda* in February 1949, in the context of the nationwide mobilisation for agrarian reform. According to *Propaganda*, Czechoslovakia had officially sought to import wine, oranges, lemons, oil and rice, but in order 'to obey American orders, De Gasperi turned a deaf ear'.[25]

Two other complaints were that 'the Marshall Plan invades our markets with products which compete with our own' – examples cited included tobacco, oil seeds, pasta, tinned tomatoes, animal feedstuffs – and that 'the Marshall Plan forces us to make customs agreements with countries such as France whose economies are not complementary with ours', hence blocking the export of products such as wine common to both.

In this context, conflict over the crucial and very delicate problem of agrarian reform was inevitable. *Propaganda* said that the Americans had deplored even the prospect of reform, with the head of the ECA Mission in Rome, Zellerbach, quoted as saying that 'even just talking about it has upset and disturbed the land-owners'. Whether Zellerbach made such a statement is not clear: no other sources refer to it, not even those from the Left and the PCI. In fact Zellerbach opposed the Left's vision of agrarian reform, but went to considerable lengths to make sure that the Italian government and land-owners understood that a reform was inevitable and could not be delayed.[26] Thirty years later, it was evident to Bolognese commentators on the Left that whatever the intentions, ERP aid to agriculture in Emilia–Romagna had favoured the traditional power blocs consolidated in the land reclamation agencies, together with the big landowners and all those who were in fact opposed to the government's land reform designs. The only agricultural co-operative to receive ERP help, it was pointed out, was one of the minority run by 'white' (i.e. Catholic) forces.[27]

ERP activities in Emilia–Romagna

Agricultural intervention did indeed dominate the picture in the areas based on Bologna. ERP summaries list the re-afforestation projects, the experiments with new techniques, the introduction of new crops and breeds and the live-stock imported. Land reclamation in the swampy zones of the Po delta was given particular prominence. Near Ferrara, 5,600 hectares were reclaimed with the ERP providing nearly half of the capital expenditure.[28]

After agriculture came the reconstruction of railways (14 per cent of the national total of ERP aid in that sector), public works in general (10 per cent), and public housing (9 per cent). From the documentation of the CIR it appears that compared to other northern regions, Emilia–Romagna generally did well in most sectors, but was of course far outdone in the proportion of counterpart funds for industry which went to the likes of Piedmont and Lombardy. While the latter obtained loans to the tune of $108.9 million, Emilia received only $11 million, the lion's share of which went to reconstruct the big electricity generating station at Piacenza on the Po. However, Emilia received 19.4 per cent of the limited support given to small and medium scale industry. By comparison it was in fifth position, behind the regions of the south, in aid awards for land reclamation, and in fourth position among the regions of the north for public works grants (still far behind the southern regions, however). As is the case in almost all ERP allocations, how specific award figures were formulated remains unknown.[29]

> The keynote throughout the Emilia region has been reconstruction. First of all the reconstruction of roads and railways, then new land reclamation products to mop up agricultural unemployment and increase the output of animal feed, of milk and meat; then the construction of a grand new auction mart (at Modena), houses and other public works.[30]

The words belong to a certain Filiberto Storoni, and come from a pamphlet entitled *Journey Through Emilia*, published by the Rome ERP Mission in May 1951. They typify an underlying ambiguity in the Marshall Plan's approach to this region, as indeed to others throughout the Peninsula: was the primary objective indeed physical reconstruction of the war damage still scarring the landscape between the Apennines and Po river, or was it the renewal and expansion of the means of production?

To the extent that the workings of the ERP grants and loans can be traced in Emilia–Romagna, there can be no doubt that the government's short-term priorities were destined to prevail over the strategic modernising impulses of the ERP Mission. Storoni's *Journey* tells of railway tracks and bridges rebuilt, of the new cattle market at Modena, of schools, kindergartens and public offices. Of industry there was no mention. The fields, orchards and land development projects dominated the picture, but with no details supplied as to the proportion of new land compared to war-damaged areas, or the relationship between public and private activities. As to evidence of results, Storoni preferred folklore:

> The reclamation efforts have already brought a certain prosperity, almost a state of euphoria. Buzzoni Volturno the butcher who was selling one animal every ten days at the start of 1950, now has gone back to selling two a week. Rolfini the fishmonger has seen his turnover increase 40 per cent in a town, Lagosanto, where fish is the staple diet of the people.[31]

Meanwhile the structural crisis in agriculture, as reported by the Bologna Chamber of Labour, went unremarked. It was to prove terminal for sectors dependent on a single traditional product such as hemp or rice.

Against the all-pervasive industrial demobilisation under way in the region, the Marshall Planners had little to offer. The evidence suggests that the majority of firms applying for ERP aid in Emilia–Romagna saw it as a straw worth grasping in a desperate situation. All those that applied, for instance, were firms anxiously awaiting moneys long owed to them by the state, either for work done, tax rebates or promised loans.[32] But hopes that

Marshall Plan moneys or machines would arrive in time to get over the emergency phase were to prove vain. Complicated mechanisms involving repeated layers of financial, technical and procedural vetting, conducted in the first instance in Rome by the CIR and its outside experts, made sure of that. To these the ERP added its own system of allocation. Requests for US-made machinery costing less than $1 million could be processed by the ERP Mission in Rome; beyond that, the entire application had to be forwarded to headquarters in the Economic Co-operation Administration, or ECA, in Washington. Only once every three months did that organisation release the necessary 'procurement authorisations'. These then eventually returned through Italian official channels to the original applicant, hopefully at the same time as the goods required were being despatched.

In its report on the third quarter of ERP activity in Italy, the CIR recognised that the procedures were slow and cumbersome, but it defended their rigour. Of twenty-nine Emilian companies that had made applications by that time, twenty-two were instructed to supply more information. Almost all were in any case destined to have their applications modified or scaled down in the name of defending 'national production', i.e. the presumed interests of other companies in other regions.[33]

A typical experience of the obstacle course faced by a company attempting to attract ERP support is provided by the case of the engineering firm Reggiane. This large-scale company based in Reggio Emilia was by far the biggest of its kind in the region, and one which had faced some of the most severe problems of physical reconstruction and reconversion. Its application – the first from Emilia–Romagna – was logged on 28 July 1948. The request was for eighty machine tools worth $1,240,000. The CIR began the work of analysing the request only in November. After a request for more information, approval was issued in March 1949, but for $968,000 worth of equipment only. After a further inspection by a government expert sent to Reggio in April, the application was apparently ready to send to Washington. By the summer, however, no progress was visible and the firm began to apply political pressure on the Minister of Industry. His bureaucrats pointed out that the firm had already received government loans for sums larger than the value of the existing machinery, therefore no further guarantees could be provided for ERP support. The question was therefore passed on to the ministry's industrial credit department, which took another eight months to issue its approval. The first machines did not arrive until November 1950.[34]

The company had protested that it was impossible to find out even how the application procedures were supposed to function. It insisted repeatedly on the urgency of its needs, pointing out the pressures it was under from its customers, the risks of being cut out of its market, the lengthening queues of applicants to the American supplier companies and the consequent increase in their prices; all to no avail. The results were that certain lines had to be discontinued, machinery wore out and new products had to be designed which did not require US-made machine tools. When these eventually arrived, they were either outdated or surplus to requirements. By this time the company was in total crisis, and was indeed put into liquidation by its government creditors in the spring of 1951. Only a long battle by the company and the entire city which depended on it enabled Reggiane eventually to be reborn.[35]

The California industrialist James Zellerbach, head of the ERP Mission in Rome, visited Bologna in October 1949 and lost no time in denouncing the complexity of the government's procedures. He demanded that 'industrial, not bureaucratic or banking criteria' be applied when submissions were examined. In response he was told by his Chamber of Commerce hosts that while ERP raw materials and goods freely available on the open market had indeed been used in the region, almost no firm had been able to acquire directly sought-after items from American output.[36]

By 1951, only twenty-seven large industrial companies in the region had benefited from ERP support. While engineering had put in the biggest number of applications, those most favoured were mining and quarrying and chemical industries. Companies involved in infrastructure support, such as telephone and transportation equipment, also benefited. The mining, chemical and food industries, it was noted, tended to request entire production systems, but the key engineering sector appeared to be satisfied with single machines or groups of machines to be inserted into existing production facilities. In this way, comment today's observers, familiar habits could be retained and the life of old machinery prolonged. Not surprisingly, there coexisted in the minds of the traditional business establishment both a desire not to be seen as outmoded and familiar forms of nostalgia. In the Chamber of Commerce's monthly, a production engineer wrote:

> [The nation's] wealth will increase if we stimulate production and expand exports . . . but departing as little as possible from the concrete facts of reality and so keeping in mind the potential of war-damaged equipment, which with its substantial, functional qualities, can be made once more a key component of [our] economic prospects . . . .[37]

The general lack of interest in the Marshall Plan's potential was evident in such writings. Besides all the obstacles, and the depressed general conditions, local experts hinted at the time that structural problems and difficulties of mentality were also at work. Many company owners were depicted as being thoughtless of the long-term challenges of modernisation and competition, and interested only in improvising for a quick return. The limits of the artisan outlook were already evident. Expansion of firms beyond the smallest scale was frowned upon, and their long-term survival was at risk from overdependence on the skills of the original founder.[38]

Emilia–Romagna was of course a region dominated by small and artisan firms, and their difficulties were proportionately greater than those of big companies long used to dealings with the organs of the state. Few possessed the resources to confront the procedural maze, or to organise a presence in Rome in the ministries and committees, or even to find out what ERP aid and the American market might have to offer them. Their intermediaries were the local Chambers of Commerce and sector organisations, but few of these proved able to supply the level of informational and logistical support necessary. A national law explicitly aimed at encouraging the modernisation of this sector, with the partial help of ERP aid, did eventually come into force in spring 1950 but with little publicity. Observers at the time and ever since have concluded that the government and the ministries were not interested in the growth of this sort of sector, that procedures guaranteeing centralisation and control – not results – remained for them the key priority, and that the Americans had very little influence on these realities.[39]

Still, for those who knew what they wanted and knew how to get it, the new law did encourage the participation of very small firms in the ERP, since it could approve loans (not grants) of up to $15,000, provided for easy and cheap repayment and promised a decision within thirty days of the application. The agricultural sector was encouraged to apply, since at these levels single machines could be imported at a time when talk of mechanisation was very much in the air. Only on closer inspection did the limits of what was on offer become apparent. American farm machinery was designed for big holdings; the smallest tractor was sixty horse-power. Although by no means unattractive to the larger landowners and agricultural contractors, these machines were useless to the mass of small holders and peasant farmers, those whose custom would eventually be monopolised by FIAT with its twenty and forty horse-power models sold on cheap credit.[40] These considerations did not discourage Emilian farmers entirely, and the region eventually benefited more than any other from this effort at agricultural modernisation. Even so the total sums allocated were no more than $600,000, and over $1.1 million worth of applications were turned down.[41]

The evolution of the Marshall Plan in its Emilian context

On the occasion of his October 1949 visit to Bologna, the head of the ERP Mission to Italy was pleased to point to the indirect results of his agency's activities. Coal and other raw materials had flowed in without difficulty, Mr Zellerbach declared; rationing had been abolished thanks to grain supplies from America, medicines sent over had eased the health situation. From the counterpart fund, 15 billion lira had been set aside for public works and housing. In his reply, the highly respected Communist Mayor of Bologna, Giuseppe Dozza, was pleased to acknowledge the 'undeniably solid facts' the Marshall Plan had brought about. But he had no difficulty in demonstrating that the region's economic crisis showed no signs of improving, and that without real investments from outside and the boost to confidence a true reconversion plan would bring, there was little chance of the ERP's efforts making much impact. Dozza surprised his audience by suggesting that only if the Left's 'social innovations' were accepted did the Marshall Plan have a real chance of success.[42]

Spring and autumn 1950 brought some relief. Seasonal work in the harvests, better energy and raw materials supplies, and a decline in strikes all contributed, and from the summer onwards the 'Korean boom' made its effects felt, as it did throughout the national economy. But the upturn was short-lived, and by the middle of 1951 the region's unresolved problems of conversion and modernisation reappeared as seriously as ever. A case in point was the Ravenna-based rubber goods firm Callegari e Ghigi, a well-founded company producing a range of items from wagon covers to boots and shoes. Faced with a sixfold surge in the cost of the raw material between the end of 1949 and the end of 1950, and a problem of overmanning dating back to the end of the war, the company decided in late 1950 to introduce new productivity systems and continuous assembly lines. Combining detailed – and secret – time-and-motion studies with the introduction of new technology, the firm managed to amortise the investment in its first new production line – with an output of 300 pairs of shoes per day – in no more than ten days. A process of expansion was started which soon took output to a level of 4,000 pairs a day, thought to be the national market's 'natural' limit of absorption. But the firm found mechanisation much easier to handle than rationalisation, where it fell back on a heavy-handed and divisive form of piece-work to stimulate production, together with such experiments as outplacing slipper sole production in a convent. Unable to go beyond the confines of the national market, or to imagine a coherent global reorganisation of its output and markets – unlike its competitor Pirelli – the firm passed through a short-lived boom before beginning in the mid-1950s a long decline towards extinction.[43]

Considering all the circumstances of the moment, the Marshall Plan's representatives in Italy remained optimistic. In a speech in the Bologna town hall in January 1951, the new head of the Rome mission, Dayton, answered his programme's leftwing critics directly:

> The sceptics may say that ERP is merely a device for causing money to flow into the pockets of the rich and not for helping the less well off elements of the Italian society. But I don't think those 5,000 citizens of Emilia who have been working full-time only in the *construction work* involved in the regional irrigation and reclamation programme will believe that nonsense. And *they* aren't rich men. [44]

Over 25,000 men would be employed in the construction sector by the ERP's agricultural efforts for the region, Dayton said, making way for the

20,000 farm workers who would eventually benefit from permanent new jobs. 'None of *them* is rich either', declared Dayton.

Soon afterwards the Information Division of the Rome Mission produced its own account of the achievements of the Marshall Plan in the region, a documentary film intended to be one of a series on 'The Regions of Italy', but which in fact – for reasons unknown – never went beyond this one product. Narrated in English, possibly for a television series on the ERP being developed in the US at that time for the ABC network, the film depicted a 'lush land, fruitful, prosperous, serene'. Traditionally rich, it was also known as 'Red Emilia', the most 'Communistic' area of Italy.[45] Into this picture, devastated by war, the Marshall Plan was shown to have brought new hope to industry and agriculture. It had rebuilt entire factories with new machinery, had reconstructed the region's railways and its principal cattle market, and had brought work to the stagnant, backward Po delta by huge land reclamation schemes featuring Caterpillar tractors and jeeps. On screen, the President of the Bologna Chamber of Commerce paid tribute to the contribution of the ERP to the region's revival.

The 'myth of the Marshall Plan' can thus be shown to have been instigated in the beginning by the Marshall Planners themselves. At the time, in 1951, the Bologna Chamber of Commerce was just as anxious to demonstrate to its members its scepticism over US recipes for modernisation as its adoption of them. Commentators in the Chamber's monthly economic bulletin were ready to give the concept of productivity its due in the American universe, but failed to see how it could function where 'the natural demographic, economic, productive and commercial environment of the United States' was lacking. In this view there was no sign of a mass market developing in Italy, while export traffic was blocked by all sorts of financial and political obstacles. The American idea of artificially stimulating markets by the use of publicity to induce new needs seemed laughable in such a context:

> In fact it is ironical . . . to talk of boosting advertising in order to create markets for mass production in countries without raw materials, poor in arable land, over-populated and so continuously full of labour in search of work, countries where capital is scarce and so are energy supplies.[46]

By the end of 1952, when this comment was written, other European economies were already showing remarkable signs of the better times to come, and even the industrial triangle of Turin, Milan and Genoa had passed the worst. But Emilia–Romagna was still thoroughly depressed. The much reduced sector of capital goods had done quite well in the year, reported the bulletin of the Bologna Chamber of Commerce, but the consumption sectors remained mired in miserable conditions.[47]

By autumn 1952, more than sixty industrial companies had closed since

1947 in Bologna alone, according to a trade union source. The same observer provided an equally disturbing picture for the agricultural sector, still dominant in the economy of the region, and in a summary noted:

> . . . declining in comparison with 1938, and with 1948–9, are the outputs of rice, hemp, grapes, silk cocoons, chestnuts, fire-wood; in 1951 there was also a decline – compared to 1949 – in the production of sugar-beet [in spite of the fact] that this item has received particular attention from the government and the land-owners as part of their war-readiness plans.[48]

The great conversion

In 1992 Pier Paolo D'Attorre asked: 'Why did [the region's] genuine industrial transition occur in the 1950s and not before?' The answer, he thought, could only be one: 'From the development of external markets, rather than from under-nourished or non-existent internal markets, came the force for the great leap forward.'[49]

As such, there was nothing exceptional about the experience of Emilia–Romagna. The entire national economy was being pulled forward by the transformation of Western Europe's prospects. However, the *forms* this development took in the area based on Bologna were quite different to those known elsewhere in Europe or in Italy. Instead of stimulating the appearance of high-technology, large-scale industrial concentrations, the new export-led demand worked to re-energise older patterns of economic activity. Far back in the nineteenth century if not earlier, small-scale industry, family and neighbourhood collaboration and organised co-operation in production and consumption all had developed as responses to the earliest challenges of industrialisation. Along the axis of the Via Emilia, wrote D'Attorre, an inheritance of 'proto-industry' remained to be used and transformed for quite new purposes. The Bolognese economic historian Carlo Poni explained what this inheritance consisted of:

> These dense local concentrations of diversified, co-ordinated activities were sustained by and fed a complex network of relationships and trade-offs encouraging the accumulation of individual and family attitudes to collaboration on the job, of cultural processes connected to acquiring skills and the needs of industrial-type activity . . . . And where spontaneous co-operation failed to function effectively, other mechanisms and devices came into action, identifiable as organised co-operation.[50]

The post-Second World War crisis shook this inheritance to its roots, but rather than killing it off, the drama of survival brought out in it quite unexpected resources of adaptation. New relationships were struck between agriculture and industry, town and country, one sector and another. Everywhere the pattern of widely-diffused small and medium-scale industry reasserted itself. The breakup of the industrial structures left by Fascism and the war forced skilled workers to become their own bosses. Those expelled from firms for political reasons after 1948 followed the same path, but they did so in collaborative not competitive fashion, exchanging knowledge and specialities, employing neighbours or men and women recruited through the Communist party or co-operative movement, to both of which they remained intensely loyal. While the Apennine hill farms emptied as the towns began to expand, Emilian agri-business was being born in the plains. Versatility, spirit of adaptation and *flexibility*, in technicians, workers and small-scale entrepreneurs alike: these were the qualities which enabled the great opportunity to be grasped when it finally came along in the mid-1950s.

The role of local institutions in this remarkable transition still provokes debate. As integral members of the communities carrying on the inheritance of 'proto-industry', the people running local government tried hard to reconcile the social and economic innovations envisaged by the 'party line' with the realities of the territories they controlled. The result was a spontaneous, almost casual, encouragement of the new kind of industrial activity.

In Modena the industrial policy of the town council – Communists in the absolute majority – began to function from 1953 onwards. Areas were set aside for the creation of artisan and small-scale industries. Such was the success of this initiative that by 1959, seventy-four companies were active in an expanded area, which became known as an 'artisan village'.[51] However, as Alberto Rinaldi makes clear in his analysis of this experience, the intentions of the town council were not so much economic as social. In the beginning the beneficiaries were artisans who had been forced out of their town-centre premises by bomb damage or slum clearance. The mayor of the town was alone in suggesting that the new industrial estate might propel the economic development of the entire area, and that the artisans on it were capable of competing at the national level in their specialised segments of the market. What no one foresaw was that the vitality of these enterprises would take them well beyond their national markets, and that their aptitude for specialisation would release them from the gravitational pull of the big national firms, whether state or privately controlled.[52]

In Modena, new activities included earth-moving machinery and small-scale hydraulic engineering. In Modena, Reggio and Parma, food-processing industries began to take on different attitudes to modernisation. Southwest of Modena, in the Apennine foothills, the ceramic tile tradition was transformed. Less than 15 miles to the north-east, in the small town of Carpi, the ancient home-based industry of straw-hat making changed within a few years into a world force in the knitted jumper, sweater and T-shirt market. Remarkably,

the underlying social mechanisms remained intact: networks linked protago-
nists at every stage of the production and distribution process, machinery was
usable in the home, and family, community and co-operative-based support
systems coped with money, with change and with the management of the
division of labour.[53]

Each part of the area knew its own experience of economic modernisation
based on the small firm and community-based industrial development. Not
until the 1970s would a region-wide recognition process lead to the start of
more comprehensive industrial policies, but throughout Emilia–Romagna
from the 1950s onwards the same closeness of town and country, of
local administrations and Communist Party, leftwing trade unions and
co-operatives, would make its weight felt. Just as the role of local administrations in developing appropriate infrastructures, zoning and rent control needs
to be appreciated, said D'Attorre, so 'recognising the peculiarities and the
potentialities of Emilia Romagna's industrialisation means understanding too
the dynamics of the new relationships between co-operatives, their members
and the market.'[54]

Conclusion: Americanisation and the myth of the Marshall Plan

Because of the strength of the Communist tradition in Italy, writes Stephen
Gundle, 'Americanisation was not the only possible model of development nor
necessarily the most desirable. But it was the one which came to be built and
in the end triumphed.'[55] But was this so in Emilia–Romagna? Since Emilia's
Communists continued to believe in the imminent disappearance of capitalism and the capitalist class in Italy, they were unprepared to face the
American challenge in all its myriad, ever-changing forms as it struck Italy
from 1948 onwards. In the national Senate the Bolognese economist
Fortunati, sitting for the PCI, declared in May 1949 that he 'wanted to make
clear . . . the irrationality of these economic paradises in which *everybody* is
supposed to start getting *better and better off* right away.'[56]

The Marshall Plan, wrote D'Attorre, helped put technical and social
modernisation on everyone's agenda and showed off the most successful
version of it with great allure. It inspired changes in mentalities, attitudes and
expectations which in Emilia–Romagna, as elsewhere, Communist doctrine
and practice found very hard to deal with. As Stephen Gundle has shown in
detail, Communist militants and sympathisers adapted by making their own
private pacts with whatever America was offering, buying the records, seeing
the films, drinking Coke in 'bars' like everyone else and in the face of militant
official anti-Americanism. In Carpi, the jumper-knitters took their sketch
pads to the cinema to copy the fashions of the stars. Finished products might
appear in American-style boxes.[57]

The ERP probably did not get the credit it deserved for helping to build

Emilia–Romagna's infrastructure and for its contribution to the eventual salvation of agriculture. As it was among other things an American weapon in the Cold War, it could of course never be openly embraced by the dominant forces in the region. But in part, the neglect was also because the ERP believed its own myths, turned a blind eye to the region's structural crisis and ignored the resentment caused by its wilful extinction of traditional outlets for trade in eastern Europe. Fifty years after the Liberation, leftwing writers of various persuasions recalled with joy the arrival of the American armies in Bologna, with their music, jeeps, chocolate, films and faith in the future.[58] The Marshall Plan would never be celebrated in such a fashion. But perhaps it was significant that the first ever historical conference promoted by the Communist Party's cultural establishment to assess the weight of America in Italy's postwar development would eventually be held in Bologna, in 1981.[59]

Acknowledgements

Parts of this chapter were first published in P.P. D'Attorre (ed.), *La ricostruzione in Emilia–Romagna*, Parma, Pratiche, 1980; for some of the additional research included in this version, I am indebted to dttssa. Deborah Succi. The chapter is dedicated to the memory of Pier Paolo D'Attorre (1951–1997), Mayor of Ravenna, 1993–7, colleague and friend.

Notes

1 Proceedings of the Hague meeting of the Netherlands Institute of International Affairs, 15–16 May 1997, in H.J. Labohm (ed.), *The Fiftieth Anniversary of the Marshall Plan in Retrospect and Prospect*, The Hague, Clingendael Institute, 1997.

2 United States National Archives and Records Administration, Washington, DC and College Park, MD (hereafter NARA), Record Group (hereafter RG) 469, ECA, Office of Information, Office of Director, Country Subject Files, 'Italy', Speech to World Affairs Council of Northern California, 30 November 1949. In fact, Communist Party membership fell in Emilia–Romagna only in 1951–2, during the worst years of the postwar depression, thus contrasting a fundamental American Cold War premise, that misery fed communism; for figures, see L. Casali and D. Gagliani, 'Movimento operaio e organizzazione di massa. Il partito comunista in Emilia Romagna (1945–1954)', in D'Attorre (ed.), *La ricostruzione*, p. 256.

3 F. Anderlini, 'Ristrutturazione industriale, classe operaia, mercato del lavoro (1937–1951)', in ibid., p. 143.

4 L. Gambi, 'L'assetto del territorio', in ibid., p. 69.

5 R. Fregna, 'Urbanistica e città: Bologna', in ibid., p. 81.

6 P.P. D'Attorre and V. Zamagni, 'Introduzione', in D'Attorre and Zamagni (eds), *Distretti, Impresa, Classe operaia. L'industrializzazione dell'Emilia Romagna*, Milan, Angeli, 1992, pp. 8–9.

7 *Emilia*, December 1949, no. 1, p. 22.

8 A. De Polzer, 'I contadini e la crisi agricola', *Emilia*, April 1950, no. 5, p. 99.

9 A. Bellettini, 'Aspetti dell'economia emiliana negli anni della ricostruzione e del primo sviluppo', in D'Attorre (ed.), *La ricostruzione*, pp. 17–18.

10 ibid.
11 Anderlini, 'Ristrutturazione industriale', p. 151; emphasis in original.
12 P.P. D'Attorre, 'L'industrializzazione di Ravenna nel contesto romagnolo', in D'Attorre (ed.), *Il 'miracolo economico' a Ravenna*, Ravenna, Longo, 1994.
13 *Cooperazione economica Italia-Stati uniti 1944–1954*, Rome, United States Embassy, n.d., pp. 18–19.
14 G. Maione, *Tecnocrati e mercanti. L'industria italiana tra dirigismo e concorrenza internazionale 1945–1950*, Milan, Sugarco, 1986, p. 238 passim.
15 R. Tremelloni, *Il Fondo Lire. L'utilizzo del Fondo Lire ERP nel 1948–49*, Rome, 1949, pp. 19–20 and 22.
16 *Un anno di ERP in Italia*, Rome, ERP Mission, February 1949, pp. 29–30, 60–2.
17 ibid., p. 29; Tremelloni, *Il Fondo Lire*, pp. 19–20.
18 P.P. D'Attorre, 'Il Piano Marshall: politica, economia, relazioni internazionali nella ricostruzione italiana', in B. Vigezzi (ed.), *L'Italia e la politica di potenza in Europa 1945–1950*, Milan, Marzorati, 1988, pp. 520–35; V. Zamagni, *Dalla periferia al centro. La seconda rinascita economica dell'Italia 1861–1990*, Bologna, Il Mulino, 1993, pp. 415–24.
19 D.W. Ellwood, 'The 1948 Elections in Italy: A Cold War Propaganda Battle', *Historical Journal of Film, Radio & Television*, 1993, no. 1.
20 D.W. Ellwood, 'Italian Modernisation and the Propaganda of the Marshall Plan', in L. Cheles (ed.), *The Art of Persuasion: Political Communication in Italy*, Manchester, Manchester University Press, 1998.
21 *Critica Economica*, 1948, no. 1, pp. 4, 11, 51 and 55.
22 F. Rodano, 'La questione del "Fondo Lire"', *Rinascita*, February 1948, no. 2, pp.74–6; and 'Il Piano Marshall e l'Italia', ibid., March 1948, no. 3, pp. 103–7.
23 *Il Piano Marshall e i comunisti*, pamphlet in series 'Problemi economici', PCI, 1949; *Propaganda*, 10 March 1949.
24 *Per la pace, il benessere popolare, le libertà democratiche*, documents of the VIIth provincial congress of the PCI, 17–20 December 1950.
25 *Propaganda*, 10 February 1949.
26 Documentation and discussion in D.W. Ellwood, 'Il Piano Marshall e il processo di modernizzazione in Italia', in E. Aga Rossi (ed.), *Il Piano Marshall e l'Europa*, Rome Instituto dell' Enciclopedia Italiana, 1983, p. 158.
27 M. Valenti, 'Il ruolo delle classi dominanti agrarie', in D'Attorre (ed.), *La ricostruzione*, p. 103.
28 *Tre anni di ERP in Italia*, Rome, ERP Mission, 1951, pp. 70–2.
29 ibid., pp. 312–15.
30 F. Storoni, *Viaggio attraverso l'Emilia*, Rome, ERP Mission, May 1951, p. 4.
31 ibid., p. 21.
32 D. Succi, 'Il Piano Marshall e le industrie dell'Emilia Romagna', unpublished paper, University of Bologna, 1996, p. 5.
33 ibid., pp. 10–11.
34 ibid., pp. 11–12.
35 ibid., and p. 29.
36 ibid., p. 13; *Giornale dell'Emilia*, 16 October 1949.
37 *La Mercanzia*, May 1949, quoted in Succi, 'Il Piano Marshall', p. 19.
38 ibid., and see sources quoted ibid., p. 19.
39 ibid., pp. 14–15.
40 ibid., pp. 16–17.
41 ibid., p. 33.
42 *Giornale dell'Emilia*, 16 October 1949.

43 L.M. Ioli, 'La vicenda industriale della Calegari & Ghigi', in D'Attorre (ed.), *Il 'miracolo economico'*, pp. 119–21.
44 Text of speech, delivered at the ERP exhibit, Salone del Podestà, Bologna, 21 January 1951, *Giornale dell'Emilia*, 22 January 1951; emphases in original.
45 For a full contextualisation of the film, see Ellwood, 'Italian Modernisation and the Propaganda of the Marshall Plan'.
46 G. Gola, 'Produttivismo: filosofia industriale', *La Mercanzia*, November-December 1952, p. 51; Succi, 'Il Piano Marshall', p. 28.
47 *La Mercanzia*, January 1953, p. 53; ibid.
48 Proceedings of the IVth Conference of the Confederal Chamber of Labour, Bologna, 28–29 September 1952, pp. 35, 37.
49 D'Attorre and Zamagni, 'Introduzione', p. 9.
50 ibid., p. 11.
51 ibid., pp. 128–9.
52 ibid., pp. 129–30.
53 L. Cicognetti and M. Pezzini, 'Dalle paglie alle maglie. Carpi: la nascita di un sistema produttivo', in D'Attorre and Zamagni (eds), *Distretti, imprese*, pp. 157–87. The presence of oral testimony makes this a particularly telling contribution.
54 D'Attorre and Zamagni, 'Introduzione', pp. 19–20.
55 S. Gundle, *I comunisti italiani tra Hollywood e Mosca*, Florence, Giunti, 1995, p. 14.
56 Senate speech of 24 May 1949; emphasis in original.
57 Interview with Luisa Cicognetti, Bologna, 14 June 1997.
58 'C'era una volta l'America', supplement to Bologna edition of *Unità* (daily newspaper of the PDS, the renamed Communist Party), 21 April 1995.
59 Proceedings in P.P. D'Attorre (ed.), *La governabilità degli Stati Uniti*, Milan, Angeli, 1983.

Part III

THE TRANSLATION AND TRANSFORMATION

10

AN AMERICANISED COMPANY IN GERMANY

The Vereinigte Glanzstoff Fabriken AG in the 1950s

Christian Kleinschmidt

Flags in black, red and gold, green, white and red, and in red and white lined the street along the approach for the guests of honour. The newly designed street sign 'Dr. Vits-Straße' shone brightly. The company police did their duty conscientiously, sporting attractive uniforms. The celebration proceeded as follows: The Cologne-Gürtzenich orchestra, led by Professor Wand, opened the proceedings. A number of speeches followed: Dr Vits [the chief executive], Professor Dr Erhard, the Federal Minister for Economic Affairs, Dr Straeter, the Minister of Economic Affairs in Northrhine-Westfalia, and Kremers, the Head of the works council. Then the orchestra rounded off this most successful affair with the Leonore overture which was warmly applauded.[1]

What at first seems to be an act of state was in fact part of the ceremony to mark the opening of a new perlon factory of the Vereinigte Glanzstoff Fabriken AG (hereafter Glanzstoff) in 1950. Glanzstoff was the largest German producer of artificial fibres and the first to start the mass production of fully synthetic fibres. As this chapter shows, top management had a strong American orientation, reflected not only in the product perlon, which was also described as 'German nylon', but also in the methods of production and sales, in further training for management and in aspects of human relations. The American influence within Glanzstoff was so great that it would have hardly been surprising, metaphorically speaking, if the star-spangled banner had been hoisted up next to the flags of West Germany and Northrhine-Westfalia.

However, this American influence was not reflected in the presentation of the company to the public nor in the official speeches on the day. The opening of the new perlon factory was celebrated primarily as a national event, as an expression of German industrial achievement and entrepreneurial spirit. In his speech Economics Minister Erhard proclaimed:

> I am very proud to take part in this celebration. Not only because my own humble advice contributed to this success, but because I can sense a spirit and a strength here, which will alone save and redeem the German people. Especially during this time of international dispute, it seems to me to be vital that we do not forget the healthy basis of every national community and state: human labour. My visit should be seen as a sign of respect to the German entrepreneurial spirit, to the strength and creativity of German managers and to the ability of German workers to work hard. This inseparable community of interest is the source of this new achievement![2]

Erhard also used the opportunity to criticise Allied plans to decartelise and dismantle German industries and companies, which also threatened Glanzstoff.[3] So far, much of the debate on the American influence in West Germany after the Second World War has focused on macroeconomic factors such as decartelisation, dismantling, the effect of Marshall Plan aid and American support for Germany's reintegration into the world market.[4] By contrast, empirical research at the microeconomic, company level has been very limited, despite the fact that some of these questions were tackled in the early 1960s by Heinz Hartmann. He investigated the influence of American firms on their German subsidiaries in terms of production techniques, management methods, organisation, personnel, marketing, accounting and so on, and identified an 'export of specific parts of an economic culture'.[5]

More recently, the question of the Americanisation of West German industry has been taken up by Volker Berghahn.[6] Referring to Hartmann's research, he sees Americanisation or 'partial' Americanisation as an expression of a new 'industrial culture', which manifests itself in entrepreneurial attitudes and behaviour towards political and economic issues, such as competition policy. On the one hand, Berghahn has identified the role of key individuals in this transformation process.[7] On the other hand, he highlighted that more widespread changes in the Federal Republic only occurred when a new generation of managers took over during the 1960s. In a recent article, Harm Schröter has also stressed the importance of generation change for Americanisation which he defines as the adoption of values, behaviour, norms and institutions by management as 'a manner of practical work'.[8] In general, it is quite common today to find the term Americanisation used as a synonym for 'modernisation', 'technological orientation', 'market liberalism' or 'mass culture'.[9]

Dissatisfaction with these rather loose definitions and the lack of empirical research has led Paul Erker to reject Americanisation as an analytic category, and Kaspar Maase to accept it only as an heuristic concept.[10] By contrast, I would like to argue in favour of retaining Americanisation as an analytic category. Even though it has often degenerated into a catch-all term, the concept itself should not necessarily be dismissed. For the purpose of this chapter, Americanisation will be understood on the one hand as the perception of and orientation towards American methods in a specific company, and on the other hand as practical implementation of these methods within the given organisation, covering both material and mental aspects. In order to identify the extent of the American influence at Glanzstoff, it is necessary to distinguish newly adopted US-style methods of production and management from previous company practice and tradition. Before studying the postwar Americanisation in detail, the chapter will therefore give an overview of the earlier history of the company, especially with respect to its relationship with the United States.

The development of Glanzstoff until 1945

Early international contacts

Founded in 1899, the Vereinigte Glanzstoff Fabriken AG had a long tradition of international relations and co-operation. This is as true of production and management methods as of the main company product, synthetic fibre. The first patent for artificial fibre was registered in England in 1855, while the production of artificial silk was developed in France in the 1870s and 1880s. During its formative years, Glanzstoff drew on this knowledge for the development of synthetic thread for the production of electric bulbs. Later, the company took up the production of synthetic silk and moved its headquarters to Elberfeld (today a suburb of Wuppertal). In the decade leading up to the First World War, annual production increased almost tenfold, from 86 tons in 1902 to 820 tons in 1912. International contacts were improved, especially with France; the first subsidiary abroad was set up in Austria in 1904 and new plants and production methods were acquired, including the production of viscose which had been patented in England. By 1914 Glanzstoff was one of the world's leading producers of artificial fibres.[11]

The First World War led to a new focus on the production of a staple fibre which after the 1930s became known as rayon. Spun together with wool or cotton to lengthen the product, it served as an important raw material for textiles. Glanzstoff's economic strength had grown from the turn of the century, but was then interrupted by the implementation of the Treaty of Versailles. The company lost foreign contacts and its position in the world market, while at the same time being subject to increasing competition in the domestic market. Glanzstoff finally regained its leading position in the production of viscose and copper silk after postwar reconstruction, rebuilding foreign relations and taking over a number of companies producing textiles and synthetic fibre. Within the German synthetic fibre industry, Glanzstoff was now in the lead. Contacts with Courtaulds in England and with Italy and Czechoslovakia, activities in Japan, the setting up of a subsidiary in the United States and the 1929 merger with the Dutch Kunstzijedefabriek in Arnheim, known as Enka and later as AKU, made Glanzstoff a more important producer than IG Farben, which had been founded in 1925.

The Great Depression, National Socialism and the policy of autarky had a mixed influence on Glanzstoff. On the one hand, there was technical advance and an increase in production with the preparation for war. Between 1933 and 1941, production at Glanzstoff increased sixfold. This was due not only to the production of rayon, but also to a new form of tyre-corduroy based on synthetic thread, which was produced on a large scale from 1937 onwards under orders from the Ministry of German Basic and Raw Materials. But on the other hand, as during the First World War, the company became increasingly isolated from the world market and from those international contacts which had been built up again so slowly during the interwar period. Their breakdown resulted, in turn, in a disruption of the international exchange of information.

During the Nazi period, international contacts were blocked by Heinz Kehrl, an important official at the Economics Ministry and also deputy chairman of Glanzstoff's supervisory board, who was quite often opposed to the company's chief executive Herrmann. Disputes between Glanzstoff's management and the National Socialists finally led to Herrmann leaving the managing board. As a result, by the end of the 1930s the balance of power at Glanzstoff had changed. Ernst Hellmut Vits was appointed to the managing board with the help of Hermann Josef Abs, who was on the managing board of the Deutsche Bank and chairman of the Glanzstoff supervisory board. Over the next thirty years, Vits was to dominate developments at Glanzstoff, together with Ludwig Vaubel. Their two main objectives were to secure Glanzstoff's leading position as a producer of artificial fibres and to pursue technical progress and innovations.

Glanzstoff and developments in artificial fibres

R&D and technological developments at Glanzstoff evolved primarily around synthetic fibre production. In this area, most of the research was carried out by IG Farben and DuPont, although it was almost impossible for German companies to follow American developments during the Nazi period. Parallel to research carried out by Wallace H. Carothers at DuPont, Hermann Staudinger of Freiburg University and Paul Schlack of IG Farben worked on the production of a true synthetic fibre. In 1934, they produced 'Pe-Ce-Faser', the first spun synthetic fibre in Germany. But in 1938, news reached German producers about an American fibre called 'nylon', 'purer than silk', strongly resistant to chemicals and of a quality high enough for

use in technical applications and textiles. While trailing their German counterparts before the First World War, two decades later American firms
assumed a leading international role in the production of artificial fibre.

Glanzstoff had already pursued a flourishing exchange of technology with
American synthetic fibre producers during the 1920s. Now, the company
contacted the European DuPont representative in London to obtain a licence
for the new fibre, but these attempts were unsuccessful. Instead, DuPont and
IG Farben reached an agreement in May 1939 which gave the latter a licence
for nylon. In return, DuPont obtained the right to produce 'Buna', a form of
synthetic rubber. IG Farben was very interested in nylon, despite having
developed an artificial fibre with similar qualities, called 'perlon'. Differences
concerned the raw materials, the production costs and especially perlon's lower
melting point at 220 degrees Celsius, compared to 250 for nylon.

Glanzstoff also remained interested in both fibres despite the earlier
setback and its own continuing research efforts. At Glanzstoff, Julius Funcke
was responsible for the development of synthetic fibres. He had joined the
company in 1927 and gained international experience during his work in
Sweden, Canada, Japan and especially in the United States, where he had been
made head of the American Glanzstoff Corporation in Elisabethton, Tennessee
in 1928. He returned to Germany as the production manager of the plants in
Breslau and Kelsterbach and, in 1940, became the head of its research and
patent department in Teltow-Seehof. Funcke recognised that, 'while for
several years the Vereinigte Glanzstoff Fabriken AG has grappled with the
problem of a true synthetic fibre, the only way forward has been to produce
DuPont's so-called nylon fibre and the IG Farben's perlon fibre.'[12]

This was indeed the option Glanzstoff had chosen. Shortly before the
outbreak of war, a small quantity of perlon silk was produced in Glanzstoff's
plant at Elsterberg for the first time. The raw materials and equipment used
had been delivered according to the terms of a licence agreement with IG
Farben. In 1943, Glanzstoff finally obtained access to the necessary technology. For information on American nylon, the company was dependent on a
critical evaluation of American scientific journals and 'technical publications
of the enemy', obtained with the help of the German army. During the war, a
further source of information was found in the analysis of American tyres and
parachutes made out of nylon silk, a material which was identified as
possessing a 'remarkable strength and durability'.[13]

The company not only tried to keep abreast of technological developments
in the United States during the war, but also showed an interest in the
country's economic developments and its vast potential as a market for artificial fibres. Already at the end of 1944, the Glanzstoff sales department noted
that the US presented unlimited possibilities for the sale of synthetic materials
for civilian use:

In the last two years the US nylon industry has made a great leap forward . . . . All preparations have been made in order to adapt nylon plants to peacetime needs within the shortest space of time. Furthermore, plans have been made to complete the technical transition for the production of civilian goods within a few weeks. Given scientific developments in nylon production, we believe that the following industries will take up the production of nylon to a degree as yet unknown: dress-making, menswear, net curtains, wall decorations, carpets, awning materials and the stocking industry.[14]

It seemed certain that the future of Glanzstoff in the postwar period was to be closely linked to the production of both nylon and perlon. As noted, even before the end of the Second World War the company had shown a considerable interest in the United States, in terms of both product and market developments. These were to continue with renewed emphasis after the cessation of hostilities. Before this, however, in the immediate postwar period Glanzstoff had to overcome a number of difficulties, including the loss of some of its production facilities and raw material shortages.

Difficult postwar reconstruction

During the last phase of the war and the immediate postwar period, production was restricted at Glanzstoff as a result of wartime bombing and Allied policy. With the division of Germany, the company lost control over two plants in the Soviet zone and in the part of the country now absorbed into Poland. However, the main Glanzstoff plants were located in the Western occupation zones and most of them resumed production in late 1945 and early 1946 with the notable exception of the 'core' plant in Oberbruch, near Aachen, which was only able to start production again in 1947. While the Obernburg and Kelsterbach plants in the US zone resumed production of artificial silk in 1946, the company's management remained wary of possible Allied restrictions. As Ludwig Vaubel observed shortly after the war:

> In the American zone the US cotton lobby is trying to establish its interests. According to the orders of the American military government in Berlin, the production of artificial fibres should be stopped completely. The regional centres are still fighting against this. Perhaps Obernburg has a greater chance due to the possibility of producing tyre thread and harvest twine but our worries are perpetual.[15]

In retrospect, these fears proved to be unfounded. In 1947 the Obernburg site produced 3,647 tons of artificial silk, in 1948, 7,840 tons, and by 1949 capacities were almost fully utilised. On the basis of an agreement between

Glanzstoff and an American firm, 25 per cent of textile yarns were exported to the United States.[16] Another of the company's major fears was related to the Allied policy of decartelisation and dismantling. In 1946, Glanzstoff was placed under Allied control. But the major focus lay on the connections with the Dutch concern AKU, with which the company had merged in 1929. In 1947, AKU representatives joined Glanzstoff's managing board. Only in 1953, when a written agreement was signed with the Dutch, were Glanzstoff's efforts to remain independent finally rewarded.[17]

The survival and success of the company under these difficult circumstances owed much to the continuity of its management after 1945 and close contact with the Allies. When the company was placed under Allied control, the British military government appointed its chief executive, Ernst Hellmut Vits, as custodian. The trust which the Allies placed in Vits is illustrated by the fact that he was the only German to be invited to join the Allied Combined Control Group as a financial advisor in 1947.[18]

Initially, efforts to restart production at Glanzstoff focused on artificial silk. Research on the development of fully synthetic fibres, interrupted briefly at the end of the war, was soon taken up again. In 1946, parts of the modified DuPont equipment, technical drawings as well as prototype machinery for the production of perlon, were transferred from the Elsterberg plant which was now located in the Soviet zone, to Obernburg. Developments at this site were to become the 'root of German synthetic fibre production'.[19] But Glanzstoff faced a number of adversities, including the difficult (re)construction of the DuPont equipment and the shortage of the necessary raw materials for the production of nylon and perlon, as a result of the priority given to other industries. While Julius Funcke, the Head of the Research Department, was sceptical about the company's hopes to produce synthetic fibres in 1946, he insisted on continuing the ongoing efforts: 'All in all, developments within this area at Glanzstoff are a considerable risk and competition is already hard. But the necessity of keeping involved in future developments and the importance of this new branch of production justify putting more resources into this area.'[20]

Subsequent developments proved him right. In the following years, Glanzstoff made a remarkable turnaround and started large-scale production of artificial fibres, inspired by the American example which the company's top managers had studied closely during several trips to the United States. Funke himself was the first to go there in 1948 and again in 1949, this time together with the chief executive, Vits. In 1950, Ludwig Vaubel visited the US and participated in Harvard's Executive Development Programme. The influence which these trips and the United States had on the company went far beyond the mass production of synthetic fibres, and concerned many other aspects of Glanzstoff's management and operations.

The influence of the American example

Technology and the scale of production

In 1948, Julius Funcke visited the United States in order to find out about possible uses of nylon and its sales in the American market. His impressions must have been favourable, because on his next trip in the following year he was accompanied by Ernst Hellmut Vits. In 1949, Funcke noted that these possibilities had increased 'rapidly' since the previous year, extending from the production of women's stockings to many other parts of the clothing industry such as women's underwear and men's socks. Funcke now saw the future for Glanzstoff's perlon production in a much more positive light than three years earlier. 'Since your return from America', he wrote to Vits in November 1949, 'Glanzstoff has become entirely *perlon-conscious*. The policy seems to be to build a larger perlon factory as soon as possible. There is no question about it – I am very happy to welcome this new development.'[21] It seems indeed that the observations made by Vits during his trip to the United States in 1949 marked a turning point in the company's production policy. Speaking in 1950, Vits remembered that:

> After Glanzstoff's anniversary I travelled to the USA and came back convinced that we should exploit the lengthy research we had done in synthetic fibres by taking up large-scale production. Earlier this year, the managing board and the supervisory board took the unanimous decision to build a perlon silk factory. The hope was to provide the German market with a synthetic material already successfully produced in America and in a number of European countries.[22]

Once some initial technical difficulties had been surmounted, the first large-scale experimental plant for perlon was set up at Obernburg in 1949. One year later, a new plant was built in Oberbruch. In a memorandum explaining the reasoning behind the construction of this new perlon factory, Vits underlined the significance of the American experience in nylon production:

> The success of our technical developments was undoubtedly one of the decisive factors in favour of building a new perlon factory. But news of the revolutionary development of nylon in the USA and the positive assessment of the economic future of synthetic fibres by large artificial fibre producers in other countries gave the final impetus to carry through the perlon project at Glanzstoff.[23]

Vits estimated that a production of two tons a day should be planned for the perlon factory, given the 25,000 tons of nylon produced per year in the USA and the continuous rise in demand. The perlon factory in Oberbruch was based on the American example to such a degree that even lighting and internal decoration followed the lines of DuPont factories.[24]

Thus, the main driver behind the construction of a new Glanzstoff plant was the observation of US producers, the American market and, most importantly, the belief of top management at Glanzstoff that these experiences could be transferred to Germany. Indeed, as subsequent developments showed, they were not mistaken about the increasing demand for articles such as women's stockings and car tyres. Until 1950, women's stockings in Germany were made out of cotton, viscose, silk or wool. The development of 'nylons' by DuPont in 1939 had a mythical quality which soon infected postwar Germany. However, the transfer of mass production and marketing methods was not the only aspect. The change was also reflected in language, cultural and behavioural patterns. Germans used the term 'German nylons' rather than 'perlons' to describe women's stockings, since they were perceived as an American phenomenon on the German market. They became a symbol of the new postwar beginning, giving clothing a lighter touch, part of 'the desire for something new and bright, or even extravagant'.[25] The term 'perlon period', *Perlonzeit* in German, was used to describe the 'economic miracle' and the early days of the growing consumer society in the Federal Republic. Nor were 'nylons' the only American innovation in women's wear to conquer German and European markets; other US-inspired improvements included, for example, ladder-free stockings.

Following the completion of the Oberbruch plant in 1950, perlon was thought to be the material of the future at Glanzstoff, used as it was for the production of women's stockings and other textiles as well as technical items. However, in the same year, the research department already pointed out that other synthetic materials such as orlon would probably gain in significance and should therefore not be neglected. Nylon production was discussed repeatedly. In 1952 Hermann Rathert, a member of the managing board, commented that having considered the pros and cons of nylon production at Glanzstoff, it seemed to be superior to perlon in certain areas even though the production method had not yet been finalised. Competition would probably force Glanzstoff into producing nylon in the near future. The company was prepared for this situation insofar as the existing machines could easily be adapted to the production of nylon.[26]

The next challenge came in the 1950s, once again from the United States, and involved the use of nylon for the manufacture of car tyres. Glanzstoff had produced tyre thread with rayon since 1937. In a DuPont circular of 1955, sent not only to Glanzstoff but also to German car producers, the American manufacturer spoke of a new corduroy lining made out of DuPont nylon called 'super cordura', which would lead to a 'sensational' improvement in tyre quality.[27] Glanzstoff reacted quickly to this latest American innovation. At a meeting in Obernburg regarding the possible construction of a nylon-corduroy factory, it was agreed that US developments meant that there was no time to lose, especially because tyre producers at home and abroad were entering sponsoring agreements with their American counterparts. After a further trip to the US in the mid-1950s, Vits decided in favour of nylon and against perlon as the most suitable material for tyre production. He observed that nylon, after having conquered the stocking industry, was now also beginning to dominate the tyre sector. Although perlon was not explicitly rejected, all those asked favoured the use of nylon.[28]

At first, nylon production at Glanzstoff was planned at one ton a day, but the projected demand soon made this amount appear too small. 'We realised', so Vits recalled later,

> that in the US nylon, next to RT-rayon, was becoming more and more important. The use of nylon in the production of tyre-corduroy and fabric in the US increased from 2,000 tons p.a. in 1951 to 13,000 tons p.a. in 1954 . . . . So, we became convinced that this was a development which we should take up in Germany.[29]

As a result of these observations and in anticipation of similar developments in the German tyre market, Glanzstoff's managing board decided in favour of an 'immediate' construction of a nylon-corduroy factory. Top managers even accepted that the new capacities might not be fully utilised at the beginning, a risk 'consciously' taken 'due to higher considerations'. Their objective and conviction was that 'we will shortly also reach the latest standard in DuPont nylon-corduroy'.[30] But once again, the orientation towards American developments was more than a question of production methods and potential markets. It also involved an improvement of storing methods for nylon's raw material, AH-salt, which followed the example of DuPont. Even in terms of pricing, Glanzstoff initially copied the US practice.

In the long-run, the decision to build a nylon-corduroy factory proved to be right, because the developments observed in the US did indeed emerge in the Federal Republic, albeit with a certain time lag. While Continental, one of the largest German tyre producers, declared in 1956 not to have an 'urgent demand' for nylon-corduroy, a few years later the car industry started to show a growing interest in the new tyres. Large automobile producers such as Mercedes-Benz began to replace rayon tyres with nylon ones in their new models, in order to meet the demands of higher speeds and improved safety.[31] As a consequence of its early move, by the end of the 1950s Glanzstoff produced 90 per cent of German tyre-corduroy, mostly using nylon, and exported 25 per cent of its output.

Sales, advertising and marketing

After the Second World War, the United States not only influenced production policy at Glanzstoff, but also the development of marketing and sales strategies. Unlike their American counterparts, German companies had paid little attention to marketing and sales during the first half of the twentieth century. Some ideas on how to strengthen sales had been articulated towards the end of the 1920s and the early 1930s. On the one hand, these ideas were a reaction to the wave of rationalisation during the interwar years, which had revealed that companies had concentrated too much on production while neglecting markets and ways to increase sales and turnover. On the other hand, business experts and entrepreneurs observed that in the United States more emphasis was placed on market analysis, demand analysis and advertising than in Germany.[32]

During the Nazi era, these methods were adopted, albeit not without controversy. In 1934 the age of market research in Germany began with the foundation of the 'Society for Consumer Research' (*Gesellschaft für Konsumforschung*), in which Ludwig Erhard (later Economics Minister) was involved. At the same time, American methods of market research and analysis were strongly criticised. A survey of the German distributive trade in 1936 observed:

> that the same businessman who recently fell for the spell of the catchword 'rationalization' and came to regret it, warmly welcomed the latest American innovation of 'market analysis'. All faith was put into market analysis – and the result was a bitter disappointment because too much had been expected, probably because those hard-working people from America had rather exaggerated.[33]

After the Second World War, these – ideologically motivated – reservations against American methods of sales and market research no longer existed. When travelling to the United States as part of the productivity missions, German industrialists and engineers observed the latest technologies and newest production methods, but learned at least as much about questions of sales and marketing. In addition, American literature on the subject was reviewed extensively. This was the background of the demand for a 'new way of thinking' which rejected the 'primacy of production'. With reference to Peter F. Drucker, who was widely read in Germany, it was noted that in Europe it was:

> relatively little understood, that marketing is a true function of business . . . . It can only receive the necessary attention if a deep-seated social prejudice is overcome according to which 'selling' is a rather lowly and 'producing' a more honourable occupation. This is the only reason why, within companies, production is seen to be the decisive element.[34]

While Drucker was also reviewed at Glanzstoff, in practice American companies such as DuPont and Dow Chemical were used as examples in sales and distribution. From 1950, Hans-Joachim Schlange-Schöningen, son of the Weimar Minister and later West German Ambassador in London, was responsible for the company's sales and exports. In a speech in 1959, he recollected how insufficient Glanzstoff's marketing and sales policy had been earlier in the decade:

> When I joined the company, and even in 1952 and 1954, my sales manager would comment 'We're in raw materials and not in advertising'. Nowadays, just a few years on, we are forced to spend millions of marks on advertising. It was said that the German public is not as easy to influence as the American. I believe that, quite to the contrary, it has never been attempted to employ this method to the maximum. I am convinced that we already have proof that if this were to be done, the success would be similar . . . .[35]

Quoting Drucker, he went on to demand: 'Markets are no longer to be had, we have to create them.' According to Schlange-Schöningen, advertising had played no role whatsoever at Glanzstoff previously. There was only production, products and sales: 'That was definitely it.' But the production of nylon-corduroy for tyres had a considerable influence on the situation at Glanzstoff: 'We had observed the procedures in North America.' The case of DuPont showed how a company had bypassed the tyre industry and directly reached the car industry, the end user, via advertising which had brought across the safety and durability of these tyres and how the renown of the name 'nylon' had also helped. This brought home the lesson that when planning investments, possibilities of influencing the market and reaching end users should also be included. 'Of course', as Schlange-Schöningen stated, 'this was a turnabout of the earlier state of affairs.'[36]

Marketing, almost previously unknown, was introduced at Glanzstoff by the end of the 1950s. Within the company and German business as a whole, marketing was more than what had traditionally been understood under the heading of 'sales'. It included the additional aspects of market research and analysis, advertising, merchandising and brought about a greater integration of these elements. The growing significance of marketing also had an influence on the Glanzstoff organisation. Communication between individual departments was increased. Those departments involved in sales, advertising and market research gained significance and became finally as important as other departments. In 1954, for example, the advertising department was taken out of the area of responsibility covered by sales and placed directly under the managing board. At the same time, an advertising commission was set up which was responsible for deciding Glanzstoff's advertising style. In this context, US advertising methods were studied, American firms and institutes visited and journals evaluated. A member of the advertising commission described an important gain from a visit to the US: 'In my opinion, Glanzstoff must now take care of long-term product sales and better represent its name, which should be inextricably linked to its products.'[37] This was to involve devising the right kind of marketing strategies and an intensification of communication between departments, especially between production and sales.

The diffusion of American sales and marketing methods is also reflected in the adoption of US terminology by the company's management. According to Schlange-Schöningen, 'we – including myself, that is – have consciously decided to use a number of American expressions. We have not been able to find any German equivalents, and I don't see why one should not use good foreign ones.'[38] This use of Americanisms illustrates that the relevant methods had not only been adopted superficially, but had reached into the core of corporate life. In this sense, they were a reflection of the transfer of business culture which, according to Heinz Hartmann, pushed 'those who employed it into a linguistically pre-determined perception of reality'.[39]

This tendency to adopt terms from the American business world increased over the subsequent years. 'Americanisms' were in daily use in business and were also part of Americanisation at Glanzstoff. As Schlange-Schöningen recollected, it was important to be *'up-to-date'*. During the 1950s, this Americanism was used not only in business but also generally, and today it belongs to the 'new' German vocabulary. At Glanzstoff, being 'up-to-date' was a challenge for management and all superiors who were supposed to be informed about the very latest developments in new methods of production and organisation.

Management training and human relations

In the early 1950s, further management training, both on and off the job, was regarded as a typically American phenomenon. The journal of the German employers federation BDA reported on German–American talks on operational management in 1952: 'It is peculiar to America that managers are continually trained on-the-job as well as outside the plant and are informed about economic and technical developments in special meetings.'[40] A book published by Ludwig Vaubel in the same year, entitled *Unternehmer gehen zur Schule* (Managers go to School), shows that Glanzstoff was 'up-to-date' in this respect, too. Vaubel, born in 1908, belonged to Glanzstoff's second management generation, as did Ernst Hellmut Vits and other members of the board. In 1934, he had joined Glanzstoff as a legal advisor and enjoyed the support of Vits and Abs, the chairman of the supervisory board. In 1939, Vaubel became head of Glanzstoff's legal department, and in 1953 he joined the managing board.

Unternehmer gehen zur Schule was an account of his participation in the thirteen-week Advanced Management Programme at the Harvard Business

School in 1950 as the 'first and only German'. The book was aimed at a broader public and filled with anecdotes about his stay in the United States.[41] Its title reflects the surprise at the fact that American managers were going back to school, which was very unusual in comparison to German practice at the time. In the United States, management training had been expanded after 1945, due to the postwar shortage in qualified management personnel. And, as Vaubel reported, at the Harvard Business School not only junior but also leading executives took part in courses on business policy, accounting, social and labour policies.

During his stay, Vaubel had informed himself about new methods of business policy, aspects of human and public relations. He concluded that these developments 'within American industry are extremely important for the whole world, not only in economic but also in political terms . . . we cannot simply ignore this development and the new methods by saying "well, that's American".' Here, Vaubel referred to the fact that, in earlier periods, the term 'American' had been synonymous in Germany with 'superficial', 'casual' or 'different', and the adoption of American methods seemed impossible. Vaubel argued against such preconceptions because he was convinced that what he had seen in America could be applied to Germany to a large extent. But, despite his enthusiasm for America he remained pragmatic: 'We must compare our achievements to foreign developments and use any new impulse to our own benefit.'[42]

Subsequently, using this rule as a guideline, Vaubel not only influenced managerial policy at Glanzstoff but also played a crucial role in the establishment of several institutions for the further training of German managers, namely the so-called 'Baden-Baden business talks' where current and future business leaders met for three weeks to discuss a wide range of subjects regarding the role of top managers.[43] These institutions also presented a forum for the discussion and industry-wide promotion of American management methods.

At Glanzstoff, management training and human relations involved better information for staff in the form of regular meetings on aspects of general economic development, on the company's sales and employment levels. These meetings, established by a resolution of the managing board in 1950, were supposed to lead to a better working climate at the management level and between all superiors and the workforce. The board was convinced that information, discussions and meetings helped improve the trust of the workforce, served as a safety valve for built-up dissatisfaction and thus promoted 'industrial peace'.[44]

In the early 1950s, in the context of the debate about the co-determination law, the issue of human relations grew in importance in Germany, especially in the area of informal corporate policy. But it did not have the same legislative status as in the US and, as the diminishing use of the term shows, it lost in significance during the course of the 1950s. Nevertheless, certain aspects of human relations appeared at Glanzstoff, in the form of on-the-job training for management, such as seminars, and departmental meetings which were held down to the level of foremen. Not only economic and technical subject matter were discussed, but also aspects of how to deal with employees and how to promote staff's decision-making ability, trust and sense of responsibility.[45] Here, as in most other aspects, the process of Americanisation at Glanzstoff aimed at finding the right solution for each individual situation, rather than copying the US practice in detail, following the suggestion of Vaubel to focus on the 'basic attitude'.[46]

Conclusion

At the end of the Second World War, Glanzstoff, like so many other major German companies, was subject to Allied and especially American plans for reconstruction. While decartelisation and dismantling determined developments in the immediate postwar period, the company gradually regained control over its operations and corporate strategy from the end of the 1940s. Subsequently, Glanzstoff increasingly followed American developments in methods of production and management. While this was based on previous experience in terms of product development, the interest in the US example was new in the areas of production, sales and personnel management.

Until 1939 Glanzstoff had produced artificial silk, and during the war the first attempts were made to produce true synthetic fibres. Contact with IG Farben and their new product perlon was just as significant as the little information which, despite the war, was obtained about the American production of nylon. From the 1930s, US companies had taken the lead in synthetic fibres and so Glanzstoff increasingly followed American developments, while not forgetting its own research. The lines on which the first perlon factory at Oberbruch was constructed in 1949–50 closely followed US examples, especially that of the market leader DuPont. This was also true of other Glanzstoff products such as 'nylons' or car tyres which were, at the same time, symbolic for the reconstruction of the German economy and the 'economic miracle'.

However, not only production, but also sales and distribution were influenced by the US experience. As the decision to construct a perlon and a nylon factory illustrates, the observation of the American market was crucial for investment decisions made at Glanzstoff. American marketing concepts were adopted. More emphasis was placed on the integration of sales, distribution and advertising, which had previously co-existed in a detached sense, and a greater co-ordination between production and sales was promoted. This also had an influence on company organisation, leading to a more important role for departments dealing with sales and advertising.

The adoption of new production and sales methods necessitated an improvement in channels of information and training on-the-job for company staff. In this area too, American developments were followed. Here, the US influence came via Vaubel's observation of management training and human relations in the USA, which then extended even beyond the company itself. Finally, a further indication of the diffusion of American methods of production and management can be found in the adoption of American business terms, which increasingly came to dominate language used at the senior management level.

Overall, these developments highlight the Americanisation of corporate policy at Glanzstoff. Even if a US model as such did not exist, the individual factors identified in the areas of production and management do present the picture of an Americanised company from the late 1940s. Americanisation at Glanzstoff was therefore not the result of a generation change. Dynamic senior managers, open to developments elsewhere in the world, had a decisive influence on the adoption of US management techniques. They had come to occupy strategic positions in the company during the 1930s and 1940s. With some of them having gained work experience abroad during the Weimar Republic, they experienced the lack of openness and of possibilities to exchange information during the war as a deficit. To them, Americanisation involved resuming prewar international relations and a return to the highest standards of artificial fibre production, both of which had been interrupted by the Nazi era.

On the other hand, the significant influence exercised by the US example on operations and management at Glanzstoff therefore supports Berghahn's more or less macroeconomic Americanisation hypothesis at a plant level. Further research is needed to show whether the case of Glanzstoff can be generalised.[47]

Acknowledgements

This chapter is based on research carried out by the author as part of his project on 'German managers' perception of foreign management and production methods between 1950 and 1980', which is sponsored by the Volkswagen Foundation. It was translated by Kirsten Petrak.

Notes

1 'Festliche Stunden im Werk Oberbruch', *Wir vom Glanzstoff*, 1950, vol. 10, no. 7.
2 L. Erhard, 'Freie Bahn für Leistung und Wettbewerb!', *Wir vom Glanzstoff*, 1950, vol. 10, no. 7. As far as the use of national pathos and of certain terms is concerned, this speech could up to this point have been delivered ten years earlier, i.e. under the Nazi regime.
3 At another occasion, however, he explicitly praised Allied and especially American support for the construction of the plant; Archives of the AKZO Nobel Faser AG, Wuppertal (hereafter AKZO Archives), L 9-4-4, Rede Bundeswirtschaftsminister Erhard bei der Eröffnungsfeier des Werks Oberbruch, 6 November 1950.

4 See, for example, the contributions in C.S. Maier (ed.), *The Marshall Plan and Germany*, New York, Berg, 1991; and I.D. Turner (ed.), *Reconstruction in Post-war Germany*, Oxford, Berg, 1989.

5 H. Hartmann, *Amerikanische Firmen in Deutschland. Beobachtungen über Kontakte und Kontraste zwischen Industriegesellschaften*, Cologne, Westdeutscher Verlag, 1963, p. 11.

6 V.R. Berghahn, *The Americanisation of West German Industry 1945–1973*, Cambridge, Cambridge University Press, 1986.

7 See especially V.R. Berghahn and P.J. Friedrich, *Otto A. Friedrich, ein politischer Unternehmer. Sein Leben und seine Zeit, 1902–1975*, Frankfurt/M., Campus, 1993.

8 H.G. Schröter, 'Zur Übertragbarkeit sozialhistorischer Konzepte in die Wirtschaftsgeschichte. Amerikanisierung und Sowjetisierung in deutschen Betrieben 1945–75', in K. Jarausch and H. Siegrist (eds), *Amerikanisierung und Sowjetisierung in Deutschland*, Frankfurt/M., Campus, 1997, pp. 147–58.

9 For example, A. Lüdtke, I. Marßolek and A. von Saldern (eds), *Amerikanisierung. Traum oder Alptraum im Deutschland des 20. Jahrhunderts*, Stuttgart, Steiner, 1996; also Jarausch and Siegrist (eds), *Amerikanisierung*, p. 22.

10 P. Erker, 'Amerikanisierung der westdeutschen Wirtschaft? Stand und Perspektiven der Forschung', in Jarausch and Siegrist (eds.), *Amerikanisierung*, pp.137–45; K. Maase, 'Amerikanisierung von unten. Demonstrative Vulgarität und kulturelle Hegemonie in der Bundesrepublik der 50er Jahre', ibid.

11 If not otherwise noted, the following summary of Glanzstoff's development until the end of the Second World War is based upon W.E. Wicht, *Glanzstoff. Zur Geschichte der Chemiefaser, eines Unternehmens und seiner Arbeiterschaft*, Neustadt/Aisch, Verlagsdruckerei Schmidt, 1992; and T. Langenbruch, *Glanzstoff 1899–1949*, Wuppertal, 1985.

12 AKZO Archives, Perlon, Verschiedenes, J.C. Funcke to H. Rathert, 5 May 1944.

13 AKZO Archives, Oberkommando der Luftwaffe, Chef der technischen Luftrüstung, Berlin, 15 October 1944.

14 AKZO Archives, Verkaufsabteilung Glanzstoff, Notiz betr. Nylon-Industrie in USA, 15 December 1944.

15 L. Vaubel, *Zusammenbruch und Wiederaufbau. Ein Tagebuch aus der deutschen Wirtschaft 1945–1949*, ed. W. Benz, Munich, Oldenbourg, 1984, p. 65.

16 These exports had to be conducted via the Joint Export/Import Agency, or JEIA, set up by the occupation authorities; see ibid., p. 202.

17 ibid., p. 242.

18 ibid., p. 18.

19 Wicht, *Glanzstoff*, p. 83. By contrast, developments at the successor companies of IG Farben were much slower.

20 AKZO Archives, D 2-2-5-7, Bericht Funcke: Stand der Produktion vollsynthetischer Seide, Borsten und Fasern, 31 December 1946, pp. 5–6.

21 AKZO Archives, D 2-2-5-7, Funcke to Vits, 23 November 1949. Emphasis in the original.

22 E. H. Vits, 'Glückliche Fahrt für Nefa-Perlon. Festrede zur feierlichen Einweihung der Perlonfabrik Oberbruch am 6.11.1950', *Wir vom Glanzstoff*, 1950, vol. 10, no. 7.

23 AKZO Archives, L 9-1, E.H. Vits, 'Die Beweggründe für die Einrichtung der Perlonseide-Fabrik in Oberbruch', 10 July 1950.

24 AKZO Archives, D 2-1-5-13, Bericht über die Besuche im Werk Oberbruch am 5/6.10.1950.

25 Sabine Weißler, 'Fahnen des Neubeginns: Perlonstrümpfe', in *Perlonzeit. Wie die Frauen ihr Wirtschaftswunder erlebten*, Berlin, Nicolaische Verlagsbuchhandlung,

1988, pp. 147–8; Anna Döpfner, 'Textiltechnik: Zwei "Karrieren"', in *Ich diente nur der Technik. Sieben Karrieren zwischen 1940 und 1950*, Berlin, 1995, p. 112.

26 AKZO Archives, D 2–2-5–7, Rathert, Notiz betr. Entwicklung bei vollsynthetischen Fasern, 14 November 1952.

27 AKZO Archives, K-13–5-8, DuPont Rdschr. v. 4.7.1955 an Glanzstoff (Abschrift).

28 AKZO Archives, L 7–7-1, Vits, Notiz für den Vorstand (Abschrift): Ergebnisse der USA-Reise, 4 August 1956.

29 E.H. Vits, 'Die Kordnylonfabrik in Obernburg hat angesponnen', *Wir vom Glanzstoff*, 1957, vol. 17, no. 5.

30 AKZO Archives, K 13–5-8, Denkschrift über die Errichtung einer Nylonkord-Fabrik in Obernburg (Entwurf), 12 October 1955.

31 AKZO Archives, K-13–5-8, Rathert, Notiz betr. Aussprache mit Prof. Nallinger von Daimler-Benz, 13 August 1959.

32 F. Blaich, 'Absatzfragen deutscher Unternehmen im 19. und in der ersten Hälfte des 20. Jahrhunderts', in *Absatzfragen deutscher Unternehmen. Gestern. heute. morgen*, Wiesbaden, Steiner, 1982, p. 5; F.J. Kropff and B.W. Randolph, *Marktanalyse. Untersuchung des Markets und Verbreitung der Reklame*, Munich, Oldenbourg, 1928, p. V.

33 G. Bergler, 'Gegenwart und Zukunft der Absatzwirtschaft', in G. Bergler and E. Schäfer (eds.), *Um die Zukunft der deutschen Absatzwirtschaft*, Berlin, Deutscher Betriebswirte-Verlag, 1936, p. 10. Rejecting certain methods on anti-American grounds while at the same time practising them under the guise of a German variation was a typical phenomenon of the Nazi era.

34 J. Jirasek and R. Münzel, *Marktorientierte Unternehmensführung. Erfahrungen aus der amerikanischen Praxis*, Stuttgart, Kohlhammer, 1962, pp. 13–14.

35 AZKO Archives, B 6–16–25, Vortrag Schlange-Schöningen zum Thema: Vertriebsorganisation und Verkaufsprobleme beim XIII. Baden-Badener Unternehmergespräch, 26 October 1959, p. 2.

36 ibid.

37 AKZO Archives, K 8–13, Ingrid Molchin, Gedanken zur Werbung, 25 November 1954, p. 3.

38 AKZO Archives, B 6–16–25, Schlange-Schöningen, Vertriebsorganisation und Verkaufsprobleme (see note 35 above), p. 7.

39 Hartmann, *Amerikanische Firmen*, p. 82.

40 'Deutsch-amerikanische Betriebsführergespräche', *Der Arbeitgeber*, 1952, no. 19, pp. 751–2.

41 L. Vaubel, *Unternehmer gehen zur Schule, Ein Erfahrungsbericht aus USA*, Düsseldorf, Droste, 1952; see also his recollection in Vaubel, *Zusammenbruch und Wiederaufbau*, p. 12.

42 Vaubel, *Unternehmer gehen zu Schule*, pp. 14–15.

43 For the role of Vaubel in the establishment of further management training in Germany and the lasting contribution of the Baden-Baden business talks, see in detail M. Kipping, 'The Hidden Business Schools: Management Training in Germany Since 1945', in V. Zamagni and L. Engwall (eds), *Management Education in an Historical Perspective*, Manchester, Manchester University Press, in press, forthcoming in 1999.

44 H.W. Flemming, 'Die Goldfisch-Kugel. Über die Grundlagen des industriellen Friedens in USA', *Der Arbeitgeber*, June 1952, p. 422.

45 AKZO Archives.

46 Vaubel, *Unternehmer gehen zur Schule*, p. 81.

47 For the case of another, at least partially Americanised company in Germany, see V. Wellhöner, *'Wirtschaftswunder', Weltmarkt, Westdeutscher Fordismus. Der Fall Volkswagen*, Münster, Westfälisches Dampfboot, 1996.

11

SELECTIVE ADAPTATION OF AMERICAN MANAGEMENT MODELS

The long-term relationship of Pechiney with the United States

Ludovic Cailluet

The literature on the Marshall Plan consistently insists on the importance of American aid to France in terms of its volume and often underlines the powerful influence of the US example on French management practices after the Second World War. Indeed, France ranked second in the list of beneficiaries of Marshall Plan funds.[1] The reference to the Marshall Plan as a starting point for the dissemination of the modern American management *credo* is partly a result of the period's fascination with the United States and of the propaganda efforts made by the Economic Co-operation Administration, or ECA, and the Association Française pour l'Accroissement de la Productivité, or AFAP.[2]

With respect to the introduction of American management models and techniques, a number of authors have recently begun to question the importance and the actual influence of the US productivity drive, stressing the continuity with the interwar period and scientific management instead.[3] Moreover, as Patrick Fridenson has shown, the Americanisation of French business has to be considered a more encompassing process than the importation of management methods alone.[4] An analysis of Americanisation in the corporate sector has to identify the numerous 'points of contact' and 'carriers' between and inside the business communities. The former are defined very broadly as opportunities to meet, whether within formal institutions or informal settings, and include cartel and marketing agreements, exchanges of technology and know-how, journeys by specialists and managers and, of course, productivity missions. 'Carriers' are organisations and, more importantly, individuals involved in the transfer process. In this respect it should be noted that affinity with US business has never been a one-way flow. Though characterised by discontinuities, French companies had activities in the USA on a respectable scale from before the First World War.[5]

This chapter will examine the contacts of the leading French aluminium and chemicals producer Pechiney with the United States since the late nineteenth century and their influence on the company's management and organisation. Such an in-depth case study is made possible by the extensive material available in the Pechiney archives, which includes travel notes, correspondence and consultancy reports, and the reaction of management to the latter. Pechiney was founded in 1855 as the Compagnie des produits chimiques et électrométallurgique d'Alais et de la Camargue, or PCAC. In 1921, it merged with its arch rival the Société électrométallurgique française, or SEMF, to form the Compagnie des produits chimiques et électrométallurgique Alais, Froges et Camargue, or AFC, better known as Pechiney; a name which it adopted officially only in 1950, but which will be used throughout this chapter.

Pechiney provides an excellent example for the long-term and complex relationship of a leading French firm with US management models. It highlights especially the crucial role of individuals as conveyors and 'translators' of American management methods into the French context. The chapter subdivides and analyses this relationship in three different phases. In a first section, it describes the roots of Pechiney's business connections with the United States in the late nineteenth century. As a result of the developments in the production process of aluminium and the oligopolistic structure of the industry, the period is dominated by exchanges of technology and international cartel agreements. The second section covers the interwar period and the Second World War. The 1930s are dominated by the influence of scientific management. Pechiney used for the first time external advisors, most of them followers of F. W. Taylor. The second part of this section looks at the impact of the war and the German occupation on the company's organisation. The third section of the chapter focuses on the immediate postwar period. It shows that the impact of the Marshall Plan was rather limited, both in financial terms and in the importation of US management models. Nevertheless, the company adapted its management and organisation to the changed environment with the help of an American consultant.

Early contacts with the US: technology and markets

An American influence on French industrial firms can be observed from the end of the nineteenth century, when the American 'model' of the modern, large-scale enterprise started to become known in Europe. Automobile, electricity and chemicals producers provide examples of this early relationship with the United States.[6] These connections and influences have taken various forms. On the one hand, the transfer of US management models concerned the shop floor level, namely the introduction of Taylorist and similar systems.

They were, for example, welcomed by the French automobile industry and applied in the 1910s, albeit with different results, at Renault and Berliet.[7] On the other hand, there was a transfer of technology and capital, for example in the case of Thomson-Houston in the electrical industry or the Gillet family business in chemicals.

Pechiney reveals a complex and slightly different example with a framework of links existing from the turn of the century. The connection between the French aluminium industry and America is due to the early industry structure of a global oligopoly and the direct contacts between individuals, namely leading technicians and industrialists. In 1886, the American C.M. Hall and the Frenchman P.L.T. Héroult patented almost simultaneously a comparable process to produce aluminium by electrolysis.[8] At first opposed in a patent dispute, the two young men started a correspondence and eventually became friends. Both were quickly associated with industrialists in their native countries and acted as a kind of bridge across the Atlantic Ocean. Héroult was associated with the Société électrométallurgique française, or SEMF, and Hall with the Pittsburgh Reduction Company.

The Chairman of the latter, A. Hunt, came to visit his French colleagues and competitors as early as 1895. He sold a license of the Hall process to the owners of the Calypso smelter near Saint-Michel-de-Maurienne in the Alps, and sent one of his engineers to monitor the new machinery and train the local staff. Considering its duration, this twelve-month experience can be considered as the first transfer of American technological know-how to the French aluminium industry. However, it ultimately failed, the company was taken over by Pechiney, and the French aluminium industry adopted the Héroult process, which proved more efficient. In the following two decades, Héroult and other SEMF executives travelled extensively in the United States to sell licenses of their electrical iron furnace. Héroult himself eventually became a US resident and, from 1901, a technical advisor to US Steel, SEMF's largest American client.[9]

At the beginning of the twentieth century, there were only five corporations of four 'nationalities' producing aluminium, using the original patents and processes. The two French rivals, PCAC and SEMF, shared the leadership with the Pittsburgh Reduction Company in the US, which later became the Aluminum Company of America, or Alcoa, and a Swiss firm, Aluminium Industrie AG. The fifth producer, British Aluminium Company, was a smaller competitor. In 1901, these five created the first international aluminium cartel which succeeded in preventing the entry of possible newcomers into the industry.[10] Despite this cartel agreement, competition was still quite fierce between the existing firms. In 1911 the managing director of Pechiney, A. Badin, who was at the same time the head of the French domestic cartel L'Aluminium Français, or L'AF, established a joint venture with the German non-ferrous metal trading company Metallgesellschaft to build an aluminium smelter in the United States, to avoid tariff barriers. Fearful of the American anti-trust legislation, Alcoa was unable to prevent the joint venture from entering its domestic market. However, in a way quite typical of the 'gentlemen's agreement culture' prevailing in the aluminium industry, the two European partners eventually associated the American producer with their venture through a technological exchange of the alternative, so-called Serpeck production process to be employed in the new plant.

Expecting a long term supply contract with Ford, Badin incorporated the joint venture locally as Southern Aluminium Company and established a bank, the Banque Franco-Américaine, to fund the project. The company's plant at Badinville 'was probably the largest, and the most ambitious, French investment in America' before 1913.[11] However, as a consequence of the outbreak of the First World War and the ensuing restrictions on capital exports imposed by the French government, as well as a certain lack of confidence in the new production process, the – unfinished – plant was sold to Alcoa in 1915.

Pechiney, after the 1921 merger with SEMF the only French aluminium producer, maintained its American connections during the interwar period, mainly through the international cartel, even though the Americans were no longer formal members of the agreement. The company's two vice-presidents, J. Level and L. Marlio, played an especially important role in this respect, establishing personal relationships with the chief executives of Alcoa and Aluminium of Canada Ltd, or Alcan, Arthur V. Davis and Edward K. Davis. Pechiney re-entered the American market in 1932 with the purchase of shares in three US aluminium manufacturers, Bohm, Fairmont and Reynolds Metals, to all of whom it provided technical support.[12] In the 1930s, Pechiney's New York-based subsidiary, International Selling Corporation, or Intsel, acted as a marketing and intelligence unit. One of its roles was to welcome and guide the missions of Pechiney engineers and executives who visited the United States almost once a year during the period.[13]

Thus, despite the disastrous end of their smelter project in 1915, the French aluminium producers maintained a strong network of contacts in the United States during the 1920s and 1930s. Through frequent visits and mutual exchanges at the top management level, they had a good knowledge of the market, management practice and the technological competence of their American competitors. However, the influence of US management models and techniques on PCAC and SEMF and their successor Pechiney remained rather limited. First of all, their main partner, Alcoa, was a much larger firm. In addition, before the First World War, it could hardly be considered an example of a sophisticated and formalised organisation.[14]

Nevertheless, the numerous contacts and exchanges with American firms through the international aluminium cartel and Intsel during the interwar period pushed the French producers to import new marketing practices and to copy the US in terms of more aggressive strategies in the downstream part of the industry, regarding rolling mills, semi-finished products and so on.[15] At

the shop floor level, however, contrary to the French automobile manufacturers, Pechiney waited until the early 1930s before experimenting with the
American model of scientific management.

Scientific management at Pechiney

One of the earliest and best known expressions of American influence in
France is the so-called scientific management movement. Henry Le Chatelier,
a professor at the Collège de France, became the main apostle of the Taylor
system from 1904 and promoted the translation of most of the American engineer's publications before the First World War.[16] In 1926, the two branches of
the scientific management movement in France, previously divided between
the disciples of Frederick W. Taylor and the French engineer Henri Fayol,
merged to form a new association, the Comité national de l'organisation
française, or CNOF. Expanding its activities, the CNOF created a training
institution known as the École d'organisation scientifique du travail, or EOST,
in 1934.[17] Despite the CNOF's undeniable impact on a generation of engineers through publications, conferences and courses, most industrialists were
more reluctant than their engineers to 'Americanise' their workshops.

While well adapted to metalworks, where it was first applied, Taylorism
appeared less appropriate for other activities. In chemicals and aluminium
plants for example, the discontinuous processes used required regularly
unplanned and unscheduled interventions of workers. The oven conductor in
an aluminium smelter, *cuviste* in French, who looked after a set of machines,
was often waiting for hours during his shift. His interventions were relatively
short but very demanding in terms of initiative and physical strength.[18] From
the point of view of the engineers, the only part of the plant where scientific
management could be of use was the one most similar to metal works, the
maintenance department. Later on, the rationalisation of offices and the
renewal of marketing structures became additional targets.

At Pechiney, the decision to implement that 'hint' of scientific management during the 1930s, was linked to the arrival of a new corporate
leadership, namely in the person of Raoul de Vitry. Its context was one of
economic crisis, since Pechiney suffered two waves of disturbances between
1929 and 1935.

During the booming second half of the 1920s, the company had integrated
upstream into electricity generation and distribution. To repay heavy investments in dams, power stations and lines, Pechiney created a new branch,
electricity, which now became a marketable product as well as a raw material.
As a consequence, the company was reorganised to accommodate the new
production and distribution activity. In the early 1930s, when the impact of
the Great Depression was first felt, the burden of debt was still important.
Since the aluminium smelting process did not allow stop-and-go production,
it was extremely difficult to respond to variations in demand by simply

closing facilities. Thus, in order to survive the slump, managers had to introduce cost-cutting measures inspired by scientific management.

These dramatic circumstances led to the employment of external advisors and to the promotion of junior engineers ready to experiment with new management methods. Appointed from 1929 to 1933, Wallace Clark was the first American consultant to enter a Pechiney plant, breaking a very strong culture of secrecy.[19] Clark was a follower of Henry L. Gantt, himself a disciple of Taylor, whose book had then just been translated with much success into French.[20] To test Clark's method, Pechiney chose the aluminium smelter at L'Argentière in the Alps. The choice was not random; L'Argentière was the largest smelter of the company and the plant manager, Jean Benoit, had a background which made him very sympathetic to the new approach.

Born in 1899, Benoit was educated as a mining engineer and joined Pechiney as chief electrician of the aluminium plant at L'Argentière in 1925. His professional progression was quite impressive. In 1929, at the early age of 30, he was made director of this very important plant and quickly acquired a reputation as productivity record breaker. Benoit was involved in the scientific management movement; he was a member of the CNOF, participated in the scientific management conference in Geneva in 1929, and later graduated from the EOST school of scientific management.

While satisfied with the rationalisation proposed by the American consultant in general, Benoit monitored Clark's intervention closely and did not follow his advice blindly. In a 1933 report, Benoit proposed a number of modifications to the consultant's recommendations in order to adapt the new procedures concerning the management of and the accounting for maintenance operations to the constraints of the plant – constraints of which he, as director, was obviously very well aware. In the subsequent years, this adapted version of Clark's American management model formed the basis for a generalised application in the whole company. Benoit's report made a strong impression on top management and was certainly the reason for his promotion to Pechiney's Paris headquarters in 1934. Until 1940, Benoit was put in charge of miscellaneous problems, from local tax to purchasing.

The French defeat in June 1940, described as a 'brilliant lesson in scientific management' by Jean Coutrot, one of the leading French Taylorists, halted for a while the rationalisation efforts at Pechiney.[21] Now the company's priority was not to improve productivity, but simply to maintain the contact between its different plants and to monitor their operations. As a consequence, the corporate structure underwent a major change.[22] During the winter of 1940, Pechiney's secretary general, Louis Jullien, devised an *ad hoc* organisation chart, which is reproduced in Figure 11.1.

This new flat structure was a very pragmatic arrangement, designed to respond to the changes in the company's environment. Following its defeat in the war, France was divided into two zones. The Northern half of the country and the Atlantic Coast were occupied by the Germans; the zone south of the

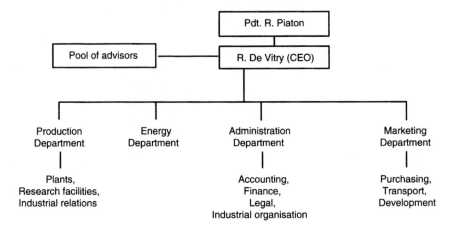

Figure 11.1 Pechiney's organisation between 1940 and 1947

Loire River was formally controlled by the French government from the spa town of Vichy. The demarcation line was an interior border controlled by German troops. Following the Allied invasion in North Africa, the Germans also occupied the previously 'free' zone in November 1942 and, after the defection of Italy to the Allies in 1943, also the former Italian occupation zone in the Alpine region, where most of Pechiney's smelters were located.

To address these geographic constraints and the resulting communication problems, the new structure aimed at shortening the links of authority and control. The prewar process departments – electrometallurgy, chemicals, mining and salina – were replaced by a single production department in order to facilitate the co-ordination between the operational units. This issue was crucial, because aluminium production required highly integrated operations. The newly created marketing and administration departments dealt mostly with the information requirements imposed by the German occupants, who received most of the company's output, and the Vichy government. Like all other French firms, Pechiney had to supply very detailed statistics, fill in a host of forms and follow an ever-increasing number of new rules.

To provide the required statistics and to maintain the relationship with the growing number of government planning and control agencies, Pechiney created an industrial organisation service, Organisation industrielle, or OI, which was placed under Jean Benoit. In addition to the management of data and government relations, Benoit was responsible for rationalisation studies. Between 1940 and 1944, his small team of in-house specialists conducted many surveys, with most of them focusing on questions of remuneration, given the wage restrictions imposed by the Vichy government. However, OI specialists also devoted considerable time and energy to studies of management accounting methods.

Of considerable importance for developments after 1945 was the dramatic increase of the functional services at Pechiney during the war. This more or less mirrored the growing number of civil servants in the Vichy government employed in planning and controlling functions.[23] The company's production decreased, but the payroll at the Pechiney head office was multiplied by a factor of more than three between 1939 and 1942, and while the company's total staff increased by 34 per cent from 1938 to 1946, the number of so-called *mensuels*, non-executive monthly paid clerks, grew by 65 per cent.

The American influence after 1945

Like the vast majority of privately owned companies in France, Pechiney benefited relatively little from the Marshall Plan. The French government used most of the American funds to pay for foodstuffs and vital raw materials or channelled them into six priority sectors identified by the country's 'Modernisation and Equipment Plan', which did not include aluminium.[24] Nevertheless, the French aluminium industry obtained Marshall Plan credits of about $1.2 million to pay for engineering services, machinery and raw material from the US. To upgrade its production facilities, Pechiney borrowed another $1.73 million from the 'Modernisation and Equipment Fund', which was mainly constituted of the so-called counterpart funds which the French government received when selling American dollar goods in France.[25]

In this way, the Marshall Plan certainly helped Pechiney obtain some financing for new machinery and, more importantly, provided access to US technology. However, in terms of the modernisation of the company's management and organisation, the European Recovery Programme of 1948 and the US productivity drive of 1949–58 were only of marginal importance. Efforts in this direction had already begun earlier, but showed nevertheless a distinct American influence.

After the liberation of the country from German occupation in 1944, one of Pechiney's priorities in terms of management was a significant reduction in the inflated administrative staff and a streamlining of operations. In a way, the idea was to reverse the modifications made to cope with the German occupation and the wartime situation. As early as December 1945 the company's chief executive, Raoul de Vitry, decided to revise the company's structure in order to improve efficiency and, in addition, asked for a rationalisation of the office organisation. This task was clearly too large for Benoit's small in-house OI team, and the decision was therefore made to prepare a comprehensive study by 'a selected specialist', in other words an external consultant.[26]

As in 1929, de Vitry decided to use Benoit's background as a productivity expert, his 'taste' for rationalisation studies and his fondness for and experience of innovative management methods. This choice demonstrates once again the vital part played by individuals as 'conveyors' of Americanisation at Pechiney. However, similar to the interwar period, Pechiney's use of the consultancy intervention led to an adaptation rather than a simple importation of US management models.

K.B. White & Co Industrial Consultants

After a quick survey, Benoit found that inflation of office staff had not only been caused by the administration of the wartime shortages and the planned economy. In March 1946, Benoit reported to de Vitry that the problems resulted from the functional structure adopted in September 1940, and he put forward a new organisation chart based on process departments. The two-page text became the base for the comprehensive organisational reform of 1948, during which Benoit played the role of a guide for the consultant.

It seems that, in the mind of the company's executives, the 'selected specialist' employed to carry out the necessary rationalisation at Pechiney had to be of American nationality. This certainly was partially due to the positive memories of the Clark experiments in the early 1930s. In addition, the Allied victory was mainly a victory of American industry and the scientific management methods it employed. Americans were seen as the most advanced organisers of their time, and many French people were impressed by direct testimonies of their military efficiency.[27]

Not surprisingly, Benoit initially contacted Wallace Clark, who however declined to return to France because of his advanced age. (He died in 1947.) Despite the lack of formal evidence, it is highly likely that Clark helped Benoit to get in touch with one of his former associates, K.B. White. An MIT graduate, White had been in charge of Clark's Paris office during the 1930s and returned to France shortly after the Second World War to operate his own industrial consultancy.[28] A possible alternative connection was White's French partner, André Pons. A graduate of the prestigious engineering school École polytechnique, Pons was a well known figure in the French scientific management movement and had also worked in the United States as a consulting engineer.[29] Benoit might have known him from before the Second World War, for example through the CNOF.

Whatever the connection, at the beginning of 1947 Pechiney formally hired K.B. White & Co to conduct a preliminary survey of the company's structure. The objective of White's assignment was to help Pechiney design new structures to replace the *ad hoc* organisation of 1940 and, in addition, to provide management tools to improve the company's efficiency. The company certainly expected a return on the costly 'investment' in the consultancy from a reduction in overheads, a rationalisation of production and the introduction of budgetary control methods.[30]

Some of K.B. White's methods must have seemed rather 'revolutionary' to most of the company directors involved in the intervention. White himself and Pons conducted interviews with the heads of the different departments, in order to 'pick their brains' about the best organisational structure and to enlist their 'political' support for the necessary changes. But they also visited various services of the Paris headquarters, three mining districts, seven chemicals and metallurgical works, two subsidiaries, a chemicals research department and a commercial warehouse, where they met local executives and engineers and observed their day-to-day relations with the local hierarchy and the head office in Paris.[31] Concurrently, an opinion poll was conducted among the youngest engineers, a total of seventeen who had been hired between 1938 and 1947.

Since the legally required establishment of an elected works committee (Comité d'entrepris) in the fall of 1945, the information of employees in the case of organisation changes had become more common in many French companies, including Pechiney. Nevertheless, such an attention to the opinion of individuals at lower hierarchical levels about the management and the organisation structure of a firm was still rare in France. This was particularly true for middle managers, the so-called *cadres*, who were not involved in the works committee.[32]

However, these habits were already changing at Pechiney. The company's top management started holding regular meetings with engineers in Paris from 1946–7 onwards. In addition, the in-house journals, created by volunteer amateur journalists from various departments during the war, were now managed by professionals from the company's industrial relations service. Pechiney's management saw these as tools to improve internal communication and to help integrate newcomers. In this respect, the interview method used by the consultancy during its survey of the company's organisation was considered 'truly American' and had a long-term influence on internal communication practices.

Some of the conclusions reached by K.B. White and detailed in the consultancy's 165-page report might have also sounded rather strange to their French clients. White developed a very American vision of the large business enterprise. Sketching an overall corporate structure, he suggested, for example, a board composed exclusively of specialists. These and other suggestions reveal a rather limited or even 'naïve' understanding of the specific characteristics of French capitalism, marked on the one hand by complex coalitions of families with extensive cross-shareholdings, and on the other by the extensive and influential networks of graduates from the country's élite higher education institutions, the so-called Grandes Écoles which spanned both the private sector and the public service. Another incongruous proposal, considering time and place,[33] was the suggestion to hire a trade unionist to cope with work relations inside the company, something which would still be considered 'revolutionary' in most French firms today.

More realistic, and in a way more relevant, was his advice to formally decentralise authority within Pechiney. For such a move to be successful, the consultant planned to give a new status to the functional services and to systematically evaluate the performance of the company's managers.[34] The practical tools he suggested in order to achieve this aim were budgetary control and individual objectives. New management and incentive procedures were to work via a staff and line organisation. In this respect, many of Pechiney's attempts to optimise its structure and practices since the crises of the 1930s were summarised in K.B. White's analysis and suggestions of 1947–8.

The intention of the consultant was to divide the company into product departments. The problem was that the plants, usually built near hydropower sources at a time when long-distance energy transportation was impossible, frequently produced many specialities. Therefore, in order to improve cost management and to decentralise authority, the consultancy proposed to introduce product-based divisions, while at the same time centralising and streamlining functional services. The reform became known as 'six-four-two', from the general order number 642 issued in March 1948.

General order no. 642

The new organisation of March 1948 was designed to avoid problems created by the former functional departments established in 1940. During the war, powerful departmental directors had created what Benoit called 'hidden headquarters'. All three departments of the wartime organisation were using their own functional specialists, for example, legal or industrial relations experts. To suppress this waste of resources, the heads of the newly created divisions were deprived of any functional staff. All of the existing functional skills were to be combined in a single, central service. As a result, continuity was preserved in the reform despite a completely different organisation chart (see Figure 11.2). There was only one new director and very few functional services were created from scratch, except the central staff relations management service.

Aluminium, or 'D-1', remained the major operational division which controlled not only smelters, finishing plants and research laboratories, but also sixteen production, distribution and marketing subsidiaries. The second most important family of products was chemicals. This was split in three divisions: D3 mineral products, D4 agricultural products and D5 organic products. The rationale was not only to cope with an actual diversification into plastics and other new products, but also to accommodate existing directors or wartime 'advisors'. This was a direct result of the organisational changes introduced during the occupation period, when de Vitry had multiplied the number of so-called 'management advisors', (conseillers de la direction). In 1947, he had to find room for each of these powerful persons in the new structure. On the other hand, de Vitry's candidate to lead the chemicals division, the 40-year-old Pierre Jouven, was considered too young to receive such an honour by the other directors and, as a consequence, was deprived of complete responsibility for the chemicals department.

But the new structure proposed by the consultant was more than a

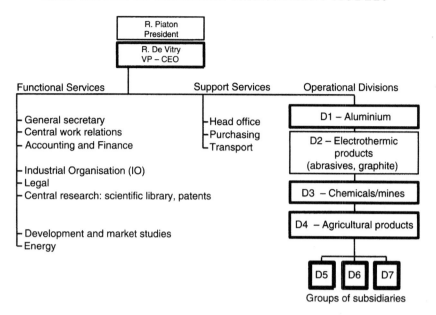

Figure 11.2 The Pechiney organisation according to the general order no. 642, March 1948

'classical' organisation chart, adapted to accommodate the senior staff management problems of Pechiney. The real innovation which helped Pechiney 'bridge the gap' between French and American management was the wide angle of the consultancy survey. For the first time, organisational matters were considered as a whole. Whereas the interwar rationalisation efforts had focused on production, K.B. White's study demonstrated that the shop floor was no longer the only 'core' of the firm. White considered a good organisation of functional and commercial services, animated by professional middle managers, to be at least as important, if not more, to the company's performance. The originality of the consultancy intervention was to combine corporate-level reorganisation with the introduction of practical Taylorist methods, in this case work simplification, which was considered a very efficient tool for cost reduction.

Indeed, from 1948 to at least 1952, the K.B. White consultancy conducted training sessions about work simplification methods at Pechiney, both in the offices and on the shop floor. Hundreds of head office clerks and managers took these courses, but they were also attended by engineers from the various plants, subsidiaries and even joint ventures of the company. Back at their workplaces, they in turn trained foremen to improve productivity at the shop floor level.[35] Through these training sessions, K.B. White exercised a long-term influence in the company as a whole which extended far beyond the head office.

The 'hybridisation' of American management methods

In general, K.B. White's recommendations regarding the reorganisation of the company were welcomed by Pechiney's managers. However, his relative ignorance of French legal constraints provoked some opposition. Pechiney's chief accountant Pierre Umdenstock, for example, complained to the company's chairman Piaton and its chief executive de Vitry about the fact that both White and Pons had completely ignored French accounting tradition and regulation. In his opinion, they considered the legally required accounting information to be 'a kind of statistics that could possibly be suppressed'.[36]

Some opposition was indeed to be expected given that the proposed reforms upset the traditional power structures at Pechiney. Thus, the budgetary control methods suggested to monitor the company's performance were a challenge to the former framework of financial information, until then strongly controlled by the accountants and the very top management. By contrast, the first plans for the introduction of budgetary controls, drawn up in 1948, foresaw the application of the new methods down to the level of foremen, a revolutionary step for such a hierarchical organisation dominated by engineers.

In fact, however, the introduction of budgetary control mechanisms was limited to the Paris head office for a decade. This was not only a response to the resistance from within the organisation, but also highlighted the primary objective, the reduction in overhead costs. In addition, department directors used budgetary controls mainly as a management information system. They were more eager to justify their decisions in terms of investments and stocks rather than to monitor the performance of their middle managers. This first attempt to adopt budgetary control shows a clear influence of the US example. But rather than a full-scale adoption of American-style methods, this was an adaptation limited by national traditions and opposition from within the existing hierarchy.

The intervention of K.B. White was not the only contact of Pechiney with the latest in American 'management science'. As early as 1945, and with increasing frequency from 1950, engineers and executives of the company travelled to the United States, a minority of them through the productivity programme.[37] Two of those who visited the United States as 'missionaries of the Marshall Plan' in 1950 were the engineers J.C. Hornus and G. Yelnik. They were deeply impressed by what they saw and learned in the USA. Subsequently, J.C. Hornus implemented some of the practices he had studied at Pechiney's American competitors when he became chief engineer of the company's manufacturing subsidiary Cégédur in the late 1950s. In the same period, G. Yelnik was promoted head of industrial relations in the aluminium department and developed extensive worker training programmes, again inspired by his American experience. Similarly, Max Duval, later to become secretary general at Pechiney, made a detailed survey of public relations practices in US companies, especially General Electric. This survey was used as the basis for the creation of such a service at Pechiney in the following years.

Participants in these trips to the United States later acted as 'conveyors' of American management models. Jean Benoit was, once again, among those who helped transfer and translate what they learned and observed through their contacts with the United States and the representatives of the productivity programme. Originally educated as an engineer, by the early 1950s Benoit had become a well-respected manager and management accounting specialist, mainly due to the production cost studies he initiated and carried out as head of Pechiney's industrial organisation service. He therefore participated in a productivity mission of French accountants and comptrollers in 1951, and returned to the US in 1953 and 1958. During this last journey, Benoit showed a particular interest in the corporate structure of General Electric, which he subsequently used as a model for the organisational reform of Pechiney in 1958.[38]

But Benoit's influence in terms of the Americanisation of French management extended well beyond his own company. His experiences at Pechiney and his trips to the United States served as a basis for many lectures he gave in the 1950s. The audiences were very eclectic, including for example the Higher Military Academy, (École de guerre); the École nationale d'administration, or ENA, established in 1945 for the training of civil servants; and many trade associations. Alongside the company's chief executive Raoul de Vitry, who helped establish INSEAD in the late 1950s, Benoit was involved in many French institutions of further management training, for example as board member of the Institut de contrôle de gestion or the Centre de recherches et d'étude des chefs d'entreprise. He also participated in the National Council of Accounting, (Conseil national de la comptabilité).

During his 35-year career, Jean Benoit was not only an 'apostle' and 'conveyor' of American management methods at Pechiney, but also a gifted 'translator'. He adapted the lessons learned from consultancy interventions and his own trips and studies, to the constraints imposed by the existing practices of the company. The fact that he exercised such an influence in French business circles was not only due to his own abilities, but also because Pechiney's management was considered by French managers to be very innovative.

Conclusion

During the first half of the century, Pechiney offers a very good example of long-term contacts and relations with the United States. However, in the period 1890–1930, the French company's links with America, which included cartels, technical agreements and frequent visits of managers and engineers, did not transform its everyday management practices. The influence of the US example was important in strategic aspects of management, for example, marketing or downstream integration; but no attempt was made to copy the American organisational model at that early stage. As the example of Alcoa before the First World War shows, the structures of the US partners in the oligopolistic international aluminium industry were in many respects comparable to those of the French firms.

American scientific management was first applied to Pechiney's plants in the early 1930s, following the Great Depression. While being introduced by an American consultancy, Wallace Clark, its introduction was not a pure importation but an adaptation to local and specific constraints of the company, and it was limited to specific parts of the organisation, namely the maintenance operations. Regarding the translation of US management methods, the French scientific management movement acted as a link, as did individuals like Jean Benoit who became a conveyor for the partial Americanisation of Pechiney in the subsequent decades.

After the Second World War, Marshall Plan funds were used mainly to buy materials and up-to-date equipment from the United States. In terms of 'Americanisation', however, the influence of the European Recovery Programme and the productivity drive on Pechiney appear to have been rather marginal. By contrast, the company's management considered it as very important to adopt a modern and 'US-like' organisation in 1948. From the first American trips of the company's engineers in 1945, the chief executive of Pechiney knew that the key to the superiority of the US competitors was their productivity. This, together with the positive experience of the Clark intervention in the 1930s, was the reason for hiring an American consultant in 1947.

The input of the K.B. White consultancy and the trips of engineers and managers were crucial for the Americanisation of Pechiney's management, for example in the case of budgetary control or industrial and public relations. The American influence was nevertheless moderated by local constraints and traditions. It was certainly the 'art' of Pechiney to translate the American management model into the French context and to adapt new tools to its own needs. This pragmatic adaptation of the US model was certainly one of the reasons for the success of the new management tools and corporate structures at Pechiney in the 1940s and 1950s, despite some internal opposition.

Thus, while the American influence on French business undoubtedly increased in the post-1945 period, the case of Pechiney has demonstrated that the Marshall Plan itself was neither a beginning nor a crucial step in the process of Americanisation. The productivity missions certainly helped promote the action of conveyors like Jean Benoit, but Pechiney's efforts to import and experiment with US management methods began long before the 1940s and continued thereafter. The partial Americanisation of Pechiney's management and structures from the 1930s through the 1950s cannot be understood without reference to the history of the aluminium industry, especially the long-term relationship of the French producers with the United

States from the late nineteenth century. Further research will have to determine to what extent this conclusion is specific to the case of Pechiney or also valid for other French companies.

Acknowledgements

The author would like to thank Patrick Fridenson and Matthias Kipping for supplying him with a number of useful references and commenting on an earlier draft. The usual disclaimer applies.

Notes

1 F.M.B. Lynch, *France and the International Economy from Vichy to the Treaty of Rome*, London, Routledge, 1997, p. 58.
2 For the 'fascination' of French managers with the United States, see L. Boltanski, 'America, America . . . Le Plan Marshall et l'importation du management', *Actes de la recherche en sciences sociales*, May 1981, vol. 38, pp. 19–41; M. Drancourt, *Mémoires de l'entreprise*, Paris, Robert Laffont, 1991, pp. 59–81; for the propaganda efforts, R.F. Kuisel, *Seducing the French: The Dilemma of Americanization*, Berkeley, University of California Press, 1993, p. 80.
3 For example, M. Margairaz, *L'État, les finances et l'économie. Histoire d'une conversion 1932–1952*, Paris, CHEFF, 1991; M. Kipping and J.-P. Nioche, 'Politique de productivité et formations à la gestion en France (1945–1960): un essai non transformé', *Entreprises et Histoire*, June 1997, no. 14, pp. 65–87.
4 P. Fridenson, 'La circulation internationale des modes managériales' in J.-P. Bouilloud and B.-P. Lecuyer (eds), *L'invention de la gestion. Histoires et pratiques*, Paris, L'Harmattan, 1994, pp. 81–9.
5 M. Wilkins, 'French Multinationals in the United States: An Historical Perspective', *Entreprises et Histoire*, May 1993, no. 3, pp. 14–29.
6 For electricity, see M. Lévy-Leboyer and H. Morsel (eds), *Histoire générale de l'électricité en France*, vol. II: *L'interconnexion et le marché, 1919–1946*, Paris, Fayard, 1994, p. 1033; for chemicals and other examples, A.D. Chandler, *Scale and Scope*, Cambridge, Mass., Harvard University Press, 1990, p. 185; Wilkins, 'French Multinationals in the United States'; and especially P. Fridenson, 'France: The Relatively Slow Development of Big Business', in A.D. Chandler *et al.* (eds), *Big Business and the Wealth of Nations*, New York, Cambridge University Press, 1997, pp. 207–45.
7 A. Moutet, 'Les origines du système de Taylor en France. Le point de vue patronal (1907–1914)', *Le mouvement social*, October–December 1975, no. 93, pp. 15–50; P. Fridenson, 'Un tournant taylorien de la société française (1904–1918)', *Annales ESC*, September–October 1987, no. 5, pp. 1031–60.
8 P. Stobart, 'Hall and Héroult. Two Remarkable Young Men of Their Times', *Cahiers d'histoire de l'aluminium*, 1987, no. 1, pp. 43–8; P. Morel (ed.), *Histoire technique de la production d'aluminium*, Grenoble, Presses Universitaires de Grenoble, 1991.
9 R. Pitaval, *Histoire de l'aluminium, métal de la victoire*, Paris, Publications minières et métallurgiques, 1946, p. 100.
10 F. Hachez, 'Le cartel international de l'aluminium du point de vue des sociétés françaises', in D. Barjot (ed.), *International Cartels Revisited, 1880–1980*, Caen, Editions du Lys, 1994.
11 M. Wilkins, 'French Multinationals in the United States'.

12 Pechiney Archives, Paris, 01–14–20477, 'Historique de nos relations avec les États-Unis', 20 August 1944.

13 Pechiney's sales in the US averaged FF25 million between 1927 and 1938, culminating at FF44 million in 1937.

14 For the organisation of Alcoa, see G.D. Smith, *From Monopoly to Competition*, Cambridge, Cambridge University Press, 1988, p. 56.

15 F. Hachez-Leroy, 'L'Aluminium Français, un outil pour l'innovation', in I. Grinberg, P. Griset and M. Le Roux (eds), *Cent ans d'innovation dans l'industrie de l'aluminium*, Paris, L'Harmattan, 1997, pp. 155–64.

16 J.M. Laux, *In First Gear: The French Automobile Industry to 1914*, Liverpool, Liverpool University Press, 1976, p. 190.

17 Kipping and Nioche, 'Politique de productivité'.

18 D.C. Ménégoz, 'Élie, cuviste à L'Argentière 1936–1951', *Cahiers d'histoire de l'aluminium*, 1997, no. 20, pp. 86–103.

19 However, during the first half of the 1930s, the company also employed the French consultant Paul Planus and, at its subsidiary Société du Duralumin, the French office of the Bedaux consultancy; see M. Kipping, 'Bridging the Gap? Consultants and Their Role in France', paper presented at a French–Japanese conference in Paris, 12–13 September 1997.

20 Clark's activities in France are not well documented. He certainly worked for Kodak-Pathé and Ugine in the 1930s and returned to the US before the war; see A. Moutet, *Les logiques de l'entreprise. L'effort de rationalisation dans l'industrie française de l'entre-deux-guerres*, Paris, Editions de l'EHESS, 1997.

21 Coutrot is quoted in Margairaz, *L'État, les finances et l'économie*, p. 497. From 1941 onwards however, Pechiney employed the Bedaux consultancy to install its system of shop floor management in all of the company's major plants; Kipping, 'Bridging the Gap?'.

22 For more detail on this and the following, see L. Cailluet, *Stratégies, structures d'organisation et pratiques de gestion de Pechiney des années 1880 à 1971*, Grenoble, Presses Universitaires de Grenoble, forthcoming.

23 The number of employees at the Ministry of Industrial Production, for example, had reached the impressive figure of 20,000 by the end of the war; P. Fridenson and A. Straus (eds), *Le capitalisme français*, Paris, Fayard, 1987, p. 76.

24 The sectors chosen for the so-called Monnet Plan of 1946 were coal, steel, energy supply, cement, agricultural machinery and transport equipment; P. Mioche, *Le Plan Monnet. Genèse et élaboration, 1941–1947*, Paris, Publications de la Sorbonne, 1987.

25 H. Morsel, 'Pechiney et le Plan Marshall', in M. Lévy-Leboyer and R. Girault (eds), *Le Plan Marshall et le relèvement économique de l'Europe*, Paris, CHEFF, 1991.

26 Pechiney Archives, 00–10–10019, Letter from J. Benoit to R. de Vitry, 17 October 1945.

27 Repiton-Préneuf, *2e DB. La campagne de France*, Paris, Imprimerie Nationale, 1994 (reprint), p. XXVIII.

28 Moutet, *Les logiques de l'entreprise*.

29 André Pons also played a role in the productivity drive in France; Kipping and Nioche, 'Politique de productivité'.

30 There is no direct evidence of K.B. White's fees in the Pechiney Archives. Nevertheless, from various sources, namely budgetary reports and balance sheets, the cost of their intervention between 1947 and 1952 can be estimated at FF65 million or 2 per cent of Pechiney's profits of the period.

31 Pechiney Archives, 00–10–10020, K.B. White & Co, Rapport no. 2: 'Rapport général de réorganisation de la Compagnie', 28 November 1947.
32 The car manufacturer Simca used a rather similar general opinion poll in 1952; Pechiney Archives, 080–6-5784, 'Rapport sur la consultation des cadres et de la maîtrise Simca à l'aide du questionnaire "Qu'en pensez vous?"', 31 July–2 August 1952.
33 During 1947–1948, the communist inspired trade union CGT led insurrectionist strikes all over the country.
34 It should be noted that in Pechiney's own terminology, no 'managers' or *cadres* appeared. Most of the field executives were engineers, whereas executives at the head office were called *employés supérieurs* or *directeurs*.
35 See A. Simon, *Issoire et Neuf-Brisach: les deux usines de la modernité pour l'industrie française de transformation de l'aluminium*, Paris, IHA, 1998.
36 Pechiney Archives, 90–3-501-IHA-2, Letters from P. Umdenstock to R. Piaton and R. de Vitry, 24 January 1948.
37 The information available at the Pechiney archives is insufficient to estimate the overall number of these visits. At least four of the reports of French productivity missions contain the names of Pechiney executives or engineers. Several young professionals also went to the United States, visiting either partner firms or competitors, including Alcoa, Kaiser, Reynolds Metals and Olin Mathieson, or attending training and academic courses.
38 For more details, see L. Cailluet, *Stratégies, structures d'organisation*.

12

LEARNING FROM AMERICA

The remodelling of Italy's public-sector steel industry in the 1950s and 1960s

Ruggero Ranieri

It is common today to view the public sector – not only but especially in Italy – as the essence of inefficiency and traditionalism. But, as the following chapter will show, such a view is not necessarily an accurate reflection of the evolution of Italian industry during the 1950s and 1960s. The chapter analyses in detail the modernisation of an important segment of the public sector steel industry in Italy, the state-owned company Finsider, after the Second World War. In the case of Finsider, the postwar remodelling was carried out largely along American lines. While highlighting the US influence, much of the literature on the modernisation of the European steel industry has so far focused almost exclusively on the technological aspect, namely the adoption of large-scale wide strip mills for the production of flat rolled steel.[1] Like for so many other European steel firms, Marshall Plan funds were indeed instrumental in facilitating the transfer of technology to Finsider. However, this Italian public sector company also carefully mastered and copied American methods in management culture, industrial relations, business strategy and organisation. During the 1950s, Finsider's large, newly built plant in Cornigliano, near Genoa, became a kind of intensive experiment in Americanisation. Finally, this chapter will also show that Cornigliano and Finsider were not an isolated experiment in Italy. Other Italian firms, in both public and private sectors, carried out similar reforms, inspired by what was called a 'neo-capitalist' ideology which became particularly influential during the early 1960s.

The chapter first sets out the context of the Americanisation of Finsider by explaining the nature and background of the company's postwar expansion, namely its relationship with the Marshall Plan as well as subsequent efforts of modernisation and expansion carried out in the early 1960s. It then looks in more detail at the actual changes, examining in particular the role of American consultants as well as the adoption of American-style training and recruitment practices, organisational design and industrial relations. Subsequently, the chapter looks at other, comparable attempts to introduce modern, often US-inspired management methods in Italian industry, also designed to help reform Italian society. In its concluding part, the chapter will briefly assess the reasons why most of these efforts, particularly in the public sector steel industry, proved a failure in the long run.

Finsider and the modernisation of Italian steel production

After the Second World War, the Italian steel industry was affected by a dispute between the public sector and most of the private steel companies. The public sector had been created in the 1930s, when the state had taken over a number of ailing steel companies, formerly under the auspices of a few large mixed banks, which had collapsed as a result of the Great Depression. In 1933, the IRI or Istituto per la Ricostruzione Industriale had been created as a state shareholding agency controlling a mixed bag of interests, both in manufacturing and in the utilities. In 1937, all state-owned assets in the steel industry – amounting to well over half of the country's entire steel-making capacity – had been consigned to a new sectoral holding company, Finsider, which was supposed to manage and restructure them. Already before the Second World War, Finsider attracted a number of talented and enterprising managers who saw an opportunity for carrying out ambitious reorganisation programmes, which had been hitherto impossible because of the tightly cartelised and restrictive environment prevailing in the trade.[2]

One of the most talented captains of industry to find a new home in the public sector was Oscar Sinigaglia, who became Chairman of Finsider after 1945. Sinigaglia started his career as a scrap merchant. During the First World War he was brought in by the government to help organise war supplies. A long-term believer in modernisation and industrial efficiency, he became a strong critic of the steel industry's mainstream establishment, which he identified as complacent and ineffective. Although he questioned the merits of state ownership in principle, to the point of proclaiming himself an economic liberal, Sinigaglia was prepared to look favourably on the IRI experiment in so far as it was conducive to rationalisation, technological progress and expansion. Together with many leading business figures of the time, from Enrico Beneduce to Attilio Bevione and later Enrico Mattei, Sinigaglia was above all a nationalist who believed that Italy should strive to take her place among the leading industrial powers.[3]

Immediately after the Second World War, under Sinigaglia's direction, Finsider produced a modernisation plan which involved concentrating output in three large-scale coastal plants. This so-called Sinigaglia plan recognised that the future lay with integrated coastal plants. With freight rates low and falling, they could draw upon the best quality supplies of raw materials available worldwide. By increasing the scale of their production they would be able to push costs down. Each of the three main coastal plants belonging to Finsider was to specialise in a different range of finished products: Bagnoli, near Naples, would be equipped for steel rods and commercial bar; Piombino, also on the Tyrrhenian coast near Livorno, for heavy products and rail; and Cornigliano, near Genoa, for thin sheet.[4]

The ensuing dispute between the public and private sector steel producers about this plan and its financing mirrored the overall debate about the appropriate direction for Italy's postwar reconstruction.[5] Sinigaglia believed that the new postwar world demanded standardisation and mass production, as well as low costs to meet increasing competition. The age of cartels and protection was on its way out, whereas the age of economies of scale and competition was on its way in. These ideas were not new, but after the war they were pursued with renewed vigour, and they could benefit from the new era of American ascendancy. The main opponents of the Sinigalia plan were a number of private firms, mainly based in the Northern region of Lombardy, the largest of which was the Falck group. These firms were particularly well versed in electrical steel production, and they had been able to enjoy the full benefit of the sellers' market prevailing during the Reconstruction. They turned out a wide variety of steel products both of common and special steel, mostly in small batches, and enjoyed good links with neighbouring customers in the steel-using trades.

The argument advanced by Falck was that Italian steel should concentrate on supplying a small, specialised mechanical industry. They saw no real scope for entering into high-volume manufacture of standardised mechanical goods, for which they believed market prospects in Italy were limited. Where standardised steel shapes were needed, for example for railways and public works, it was much more convenient to import them from Northern Europe. Falck did not believe that basic steel-making in Italy would be able to overcome the handicap of having to import the essential raw materials. On the other hand, specialised steel-making could exploit a pool of skilled and comparatively cheap labour, as well as plentiful supplies of hydroelectric energy in the Alpine regions. It followed that Italy would remain a highly dualistic country, with industry concentrated in a few regions of the North. As a result, state interventionism would be curtailed, while dependency on key foreign inputs would be made permanent and institutionalised by national and international producers' cartels.[6]

Sinigaglia's position, on the other hand, was that Italy should develop a strong mechanical sector able to export mass-produced goods. Sinigaglia wanted to step up production of 'ships, boilers, machine tools, metal shapes', targeting foreign markets, particularly those of developing countries. This could only be secured by a 'strong and healthy steel industry', developed along the terms described above, and with an output well above the prewar level. Finsider's immediate postwar projections, in fact, were in the order of

4 million tons to be achieved in 1951–52. In Sinigaglia's opinion, an array of relatively small-scale scrap-dependant producers did not add up to a serious steel industry and would only be capable of meeting a fraction of the country's needs.[7]

Altogether, Finsider's projections appear to have been rather sound. Industrial capacity in Italy had expanded considerably during the late 1930s and, as far as engineering was concerned, during the war as well. Exports of a variety of engineering goods increased considerably in the years after 1945, benefiting among other things from the temporary demise of German competition. Also, there was the problem of the South, still a poor rural area; ambitious schemes for its development were being drawn up by state-sector managers and technocrats.[8]

The outlook of Finsider's modernisers was therefore essentially a national one, both in the sense that they believed the national market was poised for expansion, and in the sense that they presented their plans as essential to the national interest. The same cannot be said for the Falck group, whose links were mainly in the North. Whereas Finsider lobbied hard to get their message across to the politicians of new democratic Italy, Falck relied on their links with the Milan-based steel-makers association, Assider, and on the support of the employers' association, Confindustria, which was also dominated by Northern firms.

Sinigaglia, on the other hand, established a close relationship with Alcide De Gasperi, Prime Minister and leader of the Christian Democratic Party, while his close collaborator, Ernesto Manuelli, garnered support among the other political parties, from the Liberals on the right to the Socialists. The Communists, and the largest, Communist-inspired trade-union, CGIL, publicly rejected the Sinigaglia plan but in fact were quite happy to endorse it locally, in so far as it brought with it new jobs. Thus the paradox was that, whereas no party was prepared to openly endorse the Sinigaglia plan, neither was there an onslaught against it, as might have been expected in the laissez-faire mood of post-fascist Italy. In fact, soon after it was put forward in early 1948, the Plan had been fully adopted as part of government policy. The new political class lacked experience, particularly in economic matters – which meant that the men in charge of large industrial holdings such as Finsider enjoyed considerable power and freedom of initiative.[9]

Sinigaglia also put to good use his personal contacts among the industrial elites. He was, for example, on very good terms with Vittorio Valletta, the dynamic Chairman of Fiat. The two met regularly in Rome on the occasion of Valletta's weekly forays from Turin to lobby politicians and government bureaucrats. Valletta had always wanted Fiat to concentrate on the mass production of cheap automobile models, affordable by consumers on fairly low incomes – something which had proved elusive in the interwar period, but was to be successfully accomplished after 1945. He was thus prepared to break the front of private industry's opposition and support Sinigaglia's plan to endow the Cornigliano plant with a wide strip mill capable of turning out large quantities of coils, since coils were essential for automobile body construction. Valletta also cultivated close links with a number of American producers and was thus able to help establish Finsider's reputation in the United States.[10]

Inevitably, the American Marshall Plan authorities were brought into the dispute over the Sinigaglia Plan. Finsider applied for a substantial loan to buy the technology needed for its massive renovation and modernisation efforts. Falck and their allies tried to thwart these attempts by seeking to convince the Americans that they should not support a state-owned company striving to acquire a monopoly. Finsider, on the other hand, pressed their case by stating that they wanted to bring down prices in order to encourage mass consumption of consumer durables, an argument which was bound to strike a sensitive chord among many New Dealers in the Marshall Plan administration. Important support for Finsider came from the American Rolling Mill Company, or ARMCO, a medium-sized steel producer based in Middletown, Ohio. ARMCO specialised in thin flat products and acted as consultants in the design and building of Cornigliano. Negotiations were long and complex. In the end, Finsider prevailed and the American loan went ahead.[11]

As a result of the Sinigaglia plan, Cornigliano was to become the largest and most modern steel works in Italy. A certain number of Finsider's most obsolete plants were either closed or downsized. The public sector as a whole, however, increased its share of steel production in Italy. Whereas in 1952 Finsider had accounted for 44 per cent of total output, it reached 50 per cent by 1957 and 60 per cent by the mid-1960s. Its share of hot-rolled and flat products, in particular, was even higher.

Completed in 1953, Cornigliano became the showcase of Finsider's modernising ambitions, in contrast with the rest of the state-owned steel sector which was less dynamic and innovative in its approach. At Bagnoli, for example, American technology was only partially adopted and American methods were resisted. For this reason, Cornigliano was separated from the rest of the holding and made into an independent company entrusted to a group of managers such as Mario Marchesi, Enrico Redaelli and Gian Lupo Osti, who carried forward Sinigaglia's ideas after his death in 1953.[12]

Cornigliano's wide strip mill was one of a handful installed in Western Europe after the war, together with its rivals at Port Talbot in Wales, Usinor and Sollac in France and Ijmuiden in Holland. Initially, it had a capacity of 500,000 metric tonnes, but very soon this was enhanced to reach 1 million tonnes. In fact, the plant's original layout had been planned in order to make this level of expansion possible at short notice. The essence of the company's strategy was to use its long-term contract with Fiat to secure a minimum base load, while directing its best efforts at marketing finished goods, such as tinplate and galvanised sheet, to a large network of customers, namely to manufacturers of consumer durables. In some cases, this entailed publicising new products as well as finding new uses for old ones. Steel-making was conceived, in other words, primarily as a profit-maximising business and not simply as servicing the rest of the manufacturing industry with intermediate goods.[13]

Before long, sales and profits soared. The 1950s and 1960s were years of rapid growth in the Italian economy and Cornigliano was at the forefront of the so-called 'economic miracle'. By 1960, it was producing 1.35 million metric tons of steel, equivalent to nearly 20 per cent of the national total and, what is more, it accounted for about half of the total for both hot and cold rolled sheet. Soon, its managers were confronted with the problem of further expansion. On the back of fast-rising demand, Italy's steel production quadrupled from 2 million tons in 1950 to 8.5 million in 1960, and it was to double again in the space of just a few years. Cornigliano, however, lay on a narrow strip of land, hemmed in by the adjoining mountains overlooking the Ligurian coastline, and it could not accommodate any further installations. Under these circumstances Finsider decided to go forward with the creation of Italsider, which was to bring together into a single company all the plants belonging to the state-owned sector, following the same criteria which had proved successful in Cornigliano. The influence of Cornigliano's top management was so commanding that they were entrusted with a key role in the merger, which was eventually carried out in 1961. A huge new plant at Taranto in Southern Italy, built between 1960 and 1964, was designed to be an essential part of Italsider.[14]

The American model and its implementation

Many commentators agree that the business culture prevailing within the steel industry in the early 1950s, indeed more generally across Italian industry, was far from advanced. Companies had traditionally been sheltered by protected and tightly cartelised markets or had enjoyed local or national monopolies for their main products. Small firms, which constituted the majority, were family-owned concerns, with a strong proprietorial culture and no proper recognition of the role and functions of professional managers. To some extent, this applied also to larger companies. Public sector companies on the other hand, were characterised by a bureaucratic, administrative ethos. There was no formal training for personnel, and accounting techniques were very haphazard. Taylorist methods had been introduced in some of the larger plants, especially in engineering, but only partially and in a very bureaucratic and authoritarian manner. They had not been accompanied by any positive move to improve industrial relations or to introduce substantial pay incentives, so that the system remained firmly based on low salaries and low productivity. Furthermore, immediately after the war companies were saddled with a ban on dismissals, coupled with an obligation to keep demobilised soldiers on the payroll. It was thought that there were about 10,000 surplus workers throughout the whole of Finsider in 1948–49. Militant unionism in some of the older establishments such as Piombino or Savona prevented management from enforcing more flexibility.[15]

Most Italian steel works turned out a variety of steel shapes in small batches. Ilva's plants, for example, either were merely geared to supply semi-finished products for the rest of the industry or they resembled large engineering shops designed on the German model, in that they were oriented towards low-volume, high valued-added niche manufacture. In the case of Terni, which specialised in high quality forgings and droppings for armaments, the steel works were part of a conglomerate, so that losses of the steel-making divisions could be compensated by gains made by others, namely by the electrical power plants which enjoyed a comfortable monopoly position.[16]

Finsider's top technicians and executives, particularly Guido Vignuzzi and Mario Marchesi, were clear in their minds that the reforms they wished to carry out implied a rejection of the German model of steel-making. 'One of our main defects', wrote Vignuzzi as early as May 1946, 'derived from the German model, is to want to produce steel everywhere and to require each plant to make ingots to feed into its own mills.' Much better, he argued, was the American model of standardising and concentrating ingot production, so that only a few standard types of semi-finished products were fed into the finishing mills. The debate between the German and US models also revolved around the choice of appropriate technology, for example whether to use Thomas converters or Siemens-Martin furnaces, or whether to go for narrow or wide strip mills. In each case, Sinigaglia's group came down in favour of the American option. Their views, however, were not unchallenged. The attachment to the German model remained strong among private producers as well as in some parts of Finsider.[17]

The centrepiece of the adoption of the American model, well beyond the mere technological dimension, was Cornigliano. Cornigliano was expressly built around the concept of standardised production of thin flat products, and it installed US-made semi-continuous process machinery. A plant of this kind could not be operated without allowing the whole production process to be carefully planned and controlled from the centre. This called for a greater role for managers, and also for a workforce that would conform to more stringent standards of regularity. Costing and marketing functions would also have to play a much larger role in order to enable the company to fend for itself in the market.

Sinigaglia had always been particularly insistent on the need for training. Already during the 1930s he had created in Genoa a school for apprenticeship and insisted on the need to raise the 'cultural level' of the technical and managerial staff. He soon recognised the need to draw on superior American experience in management, strategy and organisation. During the Marshall Plan talks, contacts with American firms had focused on the technical and engineering side, but Sinigaglia clearly saw the need to extend them. In 1951, during an important meeting to define details of the construction of Cornigliano, he was on record as observing that one should copy ARMCO's performance-related pay structure in an attempt to wean the more skilled operatives away from militant trade unionism. It was also important, he added, to copy ARMCO's marketing and publicity techniques.[18]

It appears, therefore, that the adoption of the American model happened in two stages. First, there was the recognition of the superiority of US technology especially – but not only – in the field of flat products. Second, there was the enthusiastic recognition that the American model came as a multiple innovation package covering a variety of business practices and structures. The package's full significance took some time to sink in and only appears to have been fully mastered in the course of the 1950s.

The role of productivity missions and American consultants

The transfer of the US model was facilitated by the first missions to the US undertaken by public sector chief executives, under the auspices of the US productivity programme. A very important one took place in 1953, with five Finsider and IRI executives, including Enrico Redaelli who was number two at Cornigliano, being subjected to a very intensive programme organised by management consultants, Booz Allen & Hamilton of New York. It included visits to ARMCO, Inland Steel, Republic Steel, Globe Tube and Steel and Pittsburgh Steel. The aim of the mission was originally to study budgetary techniques in US firms. Soon, however, it was broadened to cover a variety of management practices.[19]

The mission's final report underlined the opinion of the participants that many American methods and techniques might be fruitfully copied in Italy.[20] In the first place, it was thought that corrective action along American lines needed to be taken to increase the level of training for existing managers, with more missions abroad, more contact with research facilities and universities, and more formal instruction within the companies. Moreover, in order to better monitor the training requirements of all the staff, suitable job descriptions for each post should be drawn up. Company organisational design should be radically reformed in the direction of a clear separation between line and staff and the empowerment of middle managers in their own sphere of responsibility. Within Italian companies, too much power was exercised by too few people, leading to limited controls, slow decision making and insufficient managerial talent. Following the American example, on the other hand, executives should be confined to executive functions and not made to interfere unduly in the company's day-to-day management.

Long-term planning should also be gradually introduced, while companies' annual budgets should become one of the key concerns of the board. Equally, it was important to introduce standard costs procedures, by improving industrial engineering, quality controls and production plans. Furthermore the wage structure should be made fairer and more predictable by the application of scientific work management schemes. Finally, it was important to question the ideological bias according to which workers were somehow irrevocably pitted against management. More effort should be put into involving workers in the firm, sharing out information, calling them to participate in regular meetings with the staff, and discussing their individual careers.

The mission's report is a very significant document since its recommendations were acted upon thoroughly by Cornigliano's and later Italsider's chief executives in the course of the following years. Cornigliano's management team was particularly keen on its American affiliations. 'We were well aware', Gian Lupi Osti declared recently, 'that Cornigliano had been made possible by the Marshall Plan . . . and that we had chosen the "American model". We were in fact convinced that industry in the US was not only more efficient, but also more democratic and inclusive than in other leading countries.'[21] The contrast was often made between the open and friendly approach of American executives and consultants, and the stiff upper lip and secretiveness which was still the trademark of older, well-established European producers, be they German, Belgian, British or French.

Attempts to introduce American-style business practices in Cornigliano relied on a very close relationship with a number of selected US firms and consultants, nurtured by frequent visits and extensive exchange programmes. Osti recalls his visits to have taken place every six months from the mid-1950s onwards – most of them to ARMCO's headquarters in Middletown. The fact that ARMCO should play a particularly crucial role in the transmission of the American model to Italy is far from surprising. Although not among the largest steel makers in the US, ARMCO had managed to establish itself as a leader in thin flat technology. It had developed the first successful wide strip mill in 1924 at Ashland, and had gone on in 1927 to acquire the company that owned the even more successful Butler mill in Pennsylvania. Building on their lead, they had been able to issue licences for sheet technology to other steel companies such as US Steel and Republic Iron and Steel. Furthermore, during the 1930s they had acquired substantial foreign operations through their subsidiary ARMCO International, selling patents and know-how to firms in Britain, France, Germany and Italy.[22]

It is not entirely clear when the first links between ARMCO and Finsider were established. ARMCO acted as a supplier of coils to Fiat during the late 1930s, and it is not unlikely that Fiat itself put ARMCO and Finsider in touch after 1945. What we do know is that somewhere between late 1947 and mid-1948 Finsider's technical plans were thoroughly reviewed and improved by ARMCO, a fact that – as mentioned above – contributed to their success in the bid for Marshall Plan funds. The way ARMCO operated was, first of all, by advising on the appropriate choice of technology and directing its clients to the appropriate plant suppliers in the US – in the case of Cornigliano, this was

Mesta Machine Company of Pittsburgh – and, second, by providing the know-how in the form of specialist engineering supervision and technical guidance, for which they charged in the form of a royalty upon production.[23]

A further stage in the relationship concerned the training and management side. Two kinds of agreements were struck between ARMCO and Cornigliano. The first gave ARMCO a general consultancy, whereby every six months an ARMCO team visited Genoa and produced a report on Cornigliano's performance. The second agreement covered training for Cornigliano's staff, to be carried out at the ARMCO headquarters. It included both ordinary workers in line for promotion as foremen as well as technical staff and young white-collar employees due to advance into management. ARMCO remained an important partner of Italy's public-sector steel industry during the Italsider phase, offering further facilities for personnel training, although by the late 1950s Finsider had also built links with US Steel, Jones & Laughlin and other companies.[24]

Organisational change: forging a modern corporation

Cornigliano organised itself along strictly functional lines, with managerial hierarchies under the control of the central office. Great care was taken to provide job descriptions for all positions and to draw a clear dividing line between staff and line. Staff functions and a personnel department in charge of the management plan were co-ordinated by the General Secretary, an administrative 'supremo' who also took control of the sales department. A considerable effort was made to ensure the closest possible integration between production and sales. Some of the products which Cornigliano marketed were new in Italy, for example, standardised galvanised sheet produced according to the Sendzmir patent. Moreover, sheet and tinplate were only made available in a limited number of standard specifications. It was necessary, therefore, to actively promote the new range of products.[25]

The Italsider merger in 1961 involved new and complex organisational problems. Because the aim of the merger was to ensure more centralisation, the option of building a multidivisional corporation was ruled out.[26] The route chosen instead was to organise the new company according to a functional model, which still allowed the creation of a limited number of separate divisions to tackle specific tasks. Thus, for example, Italsider's exports were entrusted to Siderexport, a separate company within the group. Similarly to US Steel, which also operated about 70 per cent of its facilities in the functional mode, Italsider concentrated staff at their headquarters in Genoa while individual plants retained only a production and a sales office. The holding company, Finsider, whose headquarters remained in Rome, was supposed to shed all of its operational functions. Thus, public-sector steel would move from being organised in a holding, which supervised a number of loosely co-ordinated companies, to a centralised corporation, flanked by a holding company acting in a purely financial capacity.

Such organisational reforms assigned a far greater importance to the marketing and planning departments and consequently led to a large number of new managerial appointments. University graduates with backgrounds in the social sciences and humanities were increasingly chosen to fill these positions. Personnel offices also initiated a number of training programmes designed to involve all members of staff. Cornigliano initially relied on the 'training within industry' framework initiated by the Marshall Plan, which included specific courses for directors, middle managers, supervisors and foremen. The need for more formal training was eventually embraced by the leadership of IRI. They created the IRI school for managers, IFAP, which took its place alongside the business school IPSOA, set up earlier by Fiat and Olivetti.[27]

Two more organisational changes need to be pointed out, both initiated by Cornigliano in accordance with American practice. The first was the creation of a 'general contractor', a company specialising in co-ordinating plant extension and renovation. This was partly a result of the massive civil engineering which had been carried out at Cornigliano. Mario Marchesi, Cornigliano's chief executive, decided that all the engineering staff should be transferred to Innocenti, the plant suppliers. Thereafter, Innocenti was merged into the public sector company Italimpianti, acting as a specialised contractor for all of IRI's steel and engineering works.[28]

The second innovation was the introduction of standard costs, which consisted of turning each production unit into a budgeting unit, thus breaking up the process of accounting, and linking each single accounting unit to the relevant operational one. A standard cost was set for each separate stage of production. The method had been in place since 1928 at Fiat, who had also done their homework in America. Cornigliano took it on from the very start and operated it effectively, speed of appraisal being supplemented with flexibility in applying corrective measures. It was reinforced by the new computerised monitoring system introduced in the late 1950s using Univac technology, the first of its kind in Italy. Within the wider Italsider group, however, time lags in corrective measures materialised, making the whole exercise of standard costs much less rewarding.[29]

Innovation in industrial relations: the impact of job analysis and evaluation

Another important element of Cornigliano's reforms consisted in the introduction of job analysis and evaluation. This term covers a variety of administrative methods used to assess the value of different jobs within the factory. The introduction of job evaluation techniques in the US owed much to scientific management's emphasis on job design and analysis, as well as to the emergence of personnel departments within large corporations.[30]

ARMCO, which provided the model for Cornigliano, had operated a system of job evaluation since 1932, even before unionisation. Although it participated in the steel industry's joint efforts, which led to a comprehensive classification scheme in 1947, the company finally decided to retain its own manual, which it considered to be more rewarding for top jobs. This was an analytical evaluation scheme, based on points rating. Each job was broken down and weighted, taking particular account of four factors, responsibility, skill, effort and working conditions. According to their rating, jobs were assigned to narrow classes, and then banded together in categories, designed to facilitate mobility. At the beginning of the 1960s, there were twenty-four job classes divided into six categories.[31]

From the point of view of Cornigliano's management, confronted with an adversarial industrial relations climate, the main aim was to achieve a pay scale which could be considered objective and value-free. At the same time, the scheme was meant to bring about a sharp break with the craft system which put a premium on the skill and experience of the individual worker and gave unions far greater control over the shop floor. Pay would now be set independently of who might be performing a task at any given time. On the advice of ARMCO, Cornigliano's management recruited among those having no previous experience in the industry, such as the unskilled workers who had worked on the construction site, marking a departure from the entrenched practice whereby steelworkers were chosen among those having personal or family ties within the trade.

Job evaluation was fairly successful in Cornigliano. One of the reasons for its relatively smooth application was that the company's management could afford to offer higher wages than the rest of industry. Moreover, managers took a proactive stance, negotiating bonuses and pay rises with separate sections of the workforce so as to match productivity increases. Job categories were referred to the existing contractual parameters, allowing for a degree of trade union involvement. Initially applied merely to the manual workers, the classification scheme was gradually extended to white collar workers.

Problems emerged in the 1960s when it was decided to extend the job evaluation scheme to Italsider's entire workforce consisting of about 50,000 employees, a tenfold increase on Cornigliano. In plants such as Piombino and Taranto, also based on continuous throughput technology, the transfer seems to have been fairly straightforward despite the presence of a strong communist-inspired trade union in Piombino. Difficulties arose, however, in some of the other Italsider shops, such as Trieste, Lovere and Savona, which were essentially engineering workshops, based on small batch production and skilled craftsmanship.[32]

One important reason for the successful adoption of job evaluation schemes at Cornigliano was the close relationship which the company's management established with the Catholic-inspired trade union CISL. Created in 1948 by a splinter faction of the Marxist-dominated CGIL, CISL had adopted an efficiency-based ideology, linking pay to productivity. To some extent it was influenced by American thinking, which it was able to meld with an attachment to Catholic social doctrine. Attempting to increase its membership and gain a wider legitimisation among the work force, it was keen to pursue a company and plant-based bargaining strategy, as opposed to the preferred national bargaining which was strongly endorsed at the time both by the CGIL and by Confindustria.[33]

The application of job analysis and evaluation called for very minute contractual agreements, and this favoured CISL's approach. More generally, during the 1950s two developments helped to loosen the tightly centralised mould of pay bargaining in Italy. On the one hand, public sector companies broke away from Confindustria, forming separate organisations, the main one of which, Intersind, included Italsider as a key member. On the other hand, a weakening of the communist CGIL, in conjunction with more buoyant economic conditions, encouraged unions to negotiate increasingly at the local and sectoral level.[34] In 1960, an agreement in principle to introduce job analysis and evaluation was reached between Italsider's management and the three national metalworker unions, acting as affiliates of all the major trade unions. Detailed negotiations were carried out in the following three years at plant level by joint management–trade union committees.

By 1962, when the national contracts came up for renewal, Italsider, together with a number of engineering firms in the public sector as well as Fiat in the private sector, was prepared to break away from the other employers and strike a deal with the unions which included both better pay conditions and the acceptance of so-called 'articulated bargaining', whereby significant elements of the pay structure and conditions were to be agreed at plant and company level. The 1962 agreement was a watershed for industrial relations in Italy, both because it marked the end of low wages and because it seemed to offer an opportunity for a more constructive dialogue between social partners. For a time, big progressive corporations like Italsider looked confidently forward to a pragmatic evolution of industrial relations according to an American model, smoothed by higher than average productivity-linked pay awards.[35]

The wider context of Americanisation in Italy

The experiments set in motion at Cornigliano and Italsider were not unique. In many ways they mirrored those attempted at Olivetti. The company's chairman, Adriano Olivetti, after having flirted with socialist and federalist ideas, had gone on to develop a 'communitarian' ideology according to which the firm and its workers were bound together by a productivity pact on the shop floor as well as by the shared intent to promote social progress in the surrounding environment. American social sciences were marshalled by Olivetti managers, who were often of academic background, to elaborate and propagate this model. Another moderniser was Enrico Mattei, who had set up the public sector chemicals and oil company ENI in 1953 and liked to portray himself as an enlightened, patriotic captain of industry. He introduced job evaluation and called in Booz Allen & Hamilton to redesign the group's hierarchy and organisation. Similar reforms were carried out in a number of firms belonging to the state-owned group of mechanical engineering firms, Finmeccanica, as well as in a few private companies such as Fiat, which had been among the first to embrace American technological as well as managerial methods.[36]

By the early 1960s Italy was enjoying her own version of the affluent society. High growth and investment rates, booming exports and rising standards of consumption were transforming a relatively poor country into an industrialised, relatively wealthy one. Politics were changing too. The 'Centro-Sinistra', an alliance between the leading Christian Democrats and the Socialists, promised to deliver a string of reforms in welfare, housing and education as well as a more broadly based political system. The reforms introduced in key firms of the public sector, such as Cornigliano, seemed to herald a new age of social partnership, mass consumption and higher productivity.[37]

What were the main elements of this so-called 'neo-capitalist' managerial thinking? Perhaps the main point was a desire to elevate the status of the firm beyond that of a mere production unit. The factory was to be recognised as an agent for rationality capable of offering solutions for the improvement of the rest of society. Commenting on Adriano Olivetti's philosophy, his biographer Giuseppe Berta has aptly observed that Olivetti considered the progresive firm as the only force acting for fairness and modernisation within a deeply conservative society. His central concern was the 'idea that capitalism should secure a wide consensus, given that it stood for efficiency and given that far-reaching social reform would only come into being when the social actors would be able to recognise the leading role that the modern corporation was playing in the country's modernisation.'[38]

Similar thoughts were expressed at the time by managers and top executives in the public sector. IRI's Pasquale Saraceno, for example, singled out large public sector corporations as vehicles for injecting an industrial, market-oriented culture into the underdeveloped South. Writing in 1963, Gian Lupo Osti stressed the fact that the modern corporation offered the 'key to economic and social progress in our time'. In the first place, he argued, its internal structure and organisation had an immediate, practical impact on the social environment, so that company executives were in fact vested with social responsibilities. Furthermore, the modern corporation fostered a sustained rise in per capita incomes, which would provide the resources needed to carry out much needed public investments across a wide number of areas.[39]

Acting in conjunction with public administration, large firms were seen by neo-capitalist reformers as prime movers in the modernisation of infrastructure and in the creation of adequate social services. Run by professional managers recruited and trained in accordance with their skills and merits, supported by the efforts of a work force sharing in the management's ethos and objectives, the modern corporation offered itself as an example of achievement as well as responsibility. On the macroeconomic level, large firms acting in concert with the state could act on long-term investment projects designed to increase mass consumption. Keynesian demand management and indicative planning would abet economic performance by smoothing out fluctuations and channelling savings into investment.

There was nothing particularly original in this outlook. It was largely an American import, reflecting the confident age of American managerialism.[40] In Italy, however, its proponents had to contend with a far more contentious environment, where dominant subcultures – whether communist 'red' or Catholic 'white' – tended to reject the wealth-creating role of capitalist enterprise and where business itself was traditionally reluctant to admit to wider social responsibilities. This gave the Italian neo-capitalists a more reforming edge and sharpened the novelty and significance of their message.

A good number of neo-capitalist reformers were public sector managers, sharing in the ambiguous nature of companies, which, at least at the time, were largely run according to market criteria but were owned by the state. Such an ambiguous status was perceived as offering professional managers a freer hand and the opportunity to mould the economic and company environment according to their rational and productive beliefs. To quote Osti again, provided managers were free from any outside interference, the public sector 'could be seen as the best incarnation of managerial capitalism . . . . What could be better for a neo-capitalist manager than to rid himself of the proprietors and keep his own decision-making power in the firm intact?' A better business practice was also meant to attract private capital into the public sector. In this respect, Cornigliano went further than most other IRI or ENI companies, by allowing the state's stake to fall to just over 50 per cent. Cornigliano's employees were also successfully enticed to become shareholders, in a move towards 'popular capitalism'.[41]

Among the business elites that embraced the neo-capitalist ideology, the modernisers of Italsider played a prominent role. Their modernising creed was sober and pragmatic, lacking the particular utopian twist associated with Adriano Olivetti. Neither was it steeped in the essentially instrumental, empire-building mode of Mattei's ENI. A number of initiatives taken at Cornigliano and Italsider testify to their reformist, neo-capitalist zeal. With the well known painter and graphic designer Eugenio Carmi as Art Director, Cornigliano set out to enhance the company's image as well as promoting the applications of steel. It sponsored a number of prestigious exhibitions and festivals, set up recreational facilities for the employees including a new theatre and a library, and published a series of manuals for the work force, as well as two company journals: *Cornigliano* followed by *Rivista Italsider*. In addition, the management set up a colony for the employees' children and built low-rent housing blocks according to the most modern standards and specifications.[42] Despite all these efforts, both the public sector steel industry and the neo-capitalist model encountered increasing difficulties from the mid-1960s onwards.

Outlook and conclusion

Cornigliano's reforms had raised high expectations. Here was a company enjoying high profits and commercial success, while promoting reforms which ran counter to established industrial practice. By the time of the creation of Italsider in 1961, many, including a new constituency of middle managers, were eager to see the experiment carried forward. This was not to be, however. In the course of a few years, some of the reforms were abandoned while others were diluted or distorted. Older-style business practices gradually reappeared, politicians began to encroach on day-to-day firm management, and public sector steel lost its profitability and embarked on a vicious spiral of debt and mismanagement.[43] These developments, a detailed description of which is beyond the scope of this chapter, were due to managerial mistakes and a changing environment.

Concerning technology, the American model began to give way during the 1960s to the Japanese model. Nippon Steel were called in as consultants for the Taranto steel works. Although Japanese technology might have had its attractions, going for the even larger scale proved misguided in a smaller and fragmented market such as Italy. Moreover, whereas there had been some cross-fertilisation with American management practices during the 1950s, no serious attempt was made to absorb the Japanese 'ethos' of teamwork and selfless dedication, nor was the adoption of larger scale accompanied by more flexible organisational structures, improved commercial facilities and human resource policies.[44]

Concerning organisational design, the building of Italsider along functional lines was not successfully accomplished. There was much resistance both within the old firms and, more importantly, within Finsider's bureaucracy. Italian managerial culture was marked by top-down decision making, little emphasis on committee work or boards, and concentration of power in the hands of the chief executive. In such a context, the merger of a number of separate plants with very different traditions and, in some cases, hundreds of miles apart into a one-divisional firm was probably asking for too much. Functions were duplicated rather than streamlined. Finsider, the financial holding company, retained a large layer of administration, especially in Finance and Personnel, thus effectively exercising supervision over Italsider's management. It was able to draw on support from managers in peripheral firms, who felt marginalised by the reforms. Gradually, the whole construction began to resemble an unwieldy, disorganised conglomerate rather than a modern corporation.[45]

As seen above, the spread of management culture following the American model was initially relatively successful. In the public sector however, the unresolved issue of ownership came to haunt the reformers. During the 1960s, the political class increasingly undermined the autonomy of company managers. Politicians became frequent visitors to the factories, made long-winded speeches and increased their influence on appointments. Wider involvement of private capital was disallowed. The whole ethos of efficiency was resisted by the politicians, who preferred patronage and clientelism.[46]

Further problems arose in the area of industrial relations. Job evaluation proved ill suited to many parts of Italsider. More importantly, its smooth application depended on management being able to retain a strong influence on job control, particularly in Italy's traditionally adversarial environment. The question was whether a union culture could develop, sufficiently flexible and accommodating to perpetuate this pattern. In the 1960s however, trade unions became increasingly militant and confrontational, especially the Catholic CISL, which reneged on its prior commitment to efficiency. Thus the fate of smooth industrial relations was sealed, particularly in large companies. The job evaluation scheme was eventually dropped.[47]

Overall, the coalition of large firms committed to raising consumption levels and modernising society soon fragmented. The Centro-Sinistra did not fulfil the hopes of their supporters and failed to raise the level and quality of social expenditure. Apart from a few isolated instances, neo-capitalist solutions never commanded wide support at the national level, nor were they encouraged by politicians pandering to the deeply rooted anti-business traditions among the electorate. Furthermore, a different kind of business culture, encouraged by the 'economic miracle', was emerging in Italy. Little concerned with notions such as corporate planning or investment in human resources, it was firmly rooted among small or medium-sized manufacturing firms. Mostly active in low or intermediate value-added sectors, they were able to ride a tide of fast productivity gains by carrying out aggressive labour policies and by exploiting favourable commercial circumstances both in domestic and foreign markets.

Notes

1 For a summary of the current research, see R. Ranieri, 'The United States and the Modernisation of Europe's Steel Industry after 1945', paper presented at a conference in Caen, 17–19 September 1997.
2 On the creation of Finsider, see F. Bonelli (ed.), *Acciaio per l'industrializzazione. Contributi allo studio del problema siderurgico italiano*, Torino, Einaudi, 1982; on the history of IRI in general, M.V. Posner and S.J. Wolf (eds), *Italian Public Enterprise*, Cambridge, Cambridge University Press, 1967.
3 On Sinigaglia see G. Toniolo, 'Oscar Sinigaglia (1877–1953)', in A. Mortara (ed.), *I Protagonisti dell'intervento pubblico in Italia*, Milano, Angeli, 1984; on his activities during the First World War, A. Carparelli, 'Uomini, idee, iniziative per una politica di riconversione in Italia', in P. Hertner and G. Mori (eds), *La transizione*

dall'economia di guerra all'economia di pace in Italia e in Germania dopo la Prima Guerra Mondiale, Bologna, Il Mulino, 1983. A very good testimony on his personality and his industrial leadership can be found in the published interview, G.L. Osti, *L'industria di Stato dall'Ascesa al Degrado. Trent'anni nel gruppo Finsider. Conversazioni con Ruggero Ranieri*, Bologna, Il Mulino, 1993.

4 For the text of the Sinigaglia plan, see Finsider, *Sistemazione della Siderurgia Italiana*, Rome, 1948; see also O. Sinigaglia, 'The Future of the Italian Iron and Steel Industry', *Banca Nazionale del Lavoro Quarterly Review*, 1948, no. 4, pp. 240–5.

5 On the dispute between Falck and Sinigaglia, see R. Ranieri, 'Assessing the Implications of Mass Production and European Integration: The Debate Inside the Italian Steel Industry (1945–1960)', in M. Dumoulin, R. Girault and G. Trausch (eds), *L'Europe du patronat de la guerre froide aux années 60*, Bern, Peter Lang, 1993.

6 G. Falck, 'Lettere Scarlatte – Una lettera di Falck', *Il Mondo*, 1949, vol. I, no. 12; M. Pozzobon, 'Le acciaierie e ferriere Lombarde Falck (1945–1948)', in AAVV, *La ricostruzione nella grande industria*, Bari, De Donato, 1978.

7 'Interrogatorio dell'ing. Oscar Sinigaglia', in Ministero della Costituente, *Rapporto della Commissione Economica Presentato all'Assemblea Costituente, II: Industria, II: Appendice alla Relazione (Interrogatori)*, Rome, 1947, pp. 5–20.

8 V. Zamagni, 'Betting on the Future. The Reconstruction of Italian Industry 1946–1952', in J. Becker and F. Knipping (eds), *Power in Europe? Great Britain, France, Italy and Germany in the Postwar World, 1945–1950*, Berlin, de Gruyter, 1986; more broadly on Italy's postwar economy, see K. Allen and A. Stevenson, *An Introduction to the Italian Economy*, London, Martin & Robertson, 1974.

9 On Finsider's network, see P. Rugafiori, 'I gruppi dirigenti della siderurgia pubblica', in ID, *Imprenditori e manager. Industria e Stato in Italia 1850–1990*, Rome, Unicopli, 1995; also R. Ranieri, 'Il Piano Marshall e la Ricostruzione della Siderurgia a ciclo integrale', *Studi Storici*, 1996, vol. 37, pp. 145–90.

10 On the meetings between Sinigaglia and Valletta, see Osti, *L'industria di stato*, pp. 129–30; on Valletta's strategy, B. Bairati, *Vittorio Valletta*, Turin, UTET, 1983; on Fiat, D. Bigazzi, 'Management Strategies in the Italian Car Industry 1906–1945: Fiat and Alfa Romeo', in S. Tolliday and J. Zeitlin (eds), *The Automobile Industry and its Workers*, Cambridge, Polity Press, 1985; and S. Musso, 'Production Methods and Industrial Relations at Fiat (1930–1990)', in H. Shiomi and K. Wada (eds), *Fordism Transformed*, Oxford, Oxford University Press, 1995.

11 A detailed account of the Marshall Plan negotiations, based on US and Italian documents, is provided in Ranieri, 'Il Piano Marshall'.

12 Osti, *L'industria di Stato*, pp. 120–21; for general information on the development of the Italian steel industry during the 1950s, see M. Balconi, *La siderurgia italiana 1945–1990. Tra controllo pubblico e incentivi di mercato*, Bologna, Il Mulino, 1991, pp. 101–17.

13 F. Amatori, 'Cicli produttivi, tecnologie, organizzazione del lavoro. La siderurgia a ciclo continuo integrale dal piano autarchico alla Italsider (1937–1961)', *Ricerche Storiche*, 1980, no. 3, pp. 557–611. The text of the agreement between Fiat and Finsider can be found in D. Velo, *La strategia Fiat nel settore siderurgico*, Torino, Editoriale Forma, 1983.

14 On the debate surrounding the construction of Taranto, see R. Ranieri, 'Assessing the implications', pp. 91–100; on the Taranto plant, V. Castronovo, 'La questione siderurgica italiana dal "piano autarchico" all'impianto di Taranto', *Analisi Storica*, 1989, nos 12–13.

15 On Italy's business environment in the 1950s, see G. Martinoli (ed.), *La formazione del lavoro*, Bari, Laterza, 1964 and G. Sapelli, 'Gli "organizzatori della produzione" tra strutture d'impresa e modelli culturali', in *Storia d'Italia*, Annali 4: *Intellettuali e potere*, Turin, Einaudi, 1981; on industrial relations at Finsider after the war, G. Giugni, *L'evoluzione della contrattazione collettiva nelle industrie siderurgica e mineraria (1953–1963)*, Milano, Giuffrè, 1964.

16 On Terni, see F. Bonelli, *Lo sviluppo di una grande impresa in Italia. La Terni dal 1884 al 1962*, Torino, Einaudi, 1975.

17 Vignuzzi is quoted extensively in Ranieri, 'Il Piano Marshall', p. 146. On the debate between the German and American model, see Osti, *L'industria di stato*, pp. 119ff.

18 Ilva Archives, Genoa, Fondo Redaelli 007–4062, fasc. 4, 'Verbale Riunione presso la Finsider sul programma di impianti e di finanziamenti dello stabilimento di Cornigliano', 6 February 1951.

19 Ilva Archives, Fondo Redaelli, 018–4080, fasc. 2, 'Concezioni Aziendali e Metodi Direzionali negli Stati Uniti', 1953. The trip started in New York with ten lectures by Booz Allen specialists, each on a different aspect of corporate management. At the end of the week-long visit to the steel companies the delegation took part in the annual conference of the American Management Association. The visit was finally rounded up by what one of the participants described as a 'courtesy' visit to the Steel Division of the MSA in Washington, where a short but 'frank' sermon was delivered to the Italians, presumably on the need to step up their production for NATO contracts. On the impact of the Technical Assistance programme in Italy, see L. Segreto, 'Americanizzare o modernizzare l'economia? Progetti americani e risposte italiane negli anni Cinquanta e Sessanta', *Passato e Presente*, 1996, vol. XIV, no. 37 and P.P. D'Attorre, 'Anche noi possiamo essere prosperi: aiuti ERP e politiche della produttivita' negli anni Cinquanta', *Quaderni Storici*, 1985, vol. 58, no. 1.

20 'Concezioni Aziendali e Metodi Direzionali negli Stati Uniti' (see note 19 above).

21 Osti, *L'industria di Stato*, pp. 186–7.

22 G. Schroeder, *The Growth of Major Steel Companies 1900–1950*, Baltimore, Johns Hopkins Press, 1953; W.T. Hogan, *Economic History of the Iron and Steel Industry in the United States*, Lexington, Lexington Books, 1971, vol. 3, pp. 854ff. and vol. 4, pp. 1795ff.

23 Ranieri, 'Il Piano Marshall'.

24 Osti, *L'industria di Stato*, pp. 208–9.

25 ibid., pp. 167ff.

26 F. Amatori, 'Forme di Impresa in prospettiva storica', in S. Zamagni (ed.), *Imprese e Mercati*, Turin, UTET, 1991; on the organisation of ARMCO and other US steel companies, see A.D. Chandler, 'The M Form: Industrial Groups, American Style', *European Economic Review*, 1982, vol. 19, pp. 3–23 and A.D. Chandler, *Strategy and Structure*, Cambridge, Mass., MIT Press, 1962, pp. 331–7.

27 See P. Bizzarri, 'Elio Uccelli. Il frutto e il seme', *Rivista IAF*, 1992, vols 17–18; and G. Gemelli, 'American Influence on European Management Education: The Role of the Ford Foundation', in R.P. Amdam (ed.), *Management, Education and Competitiveness*, London, Routledge, 1996; for further details on the business practices at Finsider, R. Ranieri, 'Introduzione: La grande siderurgia in Italia. Dalla scommessa sul mercato all'industria dei partiti', in Osti, *L'industria di Stato*, pp. 42–72.

28 Osti, *L'industria di Stato*, p. 159.

29 For details on these and further measures, see Amatori, 'Cicli produttivi', pp. 604–5; on standard costs in general, H.T. Johnson and R.S. Kaplan, *Relevance*

Lost: The Rise and Fall of Management Accounting, Boston, Harvard Business School Press, 1987; on computerisation at Cornigliano, A. Baldissera *et al.*, 'Sistemi informativi e trasformazioni organizzative in un grande stabilimento metallurgico', *Quaderni di Sociologia*, 1972, vol. XXI, no. 3, pp. 249–346.

30 M. Quaid, *Job Evaluation: The Myth of Equitable Assessment*, Toronto, University of Toronto Press, 1993.

31 On job evaluation at Cornigliano and the influence of the ARMCO model, see Amatori, 'Cicli produttivi', pp. 602–3; G. Ottolenghi, *Analisi e Valutazione del Lavoro*, Milano, Etas Kompass, 1966; F. Cai, 'L'esperienza italiana sulla job evaluation. Il caso Italsider', in AAVV, *Ascesa e crisi del riformismo in fabbrica. Le qualifiche in Italia dalla job evaluation all'inquadramento unico*, Bari, De Donato, 1976; on the practice in the American steel industry, J. Stieber, *The Steel Industry's Wage Structure*, Cambridge, Mass., Harvard University Press, 1959; H.J. Harris, *The Right to Manage: Industrial Relation Policies of American Business in the 1940s*, Madison, The University of Wisconsin Press, 1982, pp. 152–4.

32 A. Fantoli, *Ricordi di un imprenditore pubblico*, intervista di S. Boffo e V. Rieser, presentazione di L. Gallino, Turin, Rosenberg & Sellier, 1995.

33 D.L. Horowitz, *The Italian Labour Movement*, Cambridge, Mass., Harvard University Press, 1963; S. Sciarra, 'L'influenza del sindacalismo americano sulla Cisl', in G. Baglioni (ed.), *Analisi della Cisl. Fatti e giudizi di una esperienza sindacale*, Rome, Edizioni Lavoro, 1980.

34 G. Contini, 'Politics, Law and Shop Floor Bargaining in Postwar Italy', in S. Tolliday and J. Zeitlin (eds), *Shop Floor and the State: Historical and Comparative Perspectives*, Cambridge, Cambridge University Press, 1985; M. Maraffi, *Politica ed economia in Italia*, Bologna, Il Mulino, 1991, pp. 205ff.

35 See G. Giugni, 'Recent Development in Collective Bargaining in Italy', *International Labour Review*, 1965, vol. 91, no. 4.; G. Turone, *Storia del sindacato in Italia, 1943–1980*, Bari, Laterza, 1981, pp. 285ff.; and, for a critical evaluation on the employers' side, F. Mortillaro, *In principio era il conflitto*, Milano, Sole 24 Ore, 1994, pp. 57–70.

36 For more details, see L. Gallino, 'Aspetti dell'evoluzione organizzativa negli stabilimenti Olivetti', in Centro Nazionale di Prevenzione e di Difesa Sociale, *Il progresso tecnologico e la societa' italiana*, vol. III, Bologna, Il Mulino, 1961; V. Ochetto, *Adriano Olivetti*, Milan, Mondadori, 1985; F. Venanzi and M. Faggiani (eds), *Eni. Una autobiografia*, Milan, Sterling & Kupfer, 1994, pp. 137–67; for a critical appreciation of this so-called 'neo-capitalist' movement, B. Trentin, 'Le dottrine neo-capitalistiche e l'ideologia delle forze dominanti nella politica economica italiana', in Istituto Gramsci, *Tendenze del Capitalismo Italiano*, Rome, Editori Riuniti, 1962, pp. 103ff.

37 P. Ginsborg, *Storia d'Italia dal dopoguerra ad oggi*, Turin, Einaudi, 1989, pp. 283–369; G. Podbielski, *Italy: Development and Crisis in the Postwar Economy*, Oxford, Clarendon, 1974.

38 G. Berta, *Le idee al potere. Adriano Olivetti tra la fabbrica e la Comunità*, Milano, Edizioni di Comunità, 1980, p. 23.

39 P. Saraceno, 'Initiative privée et action publique dans les plans d'industrialisation des régions sous-développées', in J.H. Habakkuk *et al.*, *Lectures on Economic Development*, Istanbul, Istanbul University Press, 1958; G.L. Osti, 'Iniziativa pubblica e sviluppo economico', *Mondo Economico*, 1963, vol. XVIII, no. 27, p. 28.

40 R.R. Locke, *The Collapse of the American Management Mystique*, Oxford, Oxford University Press, 1996, pp. 17–54.

41 The quote is from the paper Osti presented at the conference 'Perché l'impresa pubblica', Club Turati, Milan, 1970, pp. 19–20; see also G. L. Osti, 'L'impresa

pubblica e il controllo di gestione', in F. Archibugi and S. Lombardini (eds), *Piano economico e Impresa Pubblica*, Turin, Boringhieri, 1963.

42 Osti, *L'industria di Stato*, pp. 184–6.

43 See, in general, J. Eisenhammer and M. Rhodes, 'The Politics of Public Sector Steel in Italy from the Economic Miracle to the Crisis of the Eighties', in Y. Meny and V. Wright (eds), *The Politics of Steel: Western Europe and the Steel Industry in the Crisis Years (1974–1984)*, Berlin, de Gruyter, 1987; on the emergence of the mini-mills from the 1960s, M. Balconi, 'The Notion of Industry and Knowledge Bases: The Evidence of Steel and Mini-Mills', *Industrial and Corporate Change*, 1993, no. 3, pp. 471–507.

44 H. Nakamura, with C. Cristofani, *Il paese del sol Calante*, Milan, Sperling & Kupfer, 1993; Balconi, *La siderurgia italiana*, p. 24.

45 Osti, *L'industria di stato*, pp. 204–13.

46 E. Gerelli and G. Bognetti (eds), *La crisi delle partecipazioni statali*, Milan, Angeli, 1981; P. McCarthy, *The Crisis of the Italian State: From the Origins of the Cold War to the Fall of Berlusconi*, London, Macmillan, 1995, pp. 81–101.

47 In general, see I. Regalia, M. Regini and E. Reyneri, 'Labour Conflicts and Industrial Relations in Italy', in C. Crouch and A. Pizzorno (eds), *The Resurgence of Class Conflict in Western Europe since 1968*, London, Macmillan, 1978; on the end of the job evaluation scheme, M. Lichtner (ed.), *L'organizzazione del lavoro in Italia*, Rome, Editori Riuniti, 1975, pp. 204–5.

INDEX

229

For Product Safety Concerns and Information please contact our EU
representative GPSR@taylorandfrancis.com Taylor & Francis Verlag GmbH,
Kaufingerstraße 24, 80331 München, Germany

Printed and bound by CPI Group (UK) Ltd, Croydon, CR0 4YY
08/05/2025
01864531-0002